TO APPRECIATE THIS BOOK TO THE FULLEST, PLEASE VISIT THE WEBSITE: WWW.BOBVILLARREAL.COM AND EXPERIENCE WHAT THE AUTHOR CALLS "READ (THE BOOK) AND VIEW (THE SITE): A NEW AND EXCITING WAY TO ENJOY A BOOK." COPYRIGHTED © 2013. CONTENT INCLUDES GOOGLE EARTH TOURS OF THE PEAKS, PHOTOS ARRANGED BY CHAPTER, GOOGLE PANORAMIO PHOTOS WITH THEIR LOCATIONS MARKED IN GOOGLE EARTH, AND SEVERAL MOVIES SHOT WITH A HAND-HELD CAMERA.

Clawing for the Stars

A Solo Climber in the Highest Andes

AN ACTION, ADVENTURE, TRAVEL MEMOIR

BY
BOB VILLARREAL

abbott press®

A DIVISION OF WRITER'S DIGEST

Abbott Press books may be ordered through booksellers or by contacting:

Abbott Press
1663 Liberty Drive
Bloomington, IN 47403
www.abbottpress.com
Phone: 1-866-697-5310

Because of the dynamic nature of the Internet, any web addresses or links contained in this book may have changed since publication and may no longer be valid. The views expressed in this work are solely those of the author and do not necessarily reflect the views of the publisher, and the publisher hereby disclaims any responsibility for them.

Any people depicted in stock imagery provided by Thinkstock are models, and such images are being used for illustrative purposes only.
Certain stock imagery © Thinkstock.

ISBN: 978-1-4582-1323-5 (sc)
ISBN: 978-1-4582-1322-8 (hc)
ISBN: 978-1-4582-1321-1 (e)

Library of Congress Control Number: 2013922689

Printed in the United States of America.

Abbott Press rev. date: 02/10/2014

CONTENTS

INTRODUCTION

I began my career of thirty climbs in the highest Andes in my mid-forties and continued to my mid-sixties. What motivated me? What was I seeking? Adventure? Danger? Something of greater meaning? Did I ever find what I sought? Perhaps the reader will come to understand what drove me on by reading each absorbing chapter.

This is a collection of short stories relating events from my most memorable climbing trips in the Great Andes mountains. They are studies of character and personality unique to me played out in exotic, faraway places that just so happened to be in the Andes. For many years, the memories of my adventures among these high and magical mountains were enough for me. But one day, my grandson asked me to write about my climbs. I wrote this book to honor his request and to honor those peaks, where so much of my thoughts still reside.

HOW TO USE THE BOOK'S WEBSITE

I invite the reader to visit my website, www.bobvillarreal.com. Its content is meant to supplement the reading of each chapter, an approach I call "Read And View: A New And Exciting Way To Enjoy A Book." © 2013. One website section contains Google Earth tours for each chapter. Taking a tour before or while reading a chapter will help the reader appreciate and understand what it was like out there. (The tours may be accessed only by a PC or by a Mac (preferably using Google Chrome. The rest of the site is viewable using any web access device.)

The next part is "Photos." This contains more than 300 pictures arranged by chapter. They are displayed chronologically as I climbed up and down the mountain. This offers yet another way to enjoy the chapters visually.

For a different set of images, the reader may access the Panoramio site, accessible from the "Panoramio and Google Earth" section. It contains many photos taken on my climbs. Upon entry, one sees several pages of unordered photographs. To the right of these pages, under the heading "Organize with Tags," are tags for peaks and countries. When a tag is left-clicked, the photos that pertain only to that peak or country are displayed. One may left-click any photo and a page appears with just that picture. To its right is a Panoramio Earth box. Enter that and one may zoom right down to the peak and where I took the picture.

Finally, the website visitor can view hand-held camcorder movies I shot on several climbs.

This unique joining of a book and website, "Read And View," will help bring the book to life for every reader.

Why climb mountains alone? Well, why any inspiration?
Why did the early explorers sail the vastness of the oceans?
Why did we explore the moon? Is it not in touching the
unknown that we find our true selves?

--From the author's personal climbing journal

PROLOGUE: THE JOURNEY BEGINS

"**G**randpa, please write a book about your climbs in the Andes. I want to read about your adventures."

I never intended to write a book about what was, for twenty-one years, my obsession, my magnificent obsession, of climbing alone some of the highest peaks in the Great Andes. I would not have done so if it were not for you, Alex.[1] In fact, I might be sitting here today with nothing but memories. Yet, I accepted your request and answered it by writing my stories just to you so that you may know what happened out there. I hope you will thrill to them just as I did as I lived them.

I began my climbing career with the rock climbing courses at the Yosemite Mountaineering School when I was 40. But rock climbing is too strenuous. It's a young man's activity. I then traveled to the Grand Tetons and climbed the major peaks there with the Exum Mountain Guides. But these forays were not enough for me. I desired more. I wanted a complete immersion in another culture, the chance to exist in a barren land, and the danger of being many miles from any other human being should misfortune present itself.

Then, in a moment of pure serendipity, a casual glance at pictures in a climbing article about the Andes drew me in until a burning intensity to climb amongst those mountains captured my imagination. Strange that one brief instant might set me on the way to pursuing Andean high places for the rest of my life, a career of thirty climbs, three with guiding companies, eight with clients and companions, and nineteen alone.

---

[1]   My grandson, born in 1994.

Why climb mountains alone? Well, why any inspiration? Why did the early explorers sail the vastness of the oceans? Why did we explore the moon? Is it not in touching the unknown that we find our true selves?

And what a wonderful time my climbing career was! I imagine it, I relive it, I wake at night remembering it, years after it all came about. I journeyed to the Andes to climb the mountains and some of them wound up climbing me -- frostbite on Aconcagua, Argentina (22,834 feet) and loss of a toe; loss of will on Tres Cruces Central, Chile (21,743 feet); snow blindness on both Illimani, Bolivia (21,201 feet) and Llullaillaco, Chile (22,109 feet), and a resulting lifelong sensitivity to light. But these moments of darkness were more than balanced by the wonderful memories -- reaching the summit of Aconcagua; viewing the Inca huts on the summit of Llullaillaco; listening to the musical notes played by my "symphony rock" high on the western slopes of Pissis, Argentina (22,293 feet).[2]

In the beginning, I realized I needed to learn the mysteries of altitude climbing from experts. So, my first climbs were with guides from the American Alpine Institute (AAI) in Bellingham, Washington. I began with several mountains in Ecuador, culminating with the highest peak in the country, Chimborazo (20,564 feet), in 1988. I was 44 at the time. The next year, I went to Bolivia with the same company and climbed Illimani. Then, I journeyed to Argentina to climb the highest peak in the Andes, Aconcagua, once more with AAI. After that trip, I felt I had the skills to try things on my own.

Was altitude climbing alone, solo, an addiction? Yes, and in an outsized way. I lived out my dreams, never the same sort most have, but ones of a peculiar bent and uncommon, of climbing alone amongst the high Andes. I loved it, every stunning second of it; I craved it, reveled in it, and required it to get through the day, the week, the month -- and I still want it today, at 69. Although on several of my climbs I guided others for a fee or accompanied friends to the peaks, I always preferred to climb by myself. And my definition of "solo" was strict: no one else on the mountain but me.

What does age have to do with it? As it turns out, a good deal, in my case. My career began when I was in my mid-forties, when most altitude climbers have ended theirs. My last climb was a solo attempt

---

2   Please see Appendix B for a list of the twelve highest peaks in the Andes.

on Tres Cruces Central, at the age of 65 in November, 2009. I found that with age comes patience, the patience not to try to reach the next camp too fast. High altitude punishes those who seek to ascend in that fashion with sickness and even death. So, the slow and determined way was usually the best for me. This manner of climbing served me well during my many years amongst the high peaks. The ultimate proof of it? I'm still standing and still here to tell my story.

This is the first time I've written a book, Alex, and you were my inspiration to do so. I have seen it through because I believe it is my duty to make a truthful accounting of what occurred and have tried, as best I can, to portray the human aspect, and convey the emotional and physical context in which everything took place. This is not a climbing guidebook but a collection of short stories, true narratives that relate events from my most memorable adventures, those of my solo climbs and those with other climbers. They are studies of character and personality unique to me as they played out in exotic, faraway places that just so happened to be in the mountains.

Why did altitude climbing mean so much to me? I can't give an answer in a sentence or a paragraph because I must confess a vacant ignorance of it all. Sometimes I ask myself if there was any substance to what I sought. I cannot put into words what I cannot feel, but I can feel what I cannot put into words. Words fail me, but my feelings still burn with a fevered intensity. Perhaps the answer lies in the stories themselves, hidden and nestled deep within them.

So, Alex, read these stories, taken from my journals as I lived the climbs. Perhaps you and others will realize that, in the end, each of us is alone in our confrontation with the unknowable and the unknown, but we may approach fuller understanding should we choose to confront life on our own terms, whether it is amongst the highest mountains of our sacred planet or the great challenges of our daily lives.

Well, are you ready to go climbing? Before reading the following chapters, I would ask you to glance at Appendix A, The High Altitude Handbook. This is the pamphlet I required my clients to read before we journeyed to a peak. It addresses many questions those new to climbing at altitude have and will prepare you in the same manner.

I hope you enjoy reading "your" book.

GOOGLE TOUR: The Tour for this Chapter is on the site. It may be viewed before, during, or after reading the Chapter.

PANORAMIO PHOTOS: To view the pictures for this Chapter, choose the tag "Ojos del Salado" in the "Panoramio and Earth" section of the site.

PHOTO: General Orientation map showing peaks chronicled in *Clawing for the Stars: A Solo Climber in the Highest Andes.* (Photo 1.1 on the website.)

When James crosses the top of a rock the size of a
small car, the monster shudders ever so slightly
but remains in place. I know this because I stand
directly underneath him, some twenty feet below,
and for seconds I freeze to the spot not knowing what
I should do, pee or flee.

I see the summit now and know we are almost there.
"Judy, what are you doing here?"
I halt in puzzlement. Judy? What?
I turn to confront what must be a new addition to our climbing team.
"What'd you say?"
James points to a nearby boulder.
"That's my sister sitting on that rock. What's she doing here?"
My altitude haze disappears in an instant. James is hallucinating!

--From the author's personal climbing journal

CHAPTER 1

Nevado Ojos del Salado, Chile:
Ghosts of the Conquistadors

PHOTO: This map shows many of the peaks and other places of interest mentioned in the chapters. Ojos del Salado is south of the Great Plateau on the border with Argentina. (Photo 1.2 on the website.)

It is incontestable. The DC-8 is one of the nastiest commercial jetliners in existence. Eleven p.m. Miami International Airport. November, 1991. I'm sitting in the infamous DC-8 "Stretch," an elongated version of the jet. This Aero-Peru flight is bound for Lima, Peru, and then on to Santiago de Chile. My intent is to climb the second highest peak in the Andes, Ojos del Salado (22,609 feet). Years ago, DC-8's garnered the reputation as the noisiest passenger jets in service. Threatened by airport bans in parts of the States, Douglas made engine changes to quiet them. Yet those planes in South American service were not changed, and they still scream like banshees at takeoff. My seat is behind the engines and I'll receive the full effect. As we taxi, the pilot revs the engines, their growling a mere taste of what's to come. When we are at the top of the runway, we receive permission to roll. But this pilot is a favorite of mine. He doesn't release the brakes, power up the engines, and let their increasing thrust propel us down the tarmac. Rather, he keeps the brakes engaged while gradually increasing power. The four engines howl as the huge ship twitches and flexes in anticipation of its leap into the heavens. The noise is unbelievable. Outside it must be 140 decibels, and

1

it's the purest sound "high" I've experienced in years. When the pilot feels he has the right engine thrust, he releases the brakes, and "Stretch" is out of the blocks rushing down the way, those engines bellowing and roaring in the nighttime air. In my mind, I hear the first officer shout, "Rotate!" "The Ride of the Valkyries"[3] blasts in my head as the pilot pulls back on the wheel and the big ship lifts away from earth, the engines still detonating with pounding explosions that send a rolling, rumbling shock wave outwards over the land. There is nothing like this airplane. There is nothing like this experience. The engine crescendo fills my head and ears and settles deep inside.

Months before, my ad seeking partners for Ojos del Salado in northern Chile ran in a popular climbing magazine. The mountain's name means, literally, sources of the salty river, the name no doubt given it by Indians traveling near it on trade caravans between Tucuman, Argentina and Copiapo, Chile finding waters from its slopes not to their liking. I know little about the mountain, except its height. Its summit is an enormous volcanic crater, the western part of it blasted away. Each climber first must relinquish his passport to the Chilean carabineros[4] at their check station to the north of the peak.[5] There are two metal huts on the northern side of the mountain, the usual route of ascent. The first, the Refugio de la Universidad de Atacama, sits at 16,730 feet. The second, the Refugio Cesar Tejos, resides at 18,860 feet. (There used to be a small hotel, the Louis Murray Lodge, located next to the carabinero station. It burned down several years ago. The Lodge and the Tejos Refugio were gifts to Chile from the Anglo-American Mining Company of South Africa. Their names commemorate two employees: Murray, a geologist, and Tejos, a helicopter pilot, both of whom died in a crash on the mountain in 1984.) A road connects the carabinero station to the first hut and continues to the second Refugio. Climbers ascend to the summit from there. A road that high on a mountain steals

---

[3] From the Richard Wagner opera "Die Walkure."
[4] The Chilean police.
[5] This inspection station has since been relocated to the southern shore of Laguna Verde.

something of the adventure and mystery for me, but the peak's height remains an attraction.

My ad caused only desultory interest. Fortunately, an altitude climber from the Midwest, James, was interested, and we decided to climb together. We agreed to meet in Santiago, spend the night, and then fly to Copiapo,[6] Chile. There, we planned to find a ride out to the peak, some 145 miles east of the city.

This is the first climb on my own. My previous three climbs were with the American Alpine Institute and their excellent guides. I reached the top of Chimborazo, Ecuador (20,720 feet); Illimani, Bolivia (21,201 feet); and Aconcagua, Argentina (the highest peak in the Andes at 22,834') with them. Now it is time to put that experience to work. I feel fortunate to be able to do so. At age 47, I don't know how long I will be able to endure the rigors of climbing at altitude.

As I sort through climbing gear in my Santiago hotel room, a call arrives from James. He's in Asuncion, Paraguay. The military shut the airport after his arrival and it's to remain closed until the following day. He says to go to Copiapo and we'll meet in a day or two. This places our climb at risk. But I'm not worried. We'll make the best of it.

Copiapo, known as Copayapu in Inca times, lies at the northernmost extension of the great central valley of Chile. Its desert location belies its richness. Irrigation has made this area perfect for grape cultivation, and the city's outskirts are home to many vineyards and their rich harvests. Agribusiness is an important part of the local economy. And the city's proximity to gold mines in the vicinity and in the Andes, to the east, means a steady stream of miners, mining engineers, and trucking companies contribute to the town's financial and economic importance. In addition, Copiapo is the western terminus of the packed gravel road connecting with San Miguel de Tucuman in Argentina. Businessmen, miners, and tourists use the road and a fair amount of trade between the two countries passes over it. The Pacific Ocean lies forty miles to the west of the city, with the little towns of Caldera and

---

[6] The city attracted worldwide attention in October, 2010, when thirty-three miners were rescued from the nearby San José mine.

Bahia Inglesa offering limited shopping, dining, and sunbathing on the beaches.

When I arrive at the Hotel San Francisco de la Selva, I ask the owner if he knows anyone who drives climbers to Ojos del Salado. He says his brother might know. A short time later, Marco Roman strides in. I know from the first moment we will be friends for years to come.[7] He speaks some English, has a wonderful smile, and possesses an engaging individuality. He says he used to drive out to the peaks, but now that he's married, with a two-year-old son, a girl on the way, and a demanding job managing several shoe stores in town, he simply does not have the time. But he has a friend he thinks might be interested in taking us out to the peak.

Within an hour, I meet Giancarlo Fiocco. He's a sturdy man, six feet, two inches tall, with a keen sense of humor. Although he is not a climber, he has the mountaineer's appetite for exploring remote places and this trip has him excited. He and his wife, Maria Ester, who have two children, Giancarlito and Catarina, own and operate the La Casona Hotel. He also has an infectious smile and striking personality, and he's eager to take us to the mountain. He graciously offers to pick up James at the airport and take us around town to buy food, water, and white gas, all the things we need on the climb but couldn't bring with us.

Next day, we meet James at the airport. To this point, I have exchanged letters with him about the climb and we talked once on the phone. There are people I meet I don't forget even though I meet them just once. Such a man is James. He has a sunny way about him and an infectious sense of humor. I take to him immediately. Normally, I am rather reserved at first with others. I have no such reservations about James. He's younger than I am, by twelve years, solidly built with an easygoing manner. He's married, with children, and is a master restorer of antique furniture. He is also a keen observer of the personality traits of others, as I came to find out at our climb's conclusion. I know this

---

[7]   In fact, Marco and the author saw each other in November, 2009, and regularly trade e-mails.

will be a good journey. My mountaineering intuition tells me this and I trust it completely. After our shopping trip, we discuss with Giancarlo the eighty-mile drive to Laguna Santa Rosa the next day. We agree upon a price to cover the two-day ride out to Ojos and the one day return back to town.

The following morning, Giancarlo arrives at 8 a.m. in his well-worn Toyota Land Cruiser, a hardy, sturdy truck, and we pile all our gear inside and on the roof, in addition to our food and fifteen five-liter plastic bottles of water. As with all the peaks in this part of the Andes, the Ojos snow line is high. We don't know how high, but suspect it will be close to 17,000 feet before we find snow to melt. The water jugs give us the flexibility to place a base camp anywhere on the peak without worrying about a water source.

When we are an hour out of town, following the Mina Marte road, James asks if we might stop. He has spotted a huge boulder he wants to climb! We watch, fascinated, as he scales this monster with no rope for protection, and only brute arm, hand, and finger strength. It's quite a performance.

Three hours later, the road becomes steeper, and the Cruiser labors as it works up a series of steep switchbacks. Giancarlo mentions we're approaching the pass, where we'll see all the peaks spread out to our front. At one place, we stop to let the truck cool. He points across a shallow valley to an old dirt road that switchbacks down from the pass. Horse-drawn wagons ferrying goods between Argentina and Chile used it in the days before automobiles.

We start once more, approach a sharp turn to the right and there, spread out below and in the distance, is the southernmost part of the high Atacama Desert, the Maricunga Salar (dry lakebed). A thousand feet below us lies the turquoise colored water of Laguna Santa Rosa. In the distance, the bulk of Tres Cruces shimmers in the high mountain air. It dominates the land, its two peaks thrusting upwards into an indigo sky, an enchanting, exhilarating sight that is mine for a lifetime. The right-most summit is Tres Cruces Sur (22,133 feet and fifth highest in the Andes). The left-most crest is Tres Cruces Central (21,743 feet and eleventh highest). And the light! It is so bright at these elevations that only my mirrored sunglasses provide relief.

PHOTO: The view from the pass. The Laguna is below us with Tres Cruces on the far horizon. (Photo 1.4 on the website.)

We drop off the pass and motor down to the lake, a lapis lazuli colored gem even bluer up close than from afar. A dirt track leads to the Laguna Santa Rosa Refugio on the western shore of the lake, a stout wooden structure resting upon a raised platform, our home for the night. My altimeter registers 12,200 feet; this is a good elevation at which to begin acclimating before we reach the higher elevations of Ojos. The setting is idyllic with the lake close by, flamingoes standing in its still, silent waters, guanaco[8] herds grazing at its margins, and the stunning views of Tres Cruces and nearby peaks and high ridges to the east. In mid-afternoon, clouds swiftly descend upon the land and a snow blizzard dusts all with a coat of white. An hour later, all is in sunshine. The lake turns alternately black, green, and dark navy as clouds play before the sun.

PHOTO: The Laguna Santa Rosa Refugio with Giancarlo's Land Cruiser alongside. (Photo 1.5 on the website.)

As the next day's sun drenches the land with its warming rays, we start the fifty-mile ride to Ojos by returning to the Mina Marte-Copiapo road and then leave it to drive over the raw landscape of the salar, heading northeast. The Marte road continues to the east and eventually bears due south, the mine itself residing a short distance after the turn, right below Cerro Copiapo (19,855 feet).[9]

In thirty minutes, we intersect the Chile-Argentina highway, Chile Highway #31, and head south, with Tres Cruces growing larger every

---

[8] The guanaco is a camelid, the size of North American deer, native to the arid, mountainous regions of the Andes.

[9] This peak has a small Incaic altar on its summit.

6

mile. The road begins to climb, and when it angles due east we pass close to the two peaks of Cruces that loom to our right. We're now on what I call the Great Plateau, at an elevation of 14,200 feet, motoring due east for the thirty-five mile drive to Ojos del Salado. It's a superb day, with early high clouds giving way to a clear sky and the warmth of the sun. My mind drifts to the two letters I have at home, those written by Pedro de Merida, an officer with the Diego de Almagro expedition from Cuzco, Peru, to Chile in 1535-1537. He wrote to the King of Spain to explain what took place on the journey. These letters are my historical narrative re-creation of the expedition. They left Cuzco in July, 1535, traveled south through Argentina, and proceeded over the San Francisco Pass, at the eastern end of the Great Plateau we are now traveling. They walked the ground at our feet on their journey to Copayapu. From there, they searched in vain for gold in the Inca Kingdom of Chile. The Indians, hundreds of years before the coming of the Spanish, conducted trade between the two Indian cultures on either side of the mountains by hauling their goods over this same ground.[10]

I stir from my reverie when the truck slows. There's a huge wall of mountain to the north, to the left of our track, its high flanks stretching east to west. Once we roll to a stop below it, Giancarlo jumps out, walks uphill, and motions us to join him.

"Look, Roberto, James. Look there," he shouts excitedly.

I look to where he points but nothing I see causes excitement. The slopes here are a light rusty color, beautiful against the clear azure sky. What's so remarkable about that?

"Look, look at dark line. See it move?"

---

[10] The two letters in their entirety appear in the author's soon to be published historical narrative, "The Chronicles of Pedro de Merida: Travels to Chile, in the Years of Our Lord 1535-1537; Being an Account of That Journey to the Farthest Most Region of the Inca Empire; As Related to His Most Catholic Majesty, King Don Philip II, Our Most Sovereign Ruler" The letters offer an historical perspective to the author's climbing stories. Spaniards and Incas preceded him on several of the big peaks, 500 years ago.

A thin line lies several hundred feet above us. Whatever it is, it grows in length and comes towards us down the slope. Giancarlo laughs and says something in Spanish I can't understand. He points to the ground at our feet. We're standing in a faint gully etched in the loose sand and small pebbles.

"Watch. Watch."

The line has lengthened. I can't tell the source and don't even know what this thing is. But there is no question it's getting longer and heading down the slope towards us. As it moves closer, it finally reveals itself.

"It little stream," yells Giancarlo. "See, it come right to us, where we stand."

It's nine inches across, and, as it comes closer, we hear it push little pebbles before it. It continues and passes through the narrow channel from which we have stepped. It chugs merrily on down the brief remaining part of the slope, there to pool at the road's edge. What is the source of this strange thing?

Giancarlo laughs again as he reads the amazement in our faces.

"The water come from inside mountain. When snow melts, it collects beneath the surface of mountain and stays there, I think in little basins. When they become full, the water pushes through the outer part of slope, and this is result," he explains. "The water source is called *ojo*, or source of water. There are several on plateau, but this first time I see one on side of this mountain."

We return to the truck and motor off, the *ojo* and little stream the sole topics of conversation. When we crest a low rise, the carabinero station springs to view. It sits on stilts that support a platform upon which reside several rooms and a cooking and eating area. Here we must relinquish our passports to the Chilean police before we climb the mountain.

After dealing with the administrative paperwork, we turn our attention to Ojos, which reaches for the heavens six miles to the south. Giancarlo offers to take us anywhere we wish to make camp, but we don't care to go much higher than we are now, at 14,300 feet. After we drive over flat ground for two miles, we call a halt when it begins to rise. This is the place for Base Camp, at 14,800 feet. Our bodies ought to handle this elevation since we spent last night at 12,000 feet, but you never know with acclimation. There is no snow here, but we have enough water with us. We wish Giancarlo well when he leaves. We won't see him for twelve days. What a grand companion the man has been.

PHOTO: Our Base Camp, with Ojos in the distance. (Photo 1.7 on the site.)

We erect the tents and throw our gear inside. Although Ojos del Salado has the two Refugios for shelter, they are above us, and we brought our tents for Base Camp and perhaps higher up. Mountains and high hills are all around us, but our immediate home resides upon undulating and bounding desert land. It's a delightful afternoon for me. My entire being seems as one with this strange yet familiar landscape -- strange since this is my first visit to this peak, familiar since the solitude is like that of other remote places and peaks I have known. I exist here, I breathe here, in harmonious tranquility with nature. The slight breezes rustled by the onrushing winds late in the day present no danger. In fact, I feel like they welcome my presence, my presence existing for only brief moments in their million year existences. At night, once the sun has set over a calm desert, winds spring up and scurry across the sands about our tents as they hurry to remote destinations unknown to us.

We spend the next two days and nights adjusting to the altitude, and James has a rough time. Although he is beset by constant headaches, he takes aspirin and insists on staying on the climb. Our rapid ascent from the Laguna to this altitude caused him to succumb to the "soroche," the notorious Andes altitude sickness. He could walk back to the carabinero station and call Giancarlo. But he decides to tough it out. I admire his grit. He's my kind of guy. It doesn't appear to be more than regular altitude sickness, so it should pass eventually. He has been at altitude several times and knows how his body reacts. He has three high Andean climbs to his credit and that makes him a good climbing companion. Fortunately, I have no problems so far. My heart rate is normal, my urine is clear, and only brief, fleeting headaches pester my mountain mood. We both have the accursed altitude cough caused by the dryness of the air. I have gum to keep my throat moist. I chew it all the way up and down every big peak.

Here at Base, I retreat within myself, in a serene search for my mountain personality. There is no need to use meditation techniques or Zen exercises to call it forth. Every adventure draws it from me and it must be present. Otherwise, the mountain will swallow me whole, leaving me no more than an apocalyptic statistic, part of the body count of another unforgiving mountain. One must take nothing for granted in these high places. At times all is in harmony; the sun shines and soft idyllic breezes waft over the sands. Yet, this seeming friendliness may turn sour quickly. When that happens, my focus has little to do with summiting but everything to do with surviving. In the end, the top means nothing. It's a jumbled collection of rocks and patches of snow sitting at a high elevation. It will be there forever, from now until the end of time. If the summit remains elusive, I can return to it some other day. My attitude is all about never showing or talking of fear, staying positive, always knowing I will walk off this peak and back to my world. My journey can be half-way to nowhere before I figure out the real meaning is returning to somewhere. And that somewhere is home and family.

Rosy stabs of light chase the darkness as I prepare for the first carry to Refugio Atacama alone. We are climbing this peak in "expedition" style, like I climb all mountains. This calls for double carries of our gear to each camp higher on the mountain. The two carries allow the body to acclimate gradually to the higher elevation of that next camp. On the first haul, I take food for the coming days, a pint of white gas, and assorted other items. When I locate a suitable spot for the higher camp, I drop what I have brought, have some water and a snack, and then return to the lower camp, there to spend the night. The second carry the following day is a heavy one. I must haul my tent, sleeping bag, stove, an extra jacket, and the remaining items to the higher camp. This is the way I climb a big mountain.

James still has headaches and wants to rest another day. I follow the road as it snakes about the landscape, but it tires me and I vow to return to Base by a more direct route over the intervening sandy hillocks. In three hours, the Refugio comes into view, a large metal ship container daubed in bright orange. There's a smaller shipping box, this one colored yellow, next to it. Another, as large as the first, has a side completely missing and large trash cans sit within it. With bunk beds and a small area to prepare food, it's comfortable and warm inside the orange box. Over low sand mounds to the west rushes a stream, melt water from a field of *nieves penitentes*[11] higher up. It tastes fine, but water flowing off elsewhere either now or in the long past must have had an unpleasant flavor, thus lending the name to the mountain. The weather remains perfect. It's cooler here than at Base Camp. At midday, the temperature reads out at forty-eight degrees, and that is pleasant at this altitude. Later, back at Base, the sun, whose strengthened brightness condenses the earth to a glowing grain of sand, sinks behind nearby peaks, and the soft light of its parting spreads upon the land a quiet and thoughtful tranquility.

When the new morning arrives, I make the second haul to Atacama while James leaves later on his first carry. I have decided to take my tent, the light blue shelter I call my Baby Blue, in case I need it higher up. Its color lightens and brightens my mood. The tent maker, Integral Designs in Canada, is one of the best in the world. This second lift to a higher camp wearies me in the extreme. But in spite of the crushing weight on my back, I push forward using the rest step, sometimes at a pace of thirty steps before pausing for one or two seconds, sometimes at a pace of but four or five before resting. My speed is always a function of pack weight, the steepness of the land, the altitude, my physical condition, and my resolve to get higher.

---

[11]   Snow penitents. These are snow formations that result from sun and wind eroding a large ice field in this very dry part of the Andes. When the Spaniards first saw these in the early 16th Century, they reminded them of penitents on pilgrimage approaching Spain's great cathedral churches on their bloodied knees.

James left this morning after I did. When he joins me at the Atacama camp an hour later, we discuss our different progress rates on the mountain. He feels better, so the extra days of rest paid off for him. We agree to continue at our different rates, with me to wait at the Tejos Refugio an extra day until he makes his second carry to it. Then we can climb to the summit together. That agreed upon, he sets off back to Base Camp. The sky remains clear; it's another agreeable day. We can only hope the weather stays benign. The nearby stream provides water for drinking and cooking my freeze-dried dinner and it saves me having to use precious fuel to melt snow.

My acclimation goes well. Here at Atacama at 16,730 feet, my heart rate is 68. At home, it's 56. As the body acclimates to the new elevation, the heart rate drops towards normal. My urine runs clear in an hour, another positive indication. A new elevation causes it to darken and indicates dehydration, among other things, and the consumption of liquids helps to alleviate the problem. The accommodations here at Atacama certainly are pleasant. It's a sturdy structure offering protection from the wind, with comfortable beds and an area for cooking. But all this relative luxury on a big mountain? It's rather incongruous in an absurd sort of way. One is not supposed to feel this pampered on a climb.

Early the following day, my trudge to the Tejos containers at 18,860 feet begins. One can drive straight to this Refugio, never lifting a boot, but doing so would destroy the romance of the climb. In fact, this mountain doesn't particularly excite me. It offers no remarkable characteristics, such as mystery or symmetry, only great height and great breadth. So it's a monster, but not an inspiring or attractive one.

As I climb over the gradually ascending sand mounds, there are but a few sounds as I climb -- the sound of my boots striking the sand and gravel, single notes in the air; the noise of my Gore-Tex windsuit as with every move of my arms and legs the fabric chafes against itself. After a while, I become so used to it that I no longer notice, and the vast silence of the slopes enwraps me once more.

At the close of a grueling four hours, Tejos comes into view. It's composed of two large shipping containers welded to one another, with enough beds to bunk twenty people. There's even a shower, though it's inoperable. A shower? A large kitchen area includes several restaurant-like booths as well as a large food preparation area. And all this comfort at near 19,000 feet! It's like heresy to my sacred mountain religion.

When I return to Atacama, James is there. He has made his second carry and lies in one of the bunks. He's never seen anything resembling these big boxes on a mountain and we marvel at the opulence. We climb together the following day to Tejos, he with a first load and me with my second. Of course, he is well ahead after an hour because of the different load weights. But this isn't a race and I wouldn't think of trying to match his pace. I'm happy for him. He's acclimating well after a rocky first few days. We meet on his way back to Atacama before I even see Tejos. At this altitude, where the least effort is a physical hardship, I still must push forward. My way lies upwards, ever upwards, in a constant striving for the unknown.

By the time I reach Tejos, I am thoroughly fatigued and eager for warm broth. There is the slightest slip of running water flowing from the ice sheet nearby. I scoop the water I need from my hastily fashioned small catch basin of rocks and sand and heat it on my stove. As the soup's warmth warms me, my thoughts return home. I've been here seven days and already I miss my wife and daughters very much. I wonder what they are doing right at this instant, right at this moment.

PHOTO: Ojos del Salado, looking south, from the Tejos Refugio. (Photo 1.14 on the site.)

Later, as I sit at the kitchen table resting head in hand, a disturbing sensation seizes me. My right temple feels larger than the left. I touch both sides again and again and compare them again and again. I have cerebral edema! Each touch confirms the truth. My right temple is bulging. It's cerebral edema! I must retreat at least a thousand feet or risk dying where I am. There's a gnawing in my gut. I must return to Atacama. I must get down from here. I must get lower![12]

My pack is stuffed full of gear in minutes as the urge to flee clutches at my throat. I feel as if I cannot breathe. Down is family. Down is safety. Down is life. Somewhere, deep within, I feel that panic is near. I sense it by the clench in my stomach. But I must not panic. I must not lose control. It requires a Herculean effort to withstand those dark forces seeking to wrench my psyche from me. I must stay calm whatever the price. I must!

"Bob, control yourself. I'm here for you." It's Robert, my Guardian Angel. He has been by my side at many stressful moments in my life.[13]

A measure of calm returns and I feel more in control. I check myself methodically, this time with a serenity that might desert me in a moment. The right temple is larger than the left; there is no doubt about it. But is a bulging temple an indication of cerebral edema? I force myself to recall everything I know about the symptoms and I examine them systematically. I don't have severe headaches, blurred vision, nausea, loss of sensation, or loss of memory. After brief minutes of evaluation, I conclude this is not cerebral edema but a manifestation of peripheral edema, a condition not immediately serious, though it might become so higher up. I won't perish after all! A measure of stoical composure asserts itself and I breathe easier as my knotted stomach muscles relax. Out here, one can go over the edge in a heartbeat. During these moments, my view of events cause grave alarm and dismay when, as it happens, it is as unthreatening an instant as might be conceived.

---

[12] High Altitude Cerebral Edema (HACE), along with High Altitude Pulmonary Edema (HAPE), are the two killers at high altitude. With HACE, there is a swelling of brain tissue from fluid leakage. With HAPE, fluid accumulates in the lungs. HACE may be treated with dexamethasone. The drug nifedipine is for HAPE. The author carried neither drug on any of his climbs. The ideal treatment for either affliction is to descend 1,000 feet lower as quickly as possible.

[13] When the author was discharged from the Marines in June, 1967, his mother told him his Guardian Angel had watched over him. "What is his name?" he asked. "Robert," she said. "And he will be with you always."

An abiding relief soothes me and the ferocious phantoms are now but a memory. Yet, the ordeal has left me exhausted emotionally.

Later, the setting sun calms my nerves as it sets off a dazzling alpenglow on the western walls of the peak. It's like the Lighthouse of Alexandria as it shines outward for miles to the west. With the fading and slow dusking of the air, the inevitable moments of night descend noiselessly upon all perceptible forms, blackening borders, blackening contours, like a continuous rain of apocryphal blackening dust. The world is everlastingly silent, the dark breathing on me, an instant when my soul, released from the impending doom of cerebral edema, blazes with a delicate feeling that certifies silence is more eloquent than sound.

The next day, James arrives at 3:30 p.m. on his second carry, overwhelmed by exhaustion. He rests as we discuss a way to the summit over mugs of my warm soup. We reject the normal route since it requires entering the summit volcanic crater and using a rope, which we don't have, to work to the top. We decide instead on a course following a long rock ridge that ascends to the summit; five large "steps," one above the other, mark its length. The problem is that large and medium size stones compose each of those steps. It will be dangerous, exhausting, and time-consuming to scramble over them. I ask if he wants to put a camp on the lowest of the steps, a Sphinx-like paw, and climb to the summit from there the following day. I have Baby Blue with me and so I have available this alternative.

PHOTO: The view of the face from the Tejos Refugio. Notice the five steps on the left skyline. (Photo 1.15 and 1.16 on the website.)

James is not keen on the camp idea. I am, since another camp will give me a better chance at the summit. So we agree to my single lift to the Sphinx, where I'll spend the night. James will follow the next day after a day of rest for him here at Tejos and we'll climb together to the top. That decided, we retreat to our bunks so that our bodies can continue to adjust to this altitude. Up here, my movements are slower. My speech is slower. My thoughts are slower.

At first light, I ply the steep and demanding ground upwards, the lower boot always the firmer until I realize my goal. The giant Sphinx paw is underfoot by noon. Here, at 19,900 feet, I'm 1,000 feet above James. The weather remains calm and peaceful. My right temple is still prominent, but symptoms of cerebral edema are absent, and for that I am thankful. I have a headache, but it leaves off after an hour. My heart rate returns to normal in two. In the evening, the sun sinks dutifully in the west as it bids the world a brief farewell. I feel good about my progress. I feel good about my chance for the summit.

James surprises me when he arrives at my lonely mountain outpost before I expect him. There is no mistaking his determination. His jaw is set and he talks excitedly about his desire for the summit. His enthusiasm ignites my own fiery zeal to climb to the top. As we move upwards at half dawn, the rocks on our route pose a dangerous challenge; several large ones teeter as if they mean to roll when we step near them. When James crosses the top of one the size of a small car, the monster shudders ever so slightly but remains in place. I know this because I stand directly underneath him, some twenty feet below, and for seconds I freeze to the spot not knowing what I should do, pee or flee. The danger soon passes and I continue upwards, vowing never to climb below him again. My climbing poles,[14] which normally provide stability, are useless on terrain such as this. My ice axe[15] is useless as well. I keep my balance with careful boot placement and the judicious use of hands and arms.

We are on the flat top of step two in an hour, move up the third step, and stand upon its rocky plateau in under an hour. The rocks that compose the first three steps are medium to large size. Those of the fourth step are the size of cantaloupes and pineapples and present less danger.

As we work our way up the side of the fourth step, I realize we've been at this torture for several hours, James leading the entire time with

---

[14] Climbing poles are modified ski poles that provide stability climbing over difficult sand and snow.

[15] The ice axe provides stability on hard ice.

me behind him thirty to forty feet. And I spent the night 1,000 feet higher than he and thus have fewer feet to the summit. He began the trip in a sorry state, but he has grown in strength and today he is pure inspiration. His fervor infects me with a great greed to push on higher, to attain the ultimate goal, as my boot steps carry me ever upwards to realize the dream. My heart thumps as though it will burst. When I lean over for brief relief, my eyes close for seconds of physical recuperation. What a brute of a mountain. What a brute of a route. My slow, painful advance continues, every step, every yard gained costing such an effort that I'm almost left shaking. My heart pounds and I'm weak from loss of breath. If I have to continue struggling in this manner much longer, I shall never reach my goal.

When we attack the side of the fifth step, James begins to slow down until, within fifteen minutes, I'm climbing at his side over the small stones and sand. We trade places; I lead until the incline lessens. In minutes, the top of the fifth step is ours. We pant and pant. We gulp and gulp. After moments, we move off once more. We are at the same pace with James five steps behind.

I see the summit now and know we are almost there.

"Judy, what are you doing here?"

I stop, puzzled. Judy? What?

I turn to confront what must be a new addition to our climbing team. "What'd you say?"

James points to a nearby boulder. "That's my sister sitting on that rock. What's she doing here?"

My altitude haze disappears in an instant. James is hallucinating!

"Okay," I blurt out. "Okay. Sit down and rest. Get some air. Drink some water."

I must determine what to do. I had a fleeting glimpse of my mother near the summit of Aconcagua years before. Her image lasted but seconds and I resumed the climb with no further problems. Sometimes these things are not serious. But sometimes they are serious and signal the onset of cerebral edema. If this is edema, I must get him 1,000 feet lower or he might suffer brain damage or die. I survey things quickly. I must have a way off. He must not die! We cannot retreat by the way we came. Our only hope is the broad northern face. Its topmost boundary is to our right only twenty feet away. Escape means pulling him to the edge and dragging him after me as we descend the thirty-five degree slope all the way back to the Refugio. To our good fortune, I see few large rocks or stones to bar our way as I peer down the immense slope's incline. Its composition is like the ground around Tejos, packed sand, several ice fields, and small stones. At its bottom, the tiny Refugio buildings are faintly in view. Would that we might possess their safety at this terrible instant.

"Please, merciful Lord," is my fervent prayer, "take this cup from me."

My planning for the coming ordeal takes but a minute. I utter one more prayerful request.

"Please, don't let him die. He has a wife and two sons."

When I turn to check on James, he's at my side!

"Bob, let's go. I'm all right."

"What? What? What happened?"

"Don't worry. I saw her on Chimborazo two years ago and I was okay then too."

"No headaches or dizziness?"

"No. We have to go. The top is right in front of us." His pat on my shoulder provides further reassurance that he is well.

What a relief! It isn't cerebral edema. Never was a prayer answered so quickly. Things have changed so rapidly it tempts disbelief. Still, I must be wary and watch him closely. On we go, now with greater urgency. In minutes, we're on the spine of the beast and then its head, with majestic views for miles and miles our just reward. A loud shrieking noise is deafening and we seek its source. It lies thirty feet away at the volcanic crater's opening and is caused by wind blowing from below out through its top in a loud roar. If we had chosen the normal route, how could we climb through the crater mouth in winds like this? As we stare into the pit, James yells that our decision to forsake the normal route was a wise one. How right he is.

PHOTO: A view to the south/southwest. Cazadero is to the right, Nacimiento to the left, and Pissis in the far distance. (Photo 1.23 on the site.)

PHOTO: The author is standing on the Chilean summit of Ojos, an elevation of 22,609'. The summit immediately to the right is the Argentine summit, three feet lower. The border between the two countries runs between the two peaks. In the distance, the Tres Cruces summits rise from the desert floor. (Photo 1.24 on the website.)

He snaps some pictures and then moves over to the summit register[16] to sign his name and turns to offer me the pen.

"No, thanks. I don't sign registers."

"Okay. I'm going down. I feel fine."

I study him carefully as he moves off and feel certain his hallucination was a momentary and unserious occurrence.

"I want to stay a minute more. I'll be close behind you."

PHOTO: The author's self photo on the top of Ojos, looking south. James has just left to begin the descent. (Photo 1.27 on the website.)

Rapture of the heights seizes me and I study minutely the world at my feet. From here high in the heavens the most striking thing is how the few nearby peaks seem shrunk to insignificance. The moment is a profound one for me, for here reside pristine cleanness of mind and happiness. Here reside Dante's nine celestial spheres. I wish he were with me to witness the brilliant coalescence of virtue and integrity that infuse the high places of our earth. He would bestow upon the scene the right observation.

The panoramas in all directions take what little breath I have. On every side, steep inclines fall from the summit towards the farthest reaches below. They fall away so suddenly I feel I am floating above all the world, severed from all earthly relationships, severed from all the earth, severed from all humanity, as if I exist on an infinitesimal island in the vast Pacific Ocean. To the north, low-lying peaks dot the landscape. To the east, Cerro El Muerto (21,286 feet) sits a mile away, with Incahuasi (21,716 feet) farther in the distance. To the southwest,

---

[16] Several peaks in the Chilean-Argentine Andes have such registers.

the five-crested Pissis (22,293 feet) shimmers forty miles distant. What a massif. What a monster. What a challenge. To the west, Tres Cruces and her twin towers thrust to the heavens and dominate their part of the Great Plateau.

I gaze below with waning enthusiasm; my desire is to retreat. I see James fifty feet lower and cast myself over the north face's rim to join him on the withdrawal. The ground is loose in places and this eases the way down. When I stop to heave for more air, I watch him intently for signs of sickness. He was correct about the fleeting nature of his condition, for he moves with more assurance than I do. At times, he descends straight down. At times, he traverses the incline. At times, he slides in the sand. A broad, down-sloping snowfield allows a sitting glissade[17] that deposits us 300 feet lower. It grants a welcome respite to our wearied calves and thighs. His entire descent serves as a magnificent example of high altitude fortitude and mountaineering perseverance.

Farther down the slope, I wander off to the northeast to retrieve my tent and gear from last night's camp. We both reach Tejos by 5 p.m. That evening, over warm freeze-dried dinners, we talk of our day.

"You were stoked today! You gave me inspiration the entire time." I emphasize this with a fist to his fist gesture.

"Well, the rocks on those steps really wore me down. Whose idea was it to climb that route, anyway?" He asks this with that sly grin I have come to know and appreciate when he's facetious.

I chuckle aloud. It was a difficult route, and dangerous too.

"Yeah, it was tough. But it's like you said up there looking into the crater's mouth. Climbing the normal route in a howling wind would have been its own sheer torture."

"Were you scared when I saw Judy?" He asks this in a slightly elevated, slightly hesitant voice, which I take as a mark of deep affection for this woman.

"Well, at first, the altitude slowed my thinking. Judy? What the . . . . Judy? That was my first reaction. When you pointed to the rock where

---

17 A controlled slide down a sand or snow slope.

you saw her, I knew what was happening. As you rested, I planned. I saw my mother on Aconcagua years before, so I had had a similar experience. It was just a slight brain distortion that was not edema. I went to the summit with no further problems. So my concern with you was whether it was something benign or something serious. My plan was to drag you down the mountain if it were serious. Man, it was a relief when you were all right."

I know how lucky we have been today. Matters might have turned ugly and unforgiving.

"And how are you?" he asks.

"I'm fine. I'm weary, but my right temple is normal once more. I didn't tell you about all that, but it's of no consequence now."

On the new day, we depart from Tejos over the open sands rather than the winding road. Small clouds play about, everywhere, above, beside, ever present, inscrutable in their way, impossible to read. Later, a turn to look at the mountain causes me to call James to confirm what I see. The little stream, spawned by the *nieves penitentes* above Refugio Atacama, tumbles down a steep incline and disappears into a large chasm with no pooling of water or exit from the basin. The water must collect in an underground aquifer that supplies Laguna Verde. We're back at Base Camp at 3 p.m. After witnessing a magnificent sunset, we sleep soundly for the first time in a week.

PHOTO: Another memorable Andean sunset. (Photo 1.29 on the site.)

Giancarlo arrives on the morning of the appointed day after spending the night at Laguna Santa Rosa. I ask if we might visit Laguna Verde ten miles away. Both agree and we arrive thirty minutes later in a scathing wind that rakes the entire expanse of the lake. It's a captivating spot for a stunningly beautiful body of water at 14,300 feet. Big peaks are nearby, especially Incahuasi (21,686 feet), just to the south. Warm springs, heated by underground aquifers, feed small pools about the lake's shoreline. The Almagro expedition stopped here for two days before beginning their march to Laguna Santa Rosa over the Great Plateau and then to Copayapu. San Francisco Pass is fifteen miles east from here, the entry point of the expedition. I imagine the ghosts of the Conquistadors and the Indians rising from the sand until the scene fades and I return to the present. We linger for several minutes and then depart for Copiapo.

PHOTO: We leave the Ojos area over the Great Plateau for the return to Copiapo. Barrancas Blancas on the right, Ojos del Salado center, El Muerto to the left. (Photo 1.30 on the website.)

As we jounce along over the uneven packed earth of the road, James turns from the front seat.

"You didn't sign the summit register. Why not? Most climbers sign registers."

"It's just a habit with me. I prefer anonymity."

In truth, I don't want to share my innermost feelings. I believe summit logs are a means of boasting and I don't wish to brag about what I do.

"I understand. I've been out here with you for two weeks and I know you like I know my own self. You think it's a boast."

I can't help but smile at his perception.

"James. You know my one disappointment?"

"What's that?"

"I didn't even get to see your sister!"[18]

At a small hillock overlooking Laguna Santa Rosa, I peer below and the present becomes the past as I portage back in time to 1536, for surrounding the Laguna are thousands of soldiers, Indians, and llamas busy in the various activities of camp life. The stay will be only a few days, since Copayapu and Chile are the intended goals. Pedro de Merida's letter has brought all this to life and I stand in mute witness to a waypoint along the road to the death of the Indian Nations at the hands of the cruel Spaniards. But at the same time, this road is also the way to the birth of Nations. There is much to mourn in the passing of any civilization. Yet, Man is indefatigable in his striving to

---

[18] James recently became a grandfather for the second time.

better himself, and from the dust of a Nation's death springs vibrant new societies like that of present-day Chile. The images fade from view and vanish amidst dust devils playing upon the Maricunga Salar's now deserted face. The quiet land lies once more in silence as we prepare to return to the new civilization bequeathed to the descendants of those early Spanish and Indian participants in one of history's most cataclysmic confrontations.

GOOGLE TOUR: The Tour for this Chapter is available on the site.

PANORAMIO: For this Chapter's photos, select the "Monte Pissis, Argentina" tag on the site.

MOVIE: In the "Watch a Movie" section, the March, 2000 movie provides glimpses of Pissis.

I am not afraid. I know this because I am certain not to see another sunrise, and this bestows a measure of stoic calm.

Our world is a vast manuscript, and those who do not travel read but a sheet.

--From the author's personal climbing journal

CHAPTER 2

Monte Pissis, Argentina: High Winds from Tartarus

PHOTO: Map showing location of Pissis. The Great Plateau is approximately twenty-five miles north from Laguna Negro Francisco. (Photo 2.1 on the website.)

We climb east towards the iron tower marking the Paso Vidal Gormaz on the Chile-Argentina border, the 4x4 truck grinding and growling through the rocks and sand of the high Chilean desert 150 miles east southeast from Copiapo, Chile. The cerulean blue of the sky, unblemished by the thick clouds of the day before, promises that today the peak will come into view.

"There, Roberto! There it is," shouts Giancarlo exultantly over the whine of the engine as the truck crests the incline of the Paso at 15,000 feet. It is March, 1994, and my first climb since I retired from Pacific Telesis, a California phone company. In the distance, twelve miles to the east, rise the five-crested summits of Pissis like a queen's diadem, the afternoon sun of the altiplano providing a golden glint to the stone and ice. I ponder its place among the Andean giants, for it has few ascents. Pissis is one of several mysterious mountains in this remote area of the Andes. Its recently measured height of 22,530 feet[19] is third highest to Aconcagua, Argentina, at 22,834 feet (Ojos del Salado, at 22,609 feet,

---

[19] The Shuttle Radar Topography Mission (SRTM), conducted in 2000, recorded the height of Pissis as 22,293 feet.

is second highest). A Polish expedition in 1937 made the first ascent by way of the northeastern slopes.

"I don't recall an attempt from the west, Giancarlo." My own words thrill me. Is my journey the first solo ascent by way of the western walls of one of the great peaks of the Andes? It seems possible. As I continue to view the giant peak, my overpowering desire is that I might stand upon the highest of those five summits.

We drive east toward the mountain; though ridges and small peaks block its view, my compass verifies our course. After driving an hour, we come to a wide, flat area. My altimeter indicates 15,900 feet. From here I can see the northwestern terraces of the mountain two miles in the distance. There are several small snow patches near at hand and, though it is high for a base camp, the site seems ideal. "Here, Giancarlo. This will be my home."

In an hour, we have off-loaded all the gear, agreed upon Giancarlo's return eleven days later, and hugged one another goodbye. In moments, his dark blue truck is out of sight, swallowed by the necrotic waste and emptiness of the desert, leaving me utterly alone. I can't suggest in simple words the feeling of my complete and total isolation and how it thrills me. It takes its tenor from the stillness of the land and shares something of the soul of that silence. Climbing alone is, for some, to tread upon the outer fringes of sanity. It is an experience and challenge beyond today's living. Daring to do the improbable brings peace of spirit and deep satisfaction. As a solo mountaineer, I am not one who has lost his reason. Such a man as I have lost all **but** his reason.

That late afternoon, I prepare for the usual night on a big peak. A thin foam mattress, to protect my back from small pebbles, lies on the tent floor. I place over it a light air mattress and then throw my sleeping bag on top. Next, I remove my boots and replace my two pairs of socks, one thin, the other heavier in weight, with dry pairs. I put on my climbing suit pants, for extra warmth, and a balaclava to protect my head and face. I am now ready to melt snow and boil water for my evening meal. At bedtime, I don an extra jacket and place the foot of the sleeping bag in my zippered windsuit jacket for more warmth during the cold night.

I wonder about this peak. What have other mountaineers encountered here through the years? I would like to know their successes and their failures. But I know absolutely nothing. This enormous peak is an enigma and its secrets shall remain a secret until my discovery. I don't know how long it will take me to climb it. As with any peak, at this altitude and with the weight on my back, it depends on snow conditions, my physical condition, the occurrence of winds and storms, the degree of acclimation I achieve, the quality of sleep at night. So many things can go wrong. But I always seek to stay positive.

It snows the first night, but the storm retreats in the early morning hours. An endless expanse of white, like an ivory-colored tablecloth, drapes the landscape. New fallen snow melts and evaporates quickly in the Andean altiplano's arid climate, but this heavy load will last several days. I feel the journey has begun. With this climb, I have launched myself into what one must call an "expedition." This is a large term for climbing high peaks far from home, where one needs a fair amount of determination and organization just to reach their vicinity, let alone hope to reach their topmost heights.

PHOTO: Looking north from Base Camp after the first night's snow storm. (Photo 2.8 on the site.)

The next two days in camp help my body begin the adjustment to the higher elevation. I always spend three nights at Base Camp before making double carries to a Camp I, double carries to a Camp II site, and the single carry to Camp III. The day following is summit-day. Climbing in this way allows my body to adjust gradually to the higher altitudes. I have set my Base Camp at a high elevation since it was the only suitable terrain we identified on the drive in. Not only that, on the approach to the peak we stayed the first night in some abandoned mining buildings at 13,700 feet, also high for the first night. I pay for these choices with constant headaches until the third night, when they mercifully loosen their grip upon me.

As I revel in the obscurity of my new home, I shrug off the comforts of civilization and my soul feels the better for it. There is unremitting peace here, so high above the everyday lives of most people, preoccupied as we are with daily pursuits that do little for the welfare or wellness of our souls. A vast amphitheater of tranquility and silence, save for the wind's soughing about nearby rocks and ridges, enwraps me, inviting me to an afternoon of soothing contemplation. The quiet is so quiet, the still so still, it seems I can hear myself think. In my yearning for solitude, I have thought long and hard about its appeal. Perhaps my years in Catholic seminary, the discipline, the isolation, the long hours spent alone, the long hours spent in prayer, the long hours spent in silence, configured my personality to seek seclusion and quiet.

Next day, the first day of fall here in the Southern Hemisphere, I seek to reach the next camp. The altitude punishes every step, for progress is agonizing to 17,600 feet. There I choose a flat area near a snowfield for Camp I and drop food and gear near a bristling field of *nieves penitentes*, the toothed ice formations that thrust skyward. The northern crown of Pissis, the highest of its summits, is barely visible from this spot, the bulk of the peak hidden by ridges of rock and sand behind camp. The return to Base Camp is uneventful.

After twelve hours, I resume the climb carrying all my remaining gear to Camp I. It starts to cloud over at noon and, the tent up, a deep rumble reverberates from low peaks nearby. At first it is only a silent, dark squall, but soon it devours half the sky and then the whole, swallowing all the Milky Way. Nothing remains of the entire Galaxy, except the dark, the fury, the apocalyptic. Enthralled as I am by the crescendoing thunderclaps and bursts of lightning flashing to the west, I fail to pay attention to the increasing danger. Because my camp resides in the open, it's in a position to receive a direct lightning strike. I gather everything metallic, shove them inside my pack, and fling it thirty feet off. The flashes and thunderheads move closer, and my stomach involuntarily tightens. I don't recall ever being in the open when lightning was playing about, and I don't wish to experience it now. I feel my isolation, my vulnerability. Oddly, there are no winds to accompany this maelstrom, just the booming and the flashing. While I continue to stare, a tremendous bright burst hits ground 200 yards away, searing my sight. My muscles constrict. I expect my tent, my Baby Blue, to be the next target. My favorite psalm, "The Lord is my Shepherd . . .," is upon my lips. It has been my comfort since the Marines. When it starts to snow, the thunder ceases and the lightning leaves off. The main storm has moved in.

Snow dances against the walls intermittently until midnight, with morning bringing clear skies and my resolve to push to a Camp II site. I depart from my normal routine of two carries to the next camp and decide to make a single haul to it. My acclimation is such that this is worth the risk. Most of the snow has melted by mid-morning and more of the great mountain comes into view the higher I climb. My steps have a spring to them and this liveliness of spirit makes the weight of my pack lighter and more bearable.

But my joy is short-lived. When I reach a ridge at 17,900 feet with the peak suddenly in full view, a large, menacing glacier lies beneath the dark blue sky. It stretches from where I stand to the distant base of the mountain, its expanse riven by a thousand small crevasses gaping in the morning sun. It flows from the north past the western slopes of the peak and through a chasm between it and a subsidiary mountain to its west and to my south. I gaze at it, my mind frozen. I need to cross this white killing ground to find a Camp II high on the flanks of Pissis if I am to have a chance to reach the summit.

PHOTO: The western walls of Pissis, on the left, with the ice field directly in front. Just under the summit of the lower peak on the right is the site of Camp II, where the wind was to flatten Baby Blue, with the author inside. (Photo 2.17 on the website.)

When I start off to cross the wide expanse, the snow is firm underfoot. But I took it for granted, as I soon sink into a soft patch and the surface breaks through at every step. At a farther point, what swims to view but a shark-fin-like undulation that conceals a deep crevasse on its opposite side. I swim by it harmlessly. But I then notice this whitened land is fraught with a school of these deadly fish. I cannot make my way over this threatening morass. One of these creatures will consume me in an instant. Instead, I resolve to climb the nearby peak. The chasm between it and Pissis will reveal the glacier's full extent. If the intervening valley is ice free, an ascent is possible. Darkened clouds envelop the mountain's midsection and drape its flanks in a grey shadow that slowly rotates in a counterclockwise manner. High above the summit, a white blanket of continuous cloud stretching entirely above the mountain is witness to the spectacle far below.

I set off with all my belongings, the slow, slogging steps taking me to 18,900 feet on the subsidiary peak and a place overlooking the space between the two mountains, hard upon the void's precipitous edge. There, with the western slopes of Pissis brooding across the abyss, I understand the truth and see things with a sharpened insight, a clearer understanding. The ice field chokes the chasm and it makes a route impassable. If I cannot reach the mountain, my attempt on its western slopes is at an end. The months of preparation bringing me here seem for nothing. Was it all in vain?

As I remain determined to make a summit attempt, my resolve is to try the normal route, the way of most of the few ascents, on the eastern side of the peak. Giancarlo can take me there when he returns. With this new plan, my disposition brightens and I spend time in pleasant contemplation of the climbing still to come. Later, the setting sun casts an alpenglow on Pissis so intense it throws a blaze across the chasm and sets the rocks at my feet on fire. I watch, very still and very collected. The sun then retreats completely and the radiance subsides with it. To the north, across the vast, empty expanse stretching thirty miles to the string of peaks residing there, my climbing obsessions come to view -- Azufre, Tres Cruces, Ojos del Salado, Nacimiento, Cazadero, and Incahuasi. This part of the Andes is full of extraordinary facts, salars, shallow lakes, exquisite birds and animals, lofty, majestic mountains, high winds, shrieking storms -- eloquent truths speaking to a climber a clear and distinct language. Everything is quiet now, composed. Still, it's a surety of the cruel laws of Nature that Heisenberg's Uncertainty Principle at the subatomic level is certainly true at the atomic, and anything untoward may happen at any second. So I remain wary. I know that one's light burns brightest just before it goes dark.

After gathering soft snow from a nearby bank to melt for my freeze-dried dinner, I stare languidly out the tent door to the east. A sudden gust of wind from the south startles my dreaming and my moment of the spirit vanishes. The wind's abrupt arrival and ferocity surprises me and Baby Blue strains against the stout cords anchoring her to the nearby rocks. Another blast soon follows, accompanied by a deep-throated boom above my precarious outpost. I hear the noise without understanding its meaning. Then, a stronger explosion, this one laden with snowy spindrift barrels across the slopes, blowing a fine ice dust like powdered glass. I zip the tent door closed and feel its blue skin about me, a stout shell of protection from the onrushing darkness and cold. Now the wind is at full throat, a maelstrom of demonic clatter; just minutes before, stillness covered the mountainside in calm and tranquility. The gale shifts and bears in against the west wall of the tent, and I apply my full weight to that side to help absorb the blows. This eases the pressure on the anchor cords that fasten me and all my possessions to the mountain. There is the throb and beat of many pagan drums in this monster, and a deep, heavy tone, like the noise of a thousand marching boots upon the yielding ground. I congratulate myself for the tent's sturdiness. I rigged the parachute cords to solid anchor rocks. It can withstand anything the mountain might throw our way. At least, that is what I tell myself.

PHOTO: Looking north from Camp II. In thirty minutes, all hell broke loose. (Photo 2.20 on the website.)

The night wears on, the wind howling and blowing with a force greater than anything I have experienced on other Andean peaks. Of all the times on all the mountains in all the world these winds choose this mountain for their mischief. Sleep is out of the question. At 10 p.m. I remain seated, propped against the tent wall with my sleeping bag drawn around me for warmth. It is impossible to light the stove to melt snow for my dinner. I can do nothing but push against the monstrous force on the other side of Baby Blue's thin skin. My antagonist is there, and I sense its cold breath against my body, devil-like, implacable, relentless. It seems the embodiment of evil in this life pitted against me for my body, my existence, my very soul. There is something mysteriously personal about a remorseless gale. Avalanches, car accidents, and earthquakes surprise a man in passing. But an enraged wind assaults its victim like a persistent enemy and seeks to run the soul right out of him. And this diabolical thing on the other side seeks me. I feel its hatred for Baby Blue and me in each terrible gust, swung at, punched up, tossed about, flung down, jumped upon.

I cannot rest even for a moment as the fight for life continues. If the wind grips my tiny shelter, we will be hurled over the precipice thirty feet away and down onto the glacier 800 feet below. The hours drag on and I cannot sleep. Heavy punches make my home quake and tremble. At 2 a.m. the gale seems to increase in force and sound, and the effort to continue hanging on weakens me. Yet, I am not alone in the tempest this night, for twice the voices of my wife and daughters call out, their cries so distinct and clear I glance to the door for confirmation of their existences here, their names upon my lips. I call to them, reach out to them. But there is no answer.[20] It takes all my mental and emotional strength to remain calm. I try to forget my discomfort by retreating within myself, trying to ignore time's passage, trying to ignore the paralyzing doubt infecting my resolve.

At 4 a.m., a sense of doom has burrowed into my soul. Twice I burst out, "This is it!" when vicious, pounding blows certainly signal the end. I am not afraid. I know this because I am certain not to see another sunrise, and this bestows a measure of stoic calm. With the last vestiges of vacant energy, in a last prayer of longed-for deliverance, I ask merciful God for merciful deliverance. I have lost the will to carry on, an ignominious abasement for a man who heretofore has been the quintessential high altitude mountaineer to himself. This is no time for questions. This is no time for regrets. Death is close to the hand. Death is close to the touch.

The light of my lamp plays upon the gyrating tent walls and casts everything inside in a grotesque light. This cannot be reality, can it? I

---

[20] No doubt this was an auditory hallucination.

have that clutch in my stomach and electric taste on my tongue one feels when about to die. I feel this will be my last night upon the earth. My life's transgressions parade before me, like desolate figures in an *auto-da-fe* processional. But which sins have led to such a calamity? I beg forgiveness there in the dark, in the cold, amid the cacophony of nature gone berserk and make peace with God and all those I hold dear. I try not to comprehend that I may believe, but to believe that I may comprehend, and I believe that my time is near upon this peak. My mountain speaks to me with the wind as it whistles over the rocks and the sand and the snow. All will be well. I shall remain here forever upon the sacred scree[21] and talus[22] of my high Andean home.

How might I have anticipated it, that one blow to unhinge Blue and me from the mountain? The truth is, there was no warning, what with the unremitting punches pounding our home. And all the while, out there in the inky depths a thousand miles to the south, one mighty Tartarean blow is sweeping across the obliging land, nothing to break its building force and speed as it rushes towards my tiny home. On it comes, like a 4000 hp GE Dash 8 diesel locomotive pulling a 200-car freight galloping across the great Mojave Desert rails seeking California ports to the west, gaining speed with every stride, until it smashes head on into our trembling abode with the crushing weight of half the South American continent as its cargo. The tremendous slam pulls the southern anchor and my shelter collapses inward, briefly sending me airborne, until the remaining anchors hold and keep us from hurtling over the edge into eternity. Everything disappears, even my capacity to think, until all crashes in a heap that causes a burning sensation in my right side. The tent flaps demoniacally in the tempest and sounds like heavy machine gun fire until I gather it about me. And there we lie, without strength, without motion, breathless from exertion. I sense death cheated in his appointed rounds, for I still breathe. As the wind continues to wail, I rest, unable to realize a thought from the mental enterprise of desiring to live. I feel Robert, my Guardian Angel,

---

[21] Sand-like small rock debris.
[22] Rock rubble.

near, and his companionship gives me renewed emotional and spiritual strength.

Later, although the sun is up, the snowless storm still bawls and beats upon our flattened forms. I must escape this place or this place will become my final place. The packing effort consumes an hour in the rampage, but, gear gathered, I begin the retreat down the mountain. I drag my heavy pack over the sand and rocks. On my back, it would serve as a counterweight and permit the avenging gusts to stagger my every step, like a broken, beaten boxer's. At one ugly moment, the determined attacker pushes me to ground and my side and chest ache as I attempt to rise amidst the gusting blows. Mercifully, my stumbles downward leave the monster behind.

On my wearied retreat back to Base Camp, now free from the incessant attacks of the wind, an astounding vision of spellbinding beauty presents itself to cheer my mood. Out to the south lies a stunning plateau of shimmering opalescent splendor, with two small ponds resting at the southern foot of the Pissis flank, one emerald green, the other iridescent blue. Beyond, and across the broad upland's length, Bonete Chico (22,169 feet and fifth highest in the Andes) and Veladero (21,155 feet) thrust their Olympian brows heavenwards. I wrench my Olympus out to record the stunning scene, but the batteries are dead, drained of life. The same occurs with my Ricoh. What are the chances of this happening? But my disposable Kodak, ever faithful, records a picture to be cherished for all my lingering days. I retrieve the small garbage bag at Camp I and continue the lonely slog back to Base, where I'll celebrate my moment of escape from what might have been a cruel fate.

I wait patiently during the days until Giancarlo's return and use some of the time to plan an ascent on the eastern side of the mountain. Perhaps it's possible to drive around the northern slopes of the peak to the eastern side. Or, will we have to retreat to Paso Vidal Gormaz, drive north to Paso Valle Ancho and approach from there? I don't know the answer. Only time will tell.

My rib cage hurts, and each cough, each deep breath, causes a stabbing pain. I consume Vicodin to quell the aching, and the hours drift by in a languorous haze. On our agreed upon date, Giancarlo's truck appears that afternoon on a low ridge to the west. He speeds towards me honking repeatedly, as much to celebrate his own safe passage over a dangerous thirty miles of off-road travel as my continued existence here. I've worried that he would not return ever since he left, and my worry intensified during the inactivity at Base Camp. All I could picture was that something happened to him since he left.

I exult at his return. "Como estas? How are you, my friend?" I shout. We hug in a warm abrazo. "Bien, amigo. I come earlier but I had flat tire. The roads show no mercy, Roberto, and I never feel safe on the altiplano even with two spare tires." He says this with the accompaniment of those wonderfully rich hand gestures unique to Italians.[23] I know the gestures well. My wife's grandparents were born in Italy and her parents use their hands often for emphasis. I've been out here for eleven days without companionship and his company thrills me. Besides, he made me a huge Italian meatball sandwich and I devour it in short order.

We talk about my plans. I remain determined to climb the peak. But the west side is clearly a challenge requiring more reflection and study before I attempt it on a future trip. Later, we decide to drive to the eastern slopes for a try on that side of the peak.

We break camp as the sun peeks over Pissis. I have some drugs in me, but the truck's bouncing and heaving over the rocks still brings occasional jabs of knifelike pain. By early afternoon, we find ourselves below the eastern side of the mountain. The wind roars, and during a stop to add water to the radiator, the truck rocks slightly.

"Let's get to 17,000 feet, Giancarlo." We try, but the slope proves too steep and the rocks too numerous. At 16,000 feet it's impossible to continue. "That is all, Roberto. We cannot go farther."

PHOTO: Base Camp site below the eastern slopes. (Photo 2.25 on the site.)

We throw my gear from the truck. The wind gusts stiffly, its bite sharpened by the cold, and I draw the parka hood more tightly about my face. Giancarlo must leave. The weather is too unpredictable out here

---

[23] There is a small Italian population in Copiapo.

and he has several hours left before he reaches safety. He angles the truck back down the slope and in minutes becomes a tiny blue speck on the landscape, as he proceeds north to Valle Ancho Pass twenty-five miles away. The way to the peak over this pass is much easier on the truck than the Vidal Gormaz Pass we used last week. His parting comment unsettles me, not for the reality of its content, but his initiation of it. "You understand if it snows, it impossible to drive here. You must walk to Mina Marte." The Mina is a South African gold mine forty miles distant and lies to the northwest of Ancho. I feel uncommonly vulnerable once more and my stomach muscles writhe in response. He won't return for another seven days. Am I tempting Fate beyond all prudence?

The wind is not as fierce as it was on the subsidiary peak, but it still slows my efforts as I pitch and anchor Blue to large rocks at each corner. Every movement of my upper body causes stabbing pain in my chest and side. As I recline inside, listening to the wind strafe the rocks and sand and feel the buffets of my tiny home, my thoughts return to the night of terror on the western slopes and an urge to flee rises within me. But run I cannot. My thoughts presently turn to my wife and daughters. What will the rest of their lives be like if I'm no longer by their side? Will my girls do the "right" thing? Will they make the "right" choices? But perhaps I overestimate my influence upon them. Of course they will go on, and of course their lives will move forward, differently than if I were with them, but their lives will move forward nonetheless.

Sleep comes fitfully with these fretful thoughts playing across my mind. A distant rumble vexes the land and a sharp, violent shimmer lights my tent walls and the black visage of the night. The growling increases, with a blustering gale as culmination. But next morning, I awake to quiet stillness. After taking painkillers, I'm on the way by 8 AM, hopeful of setting camp as high above 18,000 feet as possible.

In three hours, I reach 17,600 feet. Rib pains jab more frequently, and every breath brings a stiletto-like stab to my upper torso. At 18,000 feet, a whipping gale from the northeast almost knocks me off my feet three times when it strikes my pack at just the right angle. It becomes increasingly difficult to maintain my balance. My pack acts as a sail, and at one point a wind burst throws me to ground, squarely on my injured side. As I lie there, the blows continue. The cold enters, first my hands, then my toes, and I feel the frosted breath of death try to siphon the warmth of life from me. I'm through. Beaten. The mountain has too many weapons and I have too few defenses. I have no more fight in me. It is time for flight.

Back at camp, within the warm confines of Blue, I reflect upon my journey. I confess a consuming yearning for desolate locations. Our world is a vast manuscript, and those who do not travel read but a sheet. That which perplexes many, being in a remote place their whereabouts unknown, perplexes me not in the least. I revel in the anonymity of my exact location, for I seek adventure.

Day after day, I await Giancarlo's return. One late morning, a tiny shadow on the wall begs for my attention. The image stirs several times and I move outside to examine it. What could it be? There, to my surprise and delight, sits a small cricket, looking perfectly comfortable in the cold, harsh surroundings. She is taking the sun, as it were, just as I. Perhaps blasted here by the fierce winds from lower Argentine elevations, she finds herself deposited at my tent against her will far from home and hearth. She is trying to survive just as I am trying to survive. And what of her family? Do they wish her return, as mine does me? Will they manage without her? Will she return to them whole to help manage their struggles? She is forward and willingly takes my outstretched finger to ride inside my tent. I treat her as my guest and place her in the folds of my fleece jacket, the most sumptuous place at my disposal. Later in the afternoon, bored with my awkward attempts at conversation, she hops into my jacket pocket, perhaps anticipating the cold of the coming night. At supper, I nudge a bit of dried fruit towards her so she might dine on it. She nibbles about the edges until satisfied and then pushes it aside. Afterward, she nestles in my jacket's warmth, protected, as the harsh cold begins to grip our world and my eyes close with her beside me.

The following morning breaks in a brooding sky and my mountain intuition conjures up an impending storm. I don't want another fight with winds that may seek to unhinge me from this side of the peak. I remember my tiny friend, and lean over to push aside the bedroom door so as not to frighten her. Her bed is empty! She left during the night as mysteriously as she arrived during the day, and I miss her.

Later in the day, the sky is darker and more threatening and it mirrors my fretful mood. What if my little friend were an omen, a forewarning of a storm coming my way? Perhaps she precedes a tempest gathering momentum over San Miguel de Tucuman to the east and heading straight for my precarious position here. I shudder at the thought of another hellish ordeal like the one on the western side of the mountain, especially with the pain now wracking my body. On any high mountain, the times are trying or the times are beneficent. At this moment, the times are trying and I feel pushed to the maximum of my physical endurance and psychological well-being.

My thoughts return to my daughters. I wish to write something to them, for I fear an attack by another windstorm that even now seems to be building in the east.

My Dearest Maria and Sarah:[24]

Death is not an easy thing for any of us to understand, but all life one day must end. Remember, only my body dies, but I shall still live. Time may take me but already you have restored it to me. I don't expect you to understand this, but I wish you to remember that the good never ends. If it did, there would be no light left to the world. But the world is full of wonderful life and light. The mountains, the rivers, the heavens are all part of it and we must enjoy them and thank God for them. I pray I might share life with you in the future, but if I do not, watch over your mother. She loves you both with deep and abiding affections. Good luck to you both. And live full and virtuous lives. I love you forever. Daddy.

---

[24] My adopted daughters, Maria Luz from Cuzco, Peru, and Sarah from Pasto, Colombia.

I fold the letter, along with one to my wife, write my address on the back, and place them in the upper pocket of my windsuit jacket. If I survive, they survive. If I perish, perhaps another climber passing this way will find the letters. Meanwhile, the vigil continues. My upper body aches at each cough and move right or left. It may be a punctured lung or a serious muscle tear. The painkillers bring brief relief. There's nothing to do but maintain a stoical nature and endure it. "Offer it up for your sins," the nuns would say. "It will reduce your stay in Purgatory."

Next morning, I witness events of a singular nature. The wan light of the clouded day retreats slowly from the heights above, from the rocks, from the sand, from the snow, as though it leaves reluctantly. For pregnant minutes, nothing in life stirs. Above, the darkened clouds remain impenetrable. On their unmoving surface there is a constant and tremulous phosphorescence. To the east, a fleeting reflection of distant lightning moves towards Blue and me. A gale of hurricane force drives before it a whitened mist of spindrift across the high desert ground. This is the storm presaged by my little companion. But fortune is once more my friend, for the blizzard keeps its distance and never reaches the mountain.

The terrain north of the peak is free of snow since there have been no storms since the night of my first day on the mountain. But what if another storm sweeps in and buries the northern approaches under a blanket of snow? Giancarlo and I already understand what I will do if this happens. I'll walk out to Mina Marte as soon as enough snow melts. It's not much of a plan, but it must suffice.

At last, after seven days of purgatory, my day of rescue arrives. God has been merciful and seen fit to spare the area further storms. Giancarlo has a clear path! I break camp slowly to ease the pain in my chest and side. He will spend the night at abandoned mine buildings near Mina Marte and leave early this morning. He should reach me around 11 a.m.

I peer intently to the north through my binoculars. Ten thirty a.m. There is nothing in view, to my studied gaze, save a great vacancy. Since I can see little detail at this distance, I look instead for flashes of sunlight that will reflect off my friend's truck front window as he maneuvers through the tortured terrain. I must see that flash! It becomes the touchstone of my total absorption and concentration.

When 11 a.m. arrives, but no Giancarlo, my stomach muscles tighten in apprehension. What if something happened to him? He might be comatose, incapacitated, dead. Perhaps he told no one else of my location. Then, something's out there . . . . There is! A flash! I'm sure of it. And again. Several minutes later, another. Like a marooned mariner stranded on an atoll who sees the outline of a rescuing vessel, I exult that luck has now turned to my favor.

I strain to find color, outline, shape, anything to confirm this is Giancarlo. The flashes continue intermittently and reassuringly. But something's wrong. The flashes come from two sources, one from the left and another from the right, at some distance from each other. Color and shape of the objects remain indistinguishable. Try as I might, I cannot tell what is out there. What I see makes no sense. Giancarlo has always traveled alone on our previous trips. Why should he change his routine now? Who it might be, there is no sure means of knowing. It could be an Argentine Army squad patrolling the border. Or maybe a contingent of miners taking readings and examining core samples. Drug smugglers? Other climbers? Whoever it is, I cannot hope to attract their attention this far away.

At a distance of twelve miles, halfway between Ancho Pass and the mountain, their forms appear as two trucks, one dark and the other light. Thirty minutes pass. One truck's color is blue! I'm hopeful. Perhaps it is Giancarlo and a friend along for an adventure. When he left, he drove straight down more than a thousand feet, entered a steep-sided ravine, and then disappeared when it snaked to the west. He reappeared thirty minutes later topping a ridge and driving north towards Valle Ancho.

I watch the vehicles approach with this memory, for they will enter the shallow chasm down below to reach me. Eight miles distant, each truck stands out in sharper detail, with both advancing toward the opening to the gulch. One is white, the other definitely blue, although it is impossible to see it clearly enough to confirm it's Giancarlo's.

Abruptly, the blue truck in the lead veers from its southerly path and angles away from the ravine opening, heading east-southeast and to my right. They're drifting past me entirely! It can only be miners or an Army patrol or climbers or smugglers and not Giancarlo. Something has happened to him! The truth of this entire, vacant affair becomes clear in an instant. I will be left now to my own devices for escape from this place. There's enough gas for the stove, plenty of five-liter water bottles, and sufficient food for a week or longer, but I'll plan to walk out tomorrow while the weather remains favorable. It will demand two days, at least, and the tent, stove, gas, pot, cup, loose food packets, and candy will go with me. I hesitate to leave, since my upper body pains will hamper the sheer physical and psychological exertion the effort will exact.

The trucks creep slowly past the mountain. I still maintain a distant hope they are friends. Soon, they disappear behind a high ridge stretching north to south and are lost to sight. Who are these guys, anyway? I expect their reappearance in twenty minutes. But forty minutes pass. Then, an hour. This is agony! Did they stop for lunch? If they are an Army patrol, perhaps they are firing off their weapons for practice. If miners, perhaps they found the Mother Lode. Who knows?

I begin to despair. The wind returns in short, hard bursts. I scan the ridge incessantly, especially its downward-sloping, southerly side, the point of their expected reappearance. Then, an object bounds over the northern part of the ridge, then another, both cresting it at full speed and heading directly towards me! It's the blue truck, with the white one following closely behind. It can only be Giancarlo, along with a friend. On they come, and my apprehension weakens and dissipates. Even if this is someone else, they must see me.

The trucks stop upon the top of the ridge. Human forms are a thin blur from here, but there is movement. Vague outlines flicker near the trucks, like desert contours distorted by a desert mirage. They must be searching my slope. I wrench my blue tent out and unfurl it; pain shoots through my chest as I wave it. The outlines continue to shimmer in the distance. They don't see me. Why don't they see me? I'm restless and weary from waving my arms and the tent. After several minutes, Baby

Blue slips from my grasp. I grab my expedition bag, seize my cooking pot, and position its bottom to reflect the sun's rays in their direction.

The trucks begin to move once more. They drop off the ridge plateau, descend the slope, and enter a gully and disappear, then reappear minutes later, now at the top of a mound of sand and small rocks. They continue to a point directly below me. Human figures are now clear through my binoculars as they each exit the trucks. They look up towards me, but there is still no recognition whatsoever. Why can't they see the flashes? Why can't they see me? Then, one figure raises his arm and gestures in my direction. Both then enter their trucks and, within seconds, are rushing upslope towards me! I feel a thickening palpitation rise in my throat. An exclamation of thanksgiving runs past my lips as Giancarlo arrives first, his engine screaming in the thin air. He jumps from his truck and strides over to where I sit. I cannot rise because of fatigue and pain.

PHOTO: Rescue! Giancarlo's truck is first up the slope. (Photo 2.31 on the website.)

"How are you, my friend? We come for you. We saw sun flashes and knew exactly where you were."

"I can't tell you how happy I am you're here. There's a sharp pain in my chest. I must see a doctor."

The second truck roars up.

"Roberto, what luck! This man my doctor in Copiapo. He wanted exploration, so he come with me."

Dr. Juan Saavedra introduces himself, in good English, and asks me to explain the problem.

"I want to examine you," he says. "It's warmer in the truck out of the wind. Take everything off above your waist."

"What do you know?" I remark, grimacing in pain. "A doctor who makes house calls in the middle of the Andes!"

"Fortunately, it isn't a perforated lung, so rest easy," he comforts. "You have aggravated muscle or cartilage which will take time to heal.

Stay on your pain pills and avoid upper body movement. You will feel the pain lessen in a week. If it persists, see your doctor at home.

"And where is that, by the way?" he asks.

"A little town, Livermore, to the east of San Francisco, California."

"What a coincidence! I've passed through it several times," he replies. "I got my degree at Stanford University." [25]

My journey at an end and back home once more, I ponder the mountain's gift to me. I went to Pissis as the world's mountaineers of long ago approached their passions, with no literary or photographic record to guide my steps. In this I am truly fortunate, for I climbed with a freshness of spirit rarely known on other peaks. And this brings a momentary reflection upon my solitary craft. Climbers, true climbers, are the strangest of people, their love of the high peaks so enduring it becomes like a religion. And should I go on doing what I do best and what I enjoy the most, then I may say I lived my life to the fullest. One day I will return to Pissis, if only to recapture, once again, that purity of the mountaineering experience.

---

[25] Dr. Saavedra was one of the physicians who examined and attended the medical needs of the rescued miners trapped in the San José mine near Copiapo in October, 2010.

GOOGLE TOUR: The tour for this Chapter is available on the site.

PANORAMIO: Select the "Llullaillaco, Chile" tag on the site.

MOVIE: The November, 1998 movie contains footage of a Llullaillaco climb.

The sky here is absent those silver needles
that weave our world together.

Altitude has a perfidious way of robbing me
of my mental abilities when I don't even know
my pocket is being picked.

--From the author's personal climbing journal

CHAPTER 3

Llullaillaco, Chile: A Case of Mistaken Identity

PHOTO: This is the map we used to find our way to Llullaillaco. (Photo 3.1 on the website.)

PHOTO: Maria Ester and Giancarlo on the verandah of their hotel, La Casona. (Photo 3.2 on the website.)

PHOTO: Giancarlo, on the left, and the author prepare for the ride to Llullaillaco at the hotel. (Photo 3.3 on the website.)

"Be careful, Roberto. It is said that the ghosts of Inca children reside on the mountain."

Maria Ester clutches my forearm to emphasize her point. She isn't trying to dissuade me from visiting the peak, only warning of its dangers other than its altitude, bad luck, and weather. Little do I know my problem is not going to be the sight of immaterial images but the loss of sight of material ones.

The date is November 4, 1994, the time 9 a.m. Giancarlo, my driver, and I are motoring to the seventh highest peak in the Andes, Llullaillaco (22,109 feet), on my first visit to the mountain, the highest known Inca worship site in the highest Andes. I look upon this trip as a birthday present. I'm now 50 years old, and reaching the summit will be a rich gift. There are two small huts on the top, built by Indians 500 years ago, and these make this mountain a precious objective for me.[26] There are many such places residing on high Andean peaks, the Inca's mountains, but this site is singular in its height and composition. We are driving north on the Pan-American Highway between Copiapo and the place we'll turn off to approach the mountain, forty-three miles north of Taltal. A mining friend of Giancarlo's in Santiago suggested proceeding to the gold mine, Mina Guanaco, and asking directions to the peak from one of the supervisors.

Five and a half hours out of Copiapo the turnoff appears on the right, and in thirty minutes we approach the entrance station of the mine. A supervisor offers to drive us to a place where the mountain comes into view and then we're on our own. As we follow him in our truck over a dirt and gravel road, the southerly direction we're traveling causes me some hesitation and I mention it to Giancarlo.

"I think we go south until someplace we go east," he answers.

He's right. A low range of foothills to the east is rugged and high enough to block any view of big peaks that must lie behind them.[27] Thirty minutes later, the road beats southeast and, in another twenty, directly east, which makes me think that matters may run right. Ten miles on, our supervisor friend slows and then stops after rounding a tight curve. He motions to the north, where, perhaps twenty miles distant rises a jumbled mass of molten rock with snowy traceries about its higher flanks. He assures us this is truly Llullaillaco. He also warns Giancarlo to stay on the road. There are several minefields on the wide salar (dry lakebed) between the mountain and Mina Escondida to the northwest, the second largest copper mine in Chile.

"Roberto, give guy cigarettes for help."

---

[26] See Dr. Johan Reinhard's unforgettable books, "The Ice Maiden" and "Inca Rituals and Sacred Mountains," in which he tells of discoveries on Llullaillaco and Ampato, as well as other Andean peaks. As he found out, there are more artifacts than the two huts on the top of Llullaillaco.

[27] This range of low peaks is the Cordillera de Domeyko.

I am happy to do so and even happier when his face lights up in a wide grin as his hand wraps around a full pack of Pall Malls. Giancarlo thanks him and the fellow drives off and waves in farewell.

"Buen suerte, amigos," he shouts over the roar of his truck's engine.

We appreciate the warning about the landmines, although we already know of the danger.[28] Giancarlo says every year the unwary have a truck blown up or, even worse, lose an arm or leg. My gaze fixes upon the mountain with growing concern as we proceed toward its fastnesses. I have no photographs or information upon which to rely. I know of the Inca ruins on the summit, and that is all I know. Our map is the common one found in the Chilean driver's guidebook, "Turistel." It doesn't show the road we now travel, but it does show locations of lagunas, mines, and peaks in the area, as well as the position of our mountain. I shift my attention from the map to the mountain and intently study its contours, its ridges, its summits -- there seem at least two that might qualify as the true summit. We stop to identify the highest point because such a luxury won't exist when I'm on the mountain. A spire to the east appears higher than one to its left or west. We drive farther and a different angle reverses the previous impression. Because landmines might lie anywhere near us, we cannot drive off-road to better survey the peak, so what we see from the road must suffice, and that is none too clear.

Might poor reconnaissance cause problems later? Perhaps, but I push the thought aside as the mountain consumes more of the front window and my attention. The peak, however, is not the sole point of interest; we have seen more guanaco in twenty minutes than on any other trip -- beautiful animals, larger than a deer, with a graceful, galloping stride. We crest a rise at 4 p.m., eighty-two miles from Mina Guanaco, and the tantalizingly blue waters of Laguna Aguas Calientes spread out below us with several dozen flamingoes standing in their characteristic one-legged pose upon its surface. Here

---

[28] The Chile military placed these mines during the Chile-Argentina War, 1978-1982, to protect Mina Escondida from possible capture. Inexplicably, the military has not seen fit to clear the salar of the danger they pose.

at 11,900 feet, the altitude sometimes tricks the eye and brain in indescribable ways. The water shimmers in the last rays of the molten sun as it prepares to drop behind the surrounding hills, and this causes a mirage-like effect that distorts the images of the large birds on the lake's surface. Horizons and distant mountains meld with the sky or each other, one can't say precisely. The mighty mountain sentinel, Llullaillaco, rising in the east, sees all, rules all, in a world it has governed for thousands of years.

On the eastern side of the Laguna dance images of abandoned buildings. It's the old borax mine Giancarlo's friend said we would find here. It will be our lodging for the night. Its wood frame structure is a continuous run of one-story rooms; the first has a bunk, mattress, and old notebooks probably left by the mine supervisor. Next to an old, but still useable, typewriter, a notebook displays a date of November, 1932. The next room seems to have been a food preparation area, the one adjacent obviously a small dining room. The enclosure after that is the head, which contains several separate shower stalls. The remainder of the construction comprises one room resembling a lounge, with bookcases on the walls, followed by five rooms, several with two bunk-bed racks, as well as mattresses, pillows, and even several blankets. All this fits our needs perfectly. Thankfully, it's quiet and still here; the silent, low mountain walls that rim the lake block the bothersome winds sweeping the altiplano.

As we unpack the truck, something occurs so swiftly we know it only when it's gone. A jet's scream startles the hushed land, the perpetrator streaking over us and then over the mountain, traveling east. There are no commercial air routes in this part of the Andes, so it's either a private jet or a military one on a secret mission. Neither of us has ever heard this modern noise of civilization in the mountains before. The sky is always absent those silver needles that weave our world together.

PHOTO: The abandoned borax mine. Giancarlo is knocking. "Anyone home?" (Photo 3.8 on the website.)

Terrible headaches from the altitude bother me during the night while Giancarlo sleeps like a baby. They leave off finally in early morning as we stir to begin the drive to a base camp. As we pack the truck, the morning sun's rays strike the higher slopes of surrounding peaks and my attention meanders south to a scene of singular interest. Cloudlets appear to dance near the summit of a mountain there, at about 15,000 feet. The more I stare, the more I learn; it's clearly a small volcano puffing steam bursts into the frosty air. Giancarlo recalls his friend mentioning this peak and we both thrill to its captivating wonder. Its name, Lastarria, rolls from the tongue with an enchanting sibilance, one of those words one wishes to hear again, and so it trips over my lips repeatedly.

PHOTO: Steam rises from Lastarria to the south. (Photo 3.9 on the website.)

As we drive the land searching for a road, we eventually discover a faint track heading higher and follow it over ground that alternates between small rocks and shallow sand. We feel like drifters on the earth before epochs began, traveling over land like that of a distant planet's. At 14,600 feet on a broad, sweeping slope rising gently toward the mountain, a comfortable spot offers itself as a base camp home. There is no snow here, but I've brought enough water from town. Gear bags, food, and water jugs off-loaded, Giancarlo and I perform our ritual of both writing down the pickup date, eleven days hence, and each gives the other his slip of paper. It's 9:30 a.m., so he ought to reach Copiapo by 5 p.m. His truck vanishes into a shallow ravine at the slope's edge and disappears from sight. I see a visual image one moment, accompanied by the engine's roar, and then the next moment merely the somber land and complete silence. His going happens so fast as to cause bereavement, and is all rather dramatic, in a romanticized way. Amidst the enormous vastness of the terrain, I am the only soul in this immense mountain empire. A brief breath of a breeze moves gently over the slope. Then all is still once more.

As soon as he leaves for the return to his world, back to Copiapo, I begin getting into my world, into the mountain. The routine remains the same on every peak -- my withdrawal to a private world of climbing fantasy. Now that I'm alone, things begin to come together -- the altitude, the situation, the surroundings. I have to leave my everyday persona back in the world and become a different person in my mountain world. Above all, I have to get into the solo groove, a place for me alone, where no one else may follow. It's just me out here, and I must either cut it and make it, or not and lose it. I have to get jacked up. Not the lunatic, raving, uncontrolled jacked up, but the calculating, cold, cool, quiet, stoical kind of jacked. No one can read me from the outside, but on the inside I am always one tightly focused individual in the mountains.

At noon, with camp in place and Baby Blue firmly anchored, I examine the mountain and my new neighborhood. The summit is out of view, blocked by intervening gendarmes[29] and high ridges. But a route reveals itself lower on the peak, at least to a possible Camp I and, higher, a Camp II, both determined by nearby snow patches I can see. Past Camp II, the route is unclear. As for my present location, to the right a humped tongue of lava ooze ends on this slope, perhaps a quarter mile from my home.[30] Its jagged, jumbled rocks immediately rule it out as a passage upwards. Farther to the right, past the lava flow, the ground rises at a sharp angle and presents an astonishing sight. One hundred or so small pennant-like flags flutter in the breeze. Landmine markers? An involuntary shiver of recognition runs down my spine. With two more days here to acclimate, there's enough time to confirm it.

A casual stare to the west and north confirms the immensity of this part of the Atacama Desert. It begins at the Pacific shoreline, ninety miles away, and rushes east, bounding over Andean plateaus and ranges, gradually rising until it slams headlong into the mountain massifs and their unyielding slopes. The vast mass of sand and earth has a personality all its own. The desert is splendid in its smiles, alluring, brash, irrational, irresponsible; a thing to love, a thing to hate. It casts enchantment, lures

---

[29] A gendarme is a pinnacle of rock on a mountain ridge or slope.

[30] This may be the result of the last eruption, in 1877.

one to unlimited trust, permits pleasure, then suddenly turns sour and unforgiving, its cruelty balanced by the magic of its immutable mystery, by the boldness of its pledge, by the ultimate pledge of its possible goodness. Some, like me, with a youthful discernment of nature and human nature, fall prey to its fascination, reconciled to live by its mercy or die by its will.

Within an hour, my headaches return. My pulse is 80 as my body struggles to acclimate. There is little to do but take aspirin, drink liquids, rest, and suffer. Later, stiff winds quickly rise in force and noise. They beat up from nothing, hastening in from somewhere. The howling continues through the night and disrupts my sleep. I'm wary of movement and lie stretched out in my bag listening to the incessant poundings of wind against Baby Blue. At times, I think the night might never end. The noise leaves off in the early hours of the new day, as do the headaches, and this provides brief hours of respite. Then, over the lofty battlements of the main summit, a faint flush of light strikes the night sky. There are still stars above, but they soon go dim. It is a new day upon the mighty Llullaillaco.

I decide to explore the slope where my home resides, and a two-hour excursion confirms the existence of the landmine field. It lies below a low pass through which tanks and armor headed for Mina Escondida could pass. The field is some 200 feet wide and 100 feet deep, with pennant flags of white and red marking each individual mine. I can't count them all, but there are at least 100 indicating the positions of the silent, unseen assassins below. I become nervous standing near this killing ground and move off for the safety of my camp.

Back here at home, I check with my small binoculars for a possible route and verify yesterday's inspection. A site for Camp I is visible, at an elevation of around 17,000 feet. Above it, the ground steepens markedly. It will be tough to put a Camp II on it. Still, I must find a way. And, what of the route from there? The slope ends several hundred feet higher on what might be a flat plateau or table. At this distance, I can see half the route and it looks to be climbable. The rest is a mystery and will remain so until I set foot upon that plateau, if indeed that is what it is.

ertainty of it all is part of my motivation for being here -- to
e unknown. It's new. It's exciting. And it's completely upon
a way to the summit. I know I can do it.

By early afternoon, the winds blast up -- the implacable winds,
tormentor of waking moments and destroyer of dreams. Yesterday
they blew from the northeast. Then, late at night, they burst in from
the southeast. Now they're barreling over the land from the northwest,
laden with warm air. In fact, inside Blue a light T-shirt is all I need
for comfort. My pulse is down to 62 and the headaches are now a
memory. Late at night, the winds hurry off and leave a few light
breezes behind.

The next day, I prepare for the first haul to Camp I, a light load
compared to the second day's carry. There isn't much weight -- seven
freeze-dried meals, one heavy fleece jacket, the ice ax, assorted snack
foods, gas, and anything else unnecessary for the night I will spend
back here at Base. This is but a brief exercise, and I have plenty of time
to reflect that my being out here is a tenuous affair. You can lose your
path any number of ways on a journey to the top, sometimes believing
the mountain gods are playing whimsical tricks, negating all you know
and understand about your climbing craft and making you think that
someplace, far away, perhaps in a parallel universe, resides your real,
knowing self. Will I lose my way on this climb? I feel confident I shall
remain on course.

The stars have wavered and been put to flight with dawn reddening
the sky when the sand feels my weight on the path to a Camp I over
the gently steepening grade. At 11:30 a.m., I find a suitable place near
a sheer snow incline. The elevation is only 16,500 feet, but it's the best
I can manage since the slopes immediately higher are too precipitous
for a site. That part of the climb will be over difficult ground, but I
trust that with my mountaineering skills I will find a satisfactory site
for the next camp. My personality allows me to remain optimistic in
the mountains. After fifteen minutes, I'm off for Base Camp and inside
Baby Blue at 2:30 p.m.

The following day, the second carry to Camp I takes longer than
the first, since on my back are Blue, sleeping bag and air mattress,

stove, two liters of water, and other items. There is also the aggravation of the high altitude cough, caused by the dry air at altitude, a hacking, wracking affair that pursues me up and down a mountain. As if that were not enough, a head cold I contracted at Base Camp causes labored breathing and mild discomfort. Once I reach camp and Blue is up, the rest of the day offers a chance to rest; tomorrow the journey to Camp II will present serious hardship. I stare at the route and take its measure; crampons will be required to deal with the snow slope, canted at thirty-five degrees and rising several hundred feet. Above it, there is little in view from here, and that will provide a test of my route-finding ability. Llullaillaco is demanding and will test all my mountaineering skills. I revel in the challenge. This entire affair hearkens back to the classical age of Andean mountaineering, when Whymper first climbed Chimborazo (20,702 feet) in 1880[31] and Mattias Zurbriggen, on the Edmund Fitzgerald expedition, made the first ascent of Aconcagua (22,834 feet) in 1897.[32] I feel like those early Andean explorers must have felt when they approached a mountain for the first time.

In the early evening, after forty minutes to melt snow, freeze-dried lasagna brightens my mountain disposition. A slight headache causes me momentary concern, but it retreats soon enough when my heart rate wanders down towards normal. When I lay out the gear for my first carry to Camp II tomorrow, I realize instantly that I have committed an error: I failed to bring my thick pile jacket up here, and it remains back at Base Camp. The altitude has altered my ability to think clearly, for the jacket appears on my list of items for a first carry. How could I miss it? I resolve to be more attentive from now on. Although the climate around this peak is warmer than the weather on the mountains to the

---

[31] For the story of this expedition, consult "Travels Amongst the Highest Andes of the Equator," by Edward Whymper (1892), by numerous publishers. The author climbed to the summit by the normal route in 1988.

[32] See "The Highest Andes" by Edmund Fitzgerald (1899), with limited editions over the years. The author reached the summit in 1991 by the challenging Polish Glacier Route.

south, like Pissis, I will still have need of extra warmth the higher I go. Nevertheless, I decide to push on for the present.

First light greets the new day in a clear sky, and all seems well for the first carry to Camp II. I'm wearing my full, bright red windsuit with bib overalls and jacket because it has turned colder. Twenty minutes out of camp, the bottom boundaries of the snow slope yield to the teeth of my crampons. Because of its steepness, I cannot climb straight up but must use the traverse technique, weaving back and forth across the incline's expanse. At the top of this obstacle, my altimeter registers a gain of 500 feet, and I have felt every foot. Since I'm off the snow and ice, I remove my crampons. I'm now back in a rock and sand gully that requires the grueling effort of moving three steps higher and sliding back one step. A stiff, freezing wind blasts in from the north and hits my pack as if it were a schooner's sail. My climbing poles provide a measure of stability, but I can't remain too long at this. My strength is wasting away. Presently, two gullies stand before me. The one to the right contains patches of snow. The one to the left is the extension of the sand and rock torture chamber I'm in now. Which couloir[33] should I choose? An inveterate high altitude masochist, my choice is for more torture. I move off to the left because I wish to avoid the snow.

Meanwhile, dark, threatening clouds block the sun. I struggle upwards until I reach a snow patch at 18,300 feet, a suitable spot for Camp II. I drop my sack with food and gear inside and weight it with rocks. I then cautiously begin the descent to Camp I. An exhilarating, sitting glissade down the snow slope outside camp has me home at 12:30 p.m. The gathering clouds obscure the mountain above Camp II as the high winds up there disturb hearing down here.

At 4:30 p.m., the storm still rages above. Then, sudden winds pull and twist Baby Blue as the tempest engulfs more of the mountain. If this continues tomorrow, it will prevent the second carry to Camp II. And all my food, except tonight's dinner, is up there, which means a stay here a day or two with two candy bars and a slice of fruit cake. Of

---

[33] A mountain gully.

course, I could go back to Base, retrieve more food and my jacket, and return here to wait things out above.

There's no lessening of the winds during the night and no means of telling what is happening higher. My feverish reverie imagines the cries of children in the cries of the wind, perhaps bemoaning their life's end here, just as Maria Ester warned me. Then, at 4:30 a.m., all becomes calm until dawn arrives. The shrieking winds have ended here at Camp I, yet above, the Camp II site remains in thick clouds. This determines my course of action -- to use today to retreat to Base Camp, get a night's sleep, my heavy jacket, and more food, and then return here to Camp I tomorrow and wait things out.

The journey down proves uneventful, except my strength begins to ebb as the lack of sleep exacts its toll. By the time I reach Base Camp, the weather turns to my favor as the clouds lift from the mountain and it becomes bathed in the warm, golden light of an alpenglow sunset. In minutes, the darkened gold of the mountain's rocks and sand becomes a fiery mass of flame. From this moment on, I will know Llullaillaco always as my "Flaming Mountain."

PHOTO: Alpenglow on the western walls of Llullaillaco, with a full moon above. (Photo 3.11 on the site.)

As the sun's rays retreat from the heavens, I hope to witness the Green Flash, a rare emerald green light that appears briefly above the setting sun as it sets. At this altitude and with the air so clear, the chances seem favorable. But it does not appear. During the long night, deep sleep never comes, but there is reward in short snatches of dream-like drifts as the night proves still and tranquil.

The new day arrives cloudless and windless, and my plan now is to proceed from Base through Camp I and reach Camp II, there to wait and see if the weather holds. This time, I have my warm jacket and two more meals to supplement my stash at Camp II. It will be physically demanding to climb all the way back that high, but I feel mentally and physically strong.

I arrive at Camp I in mid-morning and load the gear there for the higher camp. The climb proves a challenge as my strength begins to fade when the apparent area of Camp II comes in sight. When I get there, however, I can't find the gear I left only days before, a further indication of high-altitude-induced confusion. After a ten-minute search, I finally locate everything and secure Baby Blue within an interesting rectangular setting of rocks and boulders that offer protection against the hardest wind blows. The calm here and above provide me a slim measure of hope. I'll haul a single load to a Camp III tomorrow if the weather remains calm. I take a brief moment to mark today's accomplishment -- a 3,700 foot elevation gain with my heart rate now at 70 and no headaches. This cheers and lightens my disposition. My thoughts turn homeward to my wife and daughters. This is the seventh day out here and I miss them. Is my younger one still having problems with her math? I can't help even when I'm at home. That new math is a mystery to my wife and me!

After a dinner of freeze-dried spaghetti, I assess my progress so far. It's true I'm here at Camp II with enough days left to reach the summit before Giancarlo returns. But the constant intrusion of the wind sets me on edge; my high altitude intuition tells me that something is soon to happen. I have learned to be extra careful at these times. My mountain instinct is always right.

I'm tucked warmly within my sleeping bag when, without warning, a howling wind rushes across the slope and rips and tears at Blue and me. The uphill side of the tent receives the worst pressure despite the protection the nearby rocks afford, so I lean against that side to reduce the strain on the anchors. The screaming and howling bring to mind the Pissis climb seven months before, and a cold sweat of remembrance dampens my face. On it goes through the night, seeming to last weeks, months, my antagonist pushing from the outside against my feeble resistance from the inside. If the situation turns more ominous, I will have to collapse the tent to cut its profile to the wind. What would it be like if this were an open position, without the scant safety of the low wall of rocks around Blue and me? I can only imagine.

The terror leaves off at 5 a.m.; the quiet provides several hours of fitful dozing. I keep asking myself if that was my intuition yesterday afternoon warning me of the night's winds. If so, I hope that was its only message. Sound sleep is a rarity on any peak at any altitude, and so far I have had little. I can ask if I'm asleep even as I'm bright-eyed awake. I hear everything, the faintest rustling of Blue from the wind or the gentle dusting of falling snow against her thin walls. My eyes are wide open, covered by the lids, yet I see the whole thing notwithstanding. There is scant pleasure from sleep at high altitude; even a quick nod brings little satisfaction.

At 9 a.m. all is silence and stillness. The winds and storms have left the mountain, and the moment is favorable for the single trip to Camp III with all my belongings. The fact that the weather has been so capricious and unpredictable causes me to hasten my preparations. This window of fair weather may close quickly with the approach of a fresh storm. My pack, which contains all I need for the higher camp, is so heavy that lifting it to my shoulders requires two maneuvers. The first is to the right knee, a bench formed with my bent right leg, and from there, over the right shoulder and onto my back. A quick survey of the route upwards confirms what I already know -- it will demand resoluteness the entire way.

I set off up the thirty-five-degree angled scree and talus slope. Now the rhythmic battle for the heights begins. At this elevation and with this weight on my back, I count out six steps. I rest and then count out six more. But the slope is so steep this is too taxing. Next I count out three steps, and rest, three steps and rest, and I keep this up the remainder of the way up the incline. I do not allow myself to stop and sit, for that will destroy the rhythm upwards and to begin it again will require too much effort. At 19,000 feet, the top of the slope is directly above me and ready to reveal its secrets.

The summit comes to view before I reach the crest of the incline. When I finally gain the top of the slope, I slump forward onto the edge of a large snow plateau. Much of this side of the mountain is now in sight. The table upon which I rest stretches nearly 300 yards north to south and 200 yards east to west. Upon its surface, a navy blue pond sparkles in the rays of the day's sun and breaks the monotony of the flat terrain. To the extreme right, or south, the northern flank of the lava flow rises 150 feet above the plateau before it plunges over the rest of the mountain and down to the plain where my Base Camp sits. I can't see the source of the jumbled rocks of lava, but it appears to lie behind the main summit to my front. And on the eastern side of the top reside the Inca buildings I wish so fervently to see.

On the ice table are several spots bare of snow with large rocks nearby that are potential sites for my camp. Since wind and storms rake the peak, those rocks are necessary anchors against the merciless wind. After I locate a suitable place and tether Baby Blue, a quick assessment of my personal condition is encouraging -- no headaches and my pulse rate is dropping closer to normal. Not only that, there's no wind and not a cloud in sight. This could change in a heartbeat, but now things are perfect for a summit attempt tomorrow.

I scan the mountain and plan a route to the top. But it seems the summit isn't far enough away. From here at 19,300 feet to the top at 22,109 feet should be a difference of 2,809 feet, but it seems closer than that. Perhaps the altitude distorts what I see. Or, it could be that the true summit is not in sight from here. Then, too, perhaps this is not the main summit. But that's absurd, I tell myself. How might it not be the true top of the mountain that I see? This kind of uncertainty is not dismaying. In fact, it is one of the attractions of high altitude mountaineering for me.

PHOTO: A look down upon the ice plateau from high on the subsidiary peak. In the distance, the southern Atacama Desert, one of the driest places in the world, stretches away to the west. (Photo 3.21 on the website.)

The excellent weather continues into the evening and through the night, and there are several soft and gentle minutes of grateful repose. I awake and prepare for the day in the dark and leave camp with the steady light of my lamp guiding my steps. Dawn spreads her welcome with pinkened rays, until a golden mantle of light covers and warms the frigid land. As I slog higher, the lava flow appears below and reveals more of its extent but not its source. Perhaps an eruption eons ago blew the top off the mountain, leaving behind this fragment now bearing my weight. My attention turns to the beauty of the ice plateau far below, the blue waters of the pond glittering in the thin mountain air. Despite the sun's clarity, it remains a frosty morning. The temperature is twenty degrees Fahrenheit. But absent a wind, the cold lacks teeth.

By 10 a.m., I'm approaching the summit, for in the near distance there's a gradual lessening of the incline's angle. It's close. Very close. And the Inca huts. They reside under the high point, some sixty feet below it on the eastern side. Inca fever runs hot. The summit is secondary; to see the small structures is my consuming passion. How did the Indians build them here, at over 22,100 feet, close to 500 years ago? A few more moves over angled rocks and I'm on the top, thus disproving Zeno's *Dichotomy* by action rather than by logic.

Argentina should stretch out before me to the east. But there is something unreal about the scene. The eastern view is incomplete, for a huge massif across a steep-sided canyon partially obstructs sight of the eastern horizon. I don't understand. What is that peak doing there? And where are the Inca buildings? Below me are not huts but a rock-lined gulch separating me from the other summit. Is this a cruel joke by the mountain gods upon a mountaineering simpleton? If it is, they must be enjoying themselves immensely at my expense. I'm standing upon the highest point on this mountain. How might an additional peak, higher than mine, exist here? I stare mutely at the scene until I comprehend what has happened. The summit I stand on is a subsidiary of the main one! And the other peak is definitely higher. A check of my altimeter shows 21,000 feet.[34] The high point of the peak opposite therefore is at least 800-1,000 feet higher. This confirms that it's the true top at 22,109 feet.

PHOTO: The true summit -- so close yet so far away. (Photo 3.24 on the website.)

---

[34]   The author recently found out that the sub-summit altitude is 21,395 feet.

I feel brief disappointment, both for failing to reach the real summit and see the huts and for failing to perform an adequate reconnaissance. It was the landmines on the approach that prevented me from doing so. But, the stunning panorama brightens my mood. The view from here is stupendously vast to the north, the southern and eastern views partially blocked by the major summit. There are no high peaks to the west, but in the northeast are several of modest height. Almost ten miles distant is Zorritas, at 14,000 feet. Twenty miles out is Guanaqueros, 16,833 feet. And barely in view, thirty miles in the distance, is Volcan Socompa, 19,849 feet.

I shift my attention to the features below and now see that the lava flow does have a beginning, a place underneath the true summit's high point. I take the time to study it all with mental notes and camera shots -- the plateau, its extension south towards the flow, the depths below my precarious perch, planning, plotting, preparing for a return one day and a new summit bid. It's a valuable occasion, since captured within my mental images and those of the camera are answers to questions as to how to reach the summit over the western slopes on a future trip.

I turn to go. The route down is in the sand and loose rocks that caused me such agony on the way up. It proves just as tiring, since seldom-used leg muscles take most of the strain. During a brief pause, a glance upwards notes four large cloud masses, like ghost riders of the sky. They float down from the north in a box-like configuration, one mass at each corner. These formations are recent, since they were nonexistent when I was at the summit. It's now a race to get to Camp III before the enemy strikes. My luck holds once again as I reach the plateau at 2 p.m., but the cloud box is now a single blackened mass of ominous size. It lightly touches the mountain's shoulder in a sign of the danger to come. At 4 p.m., clouds envelop the tip of the subsidiary summit while the remainder streams out to the south. There are no winds to accompany this new threat, yet I view it with dreaded anticipation, since it's the nature of things that such clouds carry all manner of airy bursts and gusts. Baby Blue and I are vulnerable on this naked ice table, which has few natural barriers to high winds racing across its surface.

I recall the steps necessary to collapse my home and lessen its profile to the wind, in case I need to do so.

I endure the long night, certain the clouds above the mountain will spawn deadly winds and heavy snow. I'm aware of occasional stirrings above, sporadic low, brief rumbles and the sound of breezes hurrying past rocky outcrops. Thoughts of violent winds devouring Blue and me capture my mind and disturb me through the long night. Then, during passing moments, I'm the quarry of a languorous indifference, not caring if the winds return, the product of an enfeebled, stressed-out psyche. But the winds never appear.

As the dawn ushers in the new day, all is calm and still. As I stare out the tent door, a wonderful brightness bathes all on the plateau in a warming radiance, the sky a marvel of purity, a marvel of sapphire. The pond sparkles like a polished stone, and its transparent clarity provides me a moment of intense, visual pleasure. The tent door faces east. I stare at the brightened scene and linger over coffee and fruitcake in languid, stilled minutes of silent recollection.

My thoughts return to my climb of the subsidiary summit. How careless of me. The reconnaissance of the peak was incomplete. I take pride in being the complete mountaineer, whose skills include knowing how to ascend a mountain in the most efficient manner by the most efficient route. And I have failed, this trip, to display the proper level of route-finding capability. Of course, I have the excuse that the landmines on the approach prevented a closer study of the mountain's characteristics. But that provides a shallow comfort. Yet there is a measure of accomplishment, since this was undoubtedly the first solo ascent of the subsidiary summit, and that is a soothing reward for my errors.

My reverie ends when I realize I haven't put on my mirrored sunglasses that protect my eyes from the intense rays of the sun reflecting off nearby ice patches. That made right, it's time to withdraw from the mountain. This part of Llullaillaco is a wondrous place. It is also a dangerous place. As my boots hurry me home, there's a twinge of reluctance to depart, but also a great relief to go. Retreat from a mountain is a struggle of a business, made so by the need to lug all I own in one carry. After a wearying six hours, I reach Base Camp at 4 p.m. My thoughts briefly return to Maria Ester. I hope she will be happy I have failed to encounter apparitions of dead Inca children.

Later that night, I eagerly anticipate the return soon to Copiapo and the next day home to my wife and daughters and feel a pleasant, satisfying happiness. Then, without warning, there are burning, stabbing pains in both my eyes! It comes on so abruptly, I cannot understand what is happening to me or why. Every flicker of the eyelids feels like sandpaper to my eyeballs. Tears stream down my cheeks. The light from my headlamp burns my eyes, and only their closure grants relief. Within moments, I recall the cause: this morning on the plateau, I looked out the door without sunglasses. The sun's rays worked off the snow and ice directly into my unprotected eyes and produced the condition feared by every high altitude mountaineer: snow blindness! I can't see! I'm blind, here in one of the remotest parts of the high Andes. The electric taste of fear courses through my mouth. I haven't felt that since the Marines. My exposure to the sun's rays was less than thirty minutes. But that was enough. No doubt the altitude affected my judgment and I forgot to put on my glasses. I committed a mortal sin in my mountaineering religion, and this is my penance. Altitude has a perfidious way of robbing me of my mental abilities when I don't even know my pocket is being picked. Is this the calamity foretold by my intuition? No doubt it is.

An imagined, familiar voice speaks warmly to me.

"Bob. Bob. Hold the line, son. You've encountered this before. Stay calm. I'm here with you. Right at your side." It's Robert, my Guardian Angel.

A stoic composure replaces the initial shock and I'm able to understand things better. I know this affliction. In my climbing apprenticeship days as I studied the craft with guiding companies, I contracted blindness returning from the summit of Illimani in Bolivia in 1990. That time I briefly removed my sunglasses to relieve the discomfort caused by the balaclava pressing the glasses' arms against my temples. We reached Base Camp late that afternoon and the burning began during the night.

For two days, I was unable to open my eyes without pain. Fortunately, our guide knew the condition and he and two others were able to assist me off the peak.

At the dawning of the new day, the sun's warmth bathes Baby Blue. Yet I see only the absence of light. It's as though night's shade covers the land; it's light outside, while black to me. I feel the sun's faint heat, but lie enshrouded in sepulchral darkness. I listen to my Walkman in the hope it will distract me from worrying about my situation. Early in the afternoon, opening my eyelids infrequently confirms there is no horizon; the sky is as one with the desert landscape. The faintness of light makes the faint images I see an additional terror. There's an occasional unprovoked tightening of my stomach muscles when I review the possibilities of what might happen, all of them negative. "What if this . . .?" "What if that . . .?" I'm now wandering the breeding place of pure, unadulterated panic.

Then, everything changes completely in an instant. I no longer see things in a negative light but through a prism of supreme hopefulness, the result of my personality's perpetual bent to optimism. Giancarlo will arrive in a few hours. It is terrifying being blind. But there will be gradual relief tomorrow evening when sight begins to return. The pain will subside. Food and water pose no problem; there's enough for me to stay here for weeks. Still, there is some anxiety, caused by the inconvenience of my blinded condition. And what if something happened to Giancarlo? There's also the pain. Even the muted shades of light within Blue cause my eyelids to flutter as the lids rasp against the tender, sunburned eyeballs. And the tears! It's endurable, however, and I resolve to stay positive about things. It might have been worse if this had happened on the ice plateau. The fact that it occurred here at Base Camp makes it the best of all possible circumstances. If I had gone blind higher on the mountain, it might have been impossible to get back down. I shudder to think of such a thing happening.

As I await Giancarlo in the dark of light, my thoughts drift back to the battles on the mountain with storms, unremitting winds, climbing the wrong summit, and now blindness. Still, I recognize this as high adventure, the kind found only in books or on the movie screen, and here I am actually living it. I await Giancarlo's return for me, knowing that at his arrival, my travails will be close to an end and my flight home a matter of days away.

Presently, the distant whine of a powerful truck engine becomes louder and louder as Giancarlo's Land Cruiser approaches my lonely desert station. I unzip Blue's door and wave at sound rather than sight.

He is now out of the truck. I hear his footfalls in the sand as he comes towards me. I find his nearness overwhelmingly moving. I expected much from him and he disappointed me not in the least.

"Roberto, my friend. What is problem?"

"I can't see. I can't see."

Without answering, he bends over, takes my hands, pulls me up, and holds me close. His warmth revives my spirits. After guiding my hesitant footsteps to the truck, he helps me inside and gathers and packs all the food, gear, and water. I feel overwhelmed by emotion, yet my eyes remain dry.

"Thank you, my friend. It is wonderful that you have come."

We arrive at La Casona in the early morning, and my eyes begin to return to normal later in the day. That afternoon, I sit outside my room and bask in the warmth of the sun.

"You are well, Roberto?"

Giancarlo's concern for my health is most welcome and appreciated.

"Yes, my friend, I am very well. And six months from now, I shall return for another climb. And next year, perhaps I will try Llullaillaco once more."

Such is the close to this journey and the promise of another yet to come. Llullaillaco will remain in my plans, for I burn with desire to see the Inca huts. I gained a wealth of information from the top of the subsidiary peak as I looked below at possible routes to the summit. At some point, that knowledge will serve my purposes well.

Oh, and Maria Ester? When I leave with Giancarlo for the airport, she has some parting words for me.

"Bob. I'm happy the spirits did not frighten you."

She raps her knuckles gently on the nearby wooden doorjamb.

"But you never know if you go there again. . . ."

This climb taught me late in life that the most precious of my five senses is that of sight, for "to see" is "to be." Although to this day I must wear dark glasses as protection against indoor and outdoor glare, in my reckoning, this is a small price to pay for grand adventure.

GOOGLE TOUR: This Chapter's tour resides on the website.

PANORAMIO: Select the "Llullaillaco, Chile" tag on the site.

MOVIES: The November, 1998 movie contains footage of a Llullaillaco climb.

Still, at times my actions come too close
to being carelessly haphazard about it, as a
drunk is careless, acting as though I have no
regard for life, not understanding in an hour
what any sane person knows in a minute.

As for the missing miner, is his body still out
there somewhere? Most likely. Perhaps he
became lost and, at the end of his strength, sank
to the earth and cloaked himself in dreams and
snow. An entire, unknown world died with him.
Who could know his failures, his fears, his loves,
his deepest thoughts, his triumphs?

--From the author's personal climbing journal

CHAPTER 4

Closing the Circle on Llullaillaco, Chile

*T*his chapter introduces my new driver, Patricio Rios. The increasing demands of his hotel, "La Casona," temporarily required Giancarlo Fiocco to take leave of his trips to the big peaks. During our seven journeys together, we had become like brothers.

After months of searching in Copiapo for a replacement, he found Patricio. He was 26 at the time and worked for his father at their electronic repair company. He was a quiet, serious man, and one in whom I developed the deepest trust. We have remained close friends over the years.

The first part tells of my solo attempt of Llullaillaco in November, 1995, and the strange and puzzling things that took place. The second part describes the trip in April, 2001, with two retired friends of mine. We journeyed to Chile so they could see the peaks that had occupied so much of my life. On our visit to Llullaillaco, we met up with some miners from Mina Escondida, the large copper mine forty miles northwest of the peak. Our conversation with them served to heighten the mystery about the events of the 1995 climb.

Here are the stories.

It's November, 1995. I hug Patricio before he turns to leave, because this moment has been tugging at me for twenty-four hours, and I'm wavering. Should I let him return to Copiapo without me? He comes back in twelve days -- a wonderful eternity out here, but an eternity just the same. Or should I mention my need to see a doctor? I tamp down my apprehension and say nothing. Pat waves and his truck soon disappears. I'm now "off the map," as always when my driver leaves. I'm nearly as lost to civilization as the renegade ivory hunter Kurtz, so far up the Congo River no one knew where he was. Only Patricio knows my location. And when the climb begins, no one in the world, not even Marlow's re-creation, could ever know my precise whereabouts.

PHOTO: Base Camp at 14,600'. (Photo 4.8 on the site.)

I try to forget my physical problem by gazing upon the giant, Llullaillaco, the mountain I have named "Flaming Mountain." This is my first trip back since my visit in November, 1994, when my errors led to climbing the subsidiary summit by mistake. That was a first solo ascent, perhaps even a first ascent of that summit. This is a chance to try for the true high point once more and to view the Inca huts on the mountain's sacred summit. As I study the route from here at 14,600 feet, the place for Camp I is visible, as is one for Camp II, both with snowfields nearby. Camp III lies behind a high ridge and is out of sight from here, yet I know its location notwithstanding. That high ridge also blocks my view of the primary summit. A few feet below the highest point, on the eastern side, lie the Indian buildings I so wish to visit.

An extensive lava flow characterizes this side of the peak. Its source sits near the summit, falls down the western side, and collects in an extended slump on my slope. Its color is much darker than the rest of the terrain, so it stands out from miles away. This lava creep will be close by above Camp III and might serve as a way to the summit. The route in view is snow-free, except for small snow patches that will supply my water needs. Indeed, there are just small amounts of snow on this side of the mountain. It's warm in this part of the Andes compared to farther south, home to the giants, Ojos del Salado, Tres Cruces, and Pissis. Here, at 11:30 a.m., a thin short-sleeve shirt and cotton pants provide sufficient warmth.

PHOTO: It's warm here at Base Camp. (Photo 4.9 on the site.)

I feel again the urgency to pass water, my physical problem. Anxiety seizes me as I must strain to force the flow. There's no pain. But it requires so much effort and time to empty my bladder I fear a deadly disease lurks within. The difficulty began on the flight to Santiago. There was little cause for concern then, or during the two days in Copiapo provisioning for the trip and visiting with friends. But yesterday morning, on the six-hour ride from Copiapo to the abandoned borax mine at 12,000 feet on the shores of Laguna Aguas Calientes, where we spent last night, my thoughts turned gloomy and dark. Is it a urinary infection or a blockage? Will it work itself out over a couple of days and all return to normal?

Down at the mine this morning, my foreboding rose from its dark recess to force upon me the truth. My God, it's prostate cancer! What else could it be? It can be only that. I wrestled the worrisome thought back to its murky resting place from which it sprang as I prepared for the ride to Base Camp. Yet it leapt upon me again as Pat followed the steep and rock-strewn track up the mountain. When he left me at Base and drove away, I thought I might never see him again. It takes discipline to seize control of my mind and emotions, and planning the climb is a means to do it. Besides setting up Baby Blue, reading, reflecting, dozing, listening to tapes, thinking, and staring at the landscape also help me keep my worry under control. The time also helps my body acclimate. At altitude, I lose myself in lethargic nothingness, a hypnotic state in which the advancing seconds and minutes are lost to meaning, lost to consciousness, like days and nights spent in the jungle, with heat so stifling and suffocating all one can do is stare languidly in a drunken state of inertia with hardly enough strength to move hand and arm to take desultory swats at mosquitoes in the Vietnamese bush.

That night, after another forced bladder evacuation, alarm is at my throat yet again. I can't remain out here with prostate cancer! I decide that if my condition is unchanged on the morning of the third day, I'll flee to Mina Escondida, the second-largest open pit copper mine in Chile, which sits thirty-five miles to the northwest. From there, I'll call Patricio to come rescue me so I can return home to see a doctor. The long night provides time to plan the route to the mine and what gear to take. Since the hike could take two to three days, I must take Baby Blue. Two liters of water, several candy bars, and other assorted snacking foods will be enough to see me through. The palpable, real danger in hiking to the Mina from here is not the distance or the arid landscape. As I have learned upon previous trips here, military landmines litter the salar that separates the mountain from the mine. There are no real roads across it, just rough tracks where vehicles have crossed over the years. Every few years an unfortunate soul loses an arm or leg out here. A safer tactic is to follow the dirt road leading north to desolate Estacion Socompa, fifteen miles to the north. It's a small station on the train line between Antofagasta, Chile, and Salta, Argentina. I can walk twenty miles west to the mine from there.

The rising sun finds me forcing urination again. There's a gnawing in my stomach. I'm right to listen to my will that the perceived good is to leave this place, this place so inhospitable to mind and body. It's the one means to save myself -- back to town, back to home! But my reason takes control and demands rational thinking. It asks: What is different during the past days? Have I changed my diet? Have I changed my drinking habits? Is there pain upon elimination? Is the urine's color normal?

Then, I understand things so quickly an involuntary gasp escapes my lips in a whistle. There **has** been a change, and I rush my expedition bag to find the pill pouch and the information I need. The pharmacy's description of the drug and its side effects reads: "May cause difficulty in urination." I contracted a cold three weeks ago and the drug prescribed to alleviate the cold symptoms is the cause of all my anxieties! The thought of death on the mountain flees in an instant. Its burden, its weight, evaporates and I spend the remainder of the day considering my way up the mountain and rejoicing in deliverance from certain destruction. The afternoon ends in the serenity of a still and exquisite beauty, as the setting sun casts a brilliant, golden alpenglow upon the mountain's massive western walls.

As I leave camp the next morning for my first carry to Camp I, I scan the length and breadth of the slope. During the night, my mountaineer's sixth sense suggested that other climbers are out here, although there is no physical evidence to confirm it. There are no tents that I can see. I climb at my accustomed pace and allow my body to acclimate gradually. Along the way, I note that the minefield I saw here in 1994 is gone and the flags removed. Perhaps that will save some guanaco. I plan to place camp at the same location I used last trip. After I labor for several hours in the sand and rocks, the general area of the campsite comes into view. It feels like a friendly place, a known place, a safe place. But I know things can change in an instant and that keeps me loose and on guard.

My altimeter reads 16,700 feet. When I swing the pack from my shoulders, something odd on the ground draws my attention. It's a dried apricot. I study it intently, trying to understand its meaning, and pluck it up to squeeze it. It's as dried apricots usually feel -- a bit tough, yet pliable and flexible. Its color is the familiar dusky orange. Llullaillaco resides in the very heart of the Atacama Desert, one of the driest places on the face of the planet. If this apricot remains in the open but a few days, the aridity, the cold, and the strength of the sun's rays at this altitude will harden and shrivel it and darken its color. But this one appears rather fresh. There **are** other climbers on the mountain. My intuition was right. I look to the slopes above and study the route to Camp II, first the ground closer to me, sweeping left to right and right to left, then looking up higher and repeating it, just as the Marines taught us. But I see no one.

PHOTO: Camp I, the author's Camp "Apricot." (Photo 4.11 on the website.)

When I return to Base Camp, I scour each yard of terrain with binoculars from Camp I to Camp II and then higher to the edge of the ice table. Still no sign of others. They must be on the table or above it and out of sight from here. What does it all mean? One thing it means is that if there are other climbers above me, I cannot claim this as a solo climb. At night, while I brood upon the mystery, there is a sudden burst of wind, and it bashes Baby Blue's walls for hours on end, as if it wishes to tear us from the peak.

The winds subsided before first light. After my second haul to Camp I, now known as my Camp "Apricot," with the remaining gear, I spent the night there, again attacked by howling winds, and the day after, today, make the first haul to Camp II and then return to Camp I. My search for the bright colors of tents, climbers' windsuits, any hint of other climbers, is fruitless. The weather is clear, with an occasional breeze. My camp (18,300 feet) sits twenty-five feet from a small fumarolic vent puffing steamy wisps of sulfur dioxide from deep within the belly of the mountain. The opening, coated with yellow residue, emits a recognizable rotten egg smell, just like the ones in Yellowstone National Park.

The next day, I stride off on the second lift to Camp II. The wind screamed all night, as though seeking to hector me back down the mountain, but it retreated early this morning. This wind pattern is perplexing. Will it develop into something more sinister higher upon the peak? With all my remaining gear on my back, which makes the second load much heavier than the first day's, the move upwards begins. Second carries are demanding and can rip a climber's determination to shreds. I force myself higher and higher, but I must stop for breath more and more. The slope turns to sand, the kind that provides no traction, the kind that causes two steps back for every one gained. I have been in this predicament on every peak, but it is especially disheartening on this steep slope. I struggle for a long time before I lose heart and traverse to the left to get off the hellish mess. I make it, but as I move to rockier ground, a ferocious wind hits me head on. I forge on, though I am losing my will to continue.

The wind slackens as suddenly as it arose, and presently I encounter more steep and loose ground, but not as severe as on the slopes below. I continue upward, but several times I think seriously about abandoning the entire climb. Yet, something keeps propelling me forward. I will not give up! My will dismisses my physical discomfort as a needless distraction. At 3 p.m., I drag myself into camp. What a carry. What a load. What an ordeal. One consolation is that I have no headaches and my body has adjusted itself magnificently to this height. I reckon myself a lucky man. Still, I am tired beyond remembrance. I have still not seen a trace of anyone or anything. If someone were above me, wouldn't they be descending by now?

The wind whips up once more. Fortunately, my home fits neatly inside a rectangular rock enclosure that rises two feet on each of its three sides. The fourth side, the open section, accommodates my tent's door. This small collection of stones forms a barrier to the fierce battering of the wind and suggests intelligent design. The Indians who placed the stone huts on the summit 500 years ago fashioned a route to the top on the eastern slopes. Perhaps they first tried this western side, but found it too steep and chose the eastern side instead as the way to the summit. Maybe this served as a storage hut for food and supplies while they were here. It's possible. There are several huts on the eastern slopes that served that purpose.[35] And how did those guys do it, anyway? How did they climb one of the highest peaks in the Andes without the gear we have today?

The stone walls fail to silence the screeching of the icy wind; it howls for hours until it leaves off at three-thirty in the morning. My look out the door flap at 4 a.m. to the northwest reveals a bright green-white phosphorescence that lights up the sky like a nuke going off at ground level, the half-bubble bursting outwards from the inner core. I view it with a swift quickening of interest. Is it atmospheric light akin to the borealis? No. It's the light cast off by Mina Escondida, where the miners are at work all day, every day. As I crawl back into my bag, my thoughts wander towards home to my wife, my girls, and my new grandson. This is my seventh day on the peak and I wonder about their health and safety. These moments can turn unsettling if I worry too much. I must trust that they are safe.

Thirty minutes after I melt snow and boil water for a warm coffee, I'm off with all my gear for the single carry to Camp III at 9 a.m. The first part of the route demands the utmost in concentration. The slope is steep and physically draining. It requires using the rest step

---

[35] See "The Ice Maiden" and "Inca Rituals and Sacred Mountains" by Johan Reinhard, for the full explanation of what he, and his archaeological teams, discovered on Llullaillaco.

technique, with a slow pace of two steps up and one step to pause. The first 400 feet out of camp are over loose sand and small stones. I recall its grueling rigors back in 1994, so this time I choose a route angling to the right that leads to a snow and ice sheet sloping menacingly at thirty degrees. I strap up my crampons and, using the two sharp prongs at each crampon toe, "front point" the ice sheet by thrusting my boot toe into the slope. Initially, I congratulate myself for this obviously brilliant mountaineering decision, until I become utterly exhausted in fifteen minutes. The awkward boot placements have weakened my legs and swinging the ice axe has weakened my arms. Besides the physical strain, this is risky business -- front pointing on ice with no rope partner and carrying a heavy load. At a spot where large rocks jut out from the slope, I'm able to sit and work the crampons off my boots. I look below. A careless misstep here will mean a roll of hundreds of feet and I must exercise care and concentration. I begin to climb the mass of rocks. It ends eventually and I'm on the rim of the broad ice plateau that rises towards Camp III, the same table that served as a camp on the climb of the subsidiary summit, which now smiles down upon me in welcome and warming memory. The elevation is 19,340 feet. I still see no sign of other climbers. Perhaps that apricot has been out here for many weeks. But if so, how could it appear so fresh?

I have arrived at the edge of a vast openness, and I feel like a lonely figure on the floor of a somber and stilled desert. There is no wind here, simply brief, hurrying breezes. Dark clouds begin forming above the ice table as I strap on the crampons once again. I must perform this task meticulously. If I secure the teeth incorrectly to the boot, they could loosen at the most inopportune moment, and that might prove disastrous.

As I set off to the southeast over the plateau, my crampons gnaw the yielding ice and snow with their razor-like incisors as they gnash my path forward; the crunch of the steel teeth chewing the ice seemingly the loudest sound in the entire Andes. The field requires concentration because of the occasional rifts and openings in its surface. An unwary step could cause a fall and, with the enormous burden on my back, I cannot risk that happening.

Thirty steps out on the ice, I have the distinct sensation that I'm not alone, and it causes a momentary uneasiness. Something is here. Something is near. There. It's behind me! I turn about to seek the source, but see only snow and ice and barren ridges across the plateau's expanse. The sense of a presence near me is so strong that there must be an image to confirm the feeling. But there is only emptiness wherever I look. I set off again and feel the strange thing catch up in minutes with new immediacy, an insistent something demanding recognition. Now the sensation comes from off to the right, near the edge of the plateau. I study every feature with an intense stare. But once more, only the cold, barren land is my reward. Is this place bewitched? By what, exactly? Stillness and silence are the lone replies from the indefatigable source of man or spirit shadowing me. I now search the table, not for a standing human form, but for a supine one. Does the strange phenomenon come from the phantom shadow of a dead climber asleep here? I've never communicated with the dead. They have been "there," in front of me, near to me, yet never attempting to communicate with me. The barrier between life and death is unbreachable.

But there in the distance! I fasten my gaze upon a solitary figure, like a standing man off to my left at the margin of the field beneath the subsidiary summit. I wave and shout, "Helloooooo! Who's there?" Perhaps he is the one who dropped the apricot! But there is no human response or movement from the lonely sentinel. I move determinedly towards it. I must know if it will answer my questions about whatever is tracking my footsteps. But as I approach closer, the hoped-for answer turns out to be the only answer: it is no more than a single, slender rock gendarme.

I'm halfway across the plateau as my search for a body continues, one erect or horizontal, or anything that will bring understanding to my situation. Whatever is here isn't menacing, like Banquo's ghost. Nor does it have a friendly aspect like Virgil, Dante's guide into the depths of the Inferno. Nor is it a make-believe climbing companion. A friend, who found himself on Pissis separated from his partner, said he found comfort in his isolation by talking to an imaginary comrade, an invisible psychological salve for his loneliness. Hermann Buhl, on his solo first ascent of Nanga Parbat in 1953, recalled afterwards that he talked often to his "invisible companion." But my experience is not like these. And it isn't Robert, my Guardian Angel; he announces himself when he wishes my attention.

There are more encounters with the peculiar thing as I continue my tramp to the southern boundary of the ice field. I've never experienced such presentiments before, such pressing assaults from a vaporous nothing. And clouds hang only above the plateau and not the rest of the mountain; what that signifies is not clear. When I'm on scree and talus again and above the flat terrain of white, I steal a quick glance back, searching with the advantage of height, seeking a figure, a body, color, movement, any sign or clue as to what is out here. What is it? Where is it? Who is it? Only white snow and pallid ice answer my earnest questions.

PHOTO: The Camp III site above the plateau. (Photo 4.15 on the site.)

PHOTO: A glance from Camp III to the plateau, the "home" of the mysterious specter. (Photo 4.16.)

The sand and small stone slope above the plateau rises gradually and I eventually find a suitable site for camp. The load on my shoulders is punishing, but it's made tolerable by the climbing poles, which disperse the weight. The elevation, 20,700 feet, means a summit-day climb tomorrow of less than 2,000 feet, which is exactly my plan. I like to keep my summit days to less than 2,500 feet in elevation gain. The weather is cooperating, since the dark clouds remain above the plateau and not above me here. Once I anchor Blue, ninety minutes have passed since my last encounter with the "sensation of nearness." Memory of it fades. My attention now must be upon summit-day and the large expenditure of effort to come. My heart rate is 84. At sea level, it's 58. It will drop in the coming hours, if my acclimation goes well.

High above me, the true summit of the mountain is now visible to the east. One possible route leaves camp, slants to the left through a phantasmagorical wonderland of strange rock formations, and leads to the bottom of a talus and scree couloir. This gully rises 1,000 feet to the south and then intersects another steep ravine heading due east that goes directly to the summit. The lower gully proved my undoing on a previous climb. The small rocks and stones moved with each step, so every three steps forward caused a slide back of one. It required total focus and a Herculean force of will to surmount it. I had neither on that day.

Another potential route is the lava flow. It sits directly south 200 yards from my camp; from the intersection point of the low and high gullies, it plunges all the way down the mountain to my Base Camp slope 6,000 feet below. It's a mass of fractured lava stones of all conceivable sizes and shapes, from small rocks to refrigerator-size stones to blocks as large as a small truck. One must climb several hundred feet up its flank and then tread its tortured back until reaching the summit gully. But I know those jumbled rocks will pose a serious hazard because they might shift when I step on them. I have unpleasant memories of routes over lava obstacles like this one. When James and I followed the five gigantic rock "steps" to the top of Ojos del Salado, the boulders shifted beneath us several times. On one occasion, I righted myself just before pitching backwards onto the stones below. And on a prior climb of Tres Cruces Sur, a rock-choked slope was nearly my undoing. I tried to traverse a short distance to the left and stepped onto the protruding lip of a massive block. As I sidestepped over it with my arms outstretched for balance, the monster slumped downwards ever so slightly as my heart rose to my throat. I hurried the remaining steps to the left and jumped free onto smaller rocks to the side.

I leave these disturbing thoughts to focus again on the ravine. My failure there on my previous climb bothers me. It beckons me forward, though, like the Sirens lured Odysseus with their sweet singing to the sandy shores of their Isle. The "sandy shore" in this case is the couloir, its belly like quicksand, but pitched at a thirty degree angle. This decides things for me. It will be the tangled lava flow.

Later in the afternoon, my heart rate is 64 and my urine has returned to its normal color, both good signs. But the location of my camp makes me worry. This incline is littered with boulders of many sizes and this keeps me nervous and on edge. These rocks have toppled downwards from the subsidiary summit onto this slope during thousands of years. When was the last fall of rocks upon the ground where Blue and I rest? The danger keeps me alert for hours.

Late in the evening, an occasional thick, beating sound causes me to look out the tent door. My eyes lose themselves in the gloom beneath the high ceiling of the heavens. There are no storm clouds, just that distant stirring that I can't understand. An hour later, the noises turn to loud booms that I recognize now as powerful winds hammering blows against the stony ramparts of the mountain's flanks. But the winds assault the higher parts of the peak and spare my little camp. The mountain's altered state reveals one of the heartless secrets of the laws of nature. A peak's mood changes quickly; one minute it has a friendly aspect, the next it displays rancorous petulance. When gale winds become the protagonist in a climber's passage, there can be but one outcome. Will the wind prevent my progress up the peak and blow summit dreams to nothing, dashing them to pieces against the rocky heights above?

I begin preparing at 6 a.m. and I'm moving an hour later, as rosy rays of light stab the darkness of the dying night. Whooshing and shrieking sounds join the maelstrom above in a demonstration of pure power only Mother Nature, the celestial conductor of this wild symphony, can arrange. The continued blows pound upon the earthen anvil of the stony heights, like a giant Vulcan fashioning his implements for the Roman gods. When I reach the lava flow, the sounds from above are at a crescendo as I stare upon the jagged flank of twisted rocks and boulders. If I try this as a route with all its jumbled stones, the high winds will pose too many problems. If I lose my balance on a loose rock, I'll be hurled against other boulders, there to lie battered and broken, pinned by the lashing gusts to the flow's side.

I change my mind and reverse my decision; the risk is too great on the lava flow with its loose rocks and jagged stones. The gully is the other choice. Its base lies several hundred yards to the east, through the field of fantastical rock forms. When I reach it, I look above and see the cause of all the noise. At the intersection of the southern and eastern ravines high above, snow-laden wind currents bash the walls of the peak, their eddies given visual definition by the snow they carry from high snow fields. They clash and writhe in contorted gyrations, one moment beating the summit slabs, the next veering away to churn and thrash, then returning to smash the unyielding mountain repeatedly. The fury. The sound. The spectacle. All this display of raw power weakens my confidence. No one can stand up to ferocity such as this.

I see my vulnerability very clearly now. The raging winds may shift direction in an instant and rush down to seize me in their airy tentacles. My mountain intuition says it is time to flee. But I fight the thought as an enemy of my will, a will determined to climb ever higher.

Then Robert, my Angel, counsels me to leave this place. It's early enough to return to Base Camp. I've tempted fate beyond prudence and am staring into eternity, into infinity. I've come to appreciate life and enjoy the very fact of existence. At moments like this one, I come too close to being carelessly haphazard about things, as a drunk is careless, acting as though I have no regard for life, not understanding in an hour what any sane person knows in a minute.

Just as I reach camp, I feel a shove, then an insistent push from behind, an icy grasp for my frail body. I believe I hear a voice whisper. *"She's coming."* Who is? *"She. She is coming!"*[36] The wind's icy fingers probe for an opening, like a wrestler seeking the place of greatest weakness. I collapse Blue, pack hurriedly, and start down. The wind hounds me and pushes at my pack. It's all I can do to keep my balance. If I am knocked over, it will be exhausting to try to rise again.

Once I'm 300 feet lower, the wind continues to howl, but differing air pressure gradients keep it at a distance. I've passed through an invisible curtain and crossed from hell to heaven in but an instant. There, twenty feet from me, the wind screams, while here there is the slightest of breezes.

I retreat several hundred more feet and reach the margin of the ice plateau. Although the real danger remains behind me, I cannot become

---

[36] Later, the author recognized this as a mild high altitude hallucination.

complacent, since looming over all here is a spectral shade, its intentions unknown and indecipherable. Once more the dark, glooming clouds hover over the snow table and give the scene a gloaming-like appearance. My crampons froth the ice as the wind continues to roar and whine in the distance. I must traverse the table and drop down the western slopes to find safety.

Presently, it turns unbelievably cold. Have I entered an air pocket? There is a distressing feeling in the fingers of my right hand, the same distressing sensation I felt on Aconcagua years before that signaled frostbite. I recognize the danger and slap my hand repeatedly against my right leg to speed the blood flow to my fingers. Frostbite! The "bite." It's one of those words of all the words in all the languages of all the nations of all the world that causes worry in the soul of the high altitude mountaineer. I must remember that Aconcagua experience. I cannot risk the loss of my fingers! Only when a measure of warmth has returned to them do I strike out once more.

I'm on the ice only ten minutes when those same odd, strange feelings of something nearby return. I turn to left and right and seek a figure to confirm what I feel is here. Yet, as before, there is nothing, merely the white, barren land in this place high above the living world. I call out once more, but there is no answer in return, simply a mocking, empty silence. At times, I feel the presence is behind me. But when I turn to confront it, there is nothing there. At other moments, it seems off to either side. But again, I see only the empty ice plateau and nothing more.

When I am half-way across the table, whatever is out here stops bothering me. But then, fifteen minutes later, it returns. I stop and stare intently all around, but I stare into nothing, into silence. There is otherworldliness to what is here, in its absence of form, in its absence of sound. At one point, I think myself mad. "Okay," I cry out, "what do you want of me?" Do I really expect a response? There is none, only the sound of my windsuit when the hood flutters in the breeze. The thing dogs my steps to the table's western edge, where I unbuckle my crampons and drop over the side for the descent back to Base Camp. The haunting sensation leaves off the pursuit and remains on the plateau, perhaps condemned to wander the ice, for reasons known but to the mountain gods of Llullaillaco.

I descend towards Camp II, down towards Camp Apricot, and then down to the ultimate safety of Base Camp. I have a momentary twinge of disappointment: a summit attempt proved impossible. But my concentration must be upon the steep inclines back down the mountain. A stumble or fall on these sections might prove catastrophic. During a brief rest stop at Camp I, I hear the shrieking high above and count myself once more the luckiest of men. Gentle zephyrs play across the slopes the last 500 feet to Base Camp and, in the fading light, faint images of the food and supply boxes at camp come into view. But something is disturbing about the distant scene. When I draw closer, things appear even worse. The place is a shambles! My storage boxes are split open and their contents litter the landscape. A bottle of soda lies thirty feet away. Another bottle is fifty feet from camp, with its lid twisted and the contents emptied. My prized stick of salami sits in the dirt, the casing ripped apart and half the stick eaten. A box of lemon cookies and a bag of potato chips lie torn, their contents scattered over the sand and rocks. Most interesting of all: three packs of Pall Mall cigarettes are unwrapped and half the contents of each one are missing!

Who or what is the culprit in this mischief? The criminals could have been several guanaco. They're strong enough to kick soda bottles and graze on my camp provisions. But the elevation might be too high. A condor? Perhaps. They're large enough, but I've yet to see one on this trip. The cunning little Andean fox? There's the incarnation of a little robber if there ever was one! Those pesky rogues can steal you blind, if you let them. But I've never seen them at this height. The strangeness of it all provides wonderful and delightful entertainment.

As I await Patricio's arrival, my thoughts return to the crossing of the ice field. I'm no longer at the high altitude of the plateau and I'm able to think quite clearly here, but things remain a mystery. The significance of the apricot at Camp I? It told me someone might be higher on the mountain and on the route. Did the possibility of others on the peak have something to do with my feeling on the ice plateau of something nearby? If so, why did the sensation present itself on just that part of the climb? What bizarre kind of peculiarity exists out here? Was the sensation I felt only for me? Or will it also bother others?

PHOTO: What was it the author felt on the ice plateau? (Photo 4.18 on the website.)

I fail to produce any answers and let it all go. After all, it's pickup day, and Patricio said he intends to leave this morning from Copiapo and arrive around 3 p.m. We'll spend the night at the borax mine and return to town tomorrow. Not surprisingly, at 2:45 p.m., I see his truck work the slopes towards me. He pulls up in thirty minutes. After a hug, I bombard him with the story of what happened on the plateau. He'll hear more of it tonight and tomorrow on the trip back to town.

PHOTO: Patricio is bearing directly for the author. (Photo 4.19.)

He also has an exciting experience to relate. After he dropped me off at Base Camp, he was forty miles west, motoring towards the Pan-American Highway for the return to Copiapo. He noticed a shaking in the truck's read end and determined it was a loose axle. He replaced a rear bearing and limped the remaining forty miles to the highway at ten miles per hour. There, he got a ride to find a mechanic in Antofagasta (the Chilean city on the Pacific Coast). What a resourceful guy!

We are ten minutes down the slope when some movements to the right draw our attention.

"Hey, what's that, Pat?"

He edges the truck closer. It's two Andean foxes sunning themselves among low-lying rocks. They seem bemused by our attention.

"They sure look healthy and well fed."

"Yeah, like they had big dinner," replies Pat. "And look, the one on left. His mouth curl on both sides. He smile!"

Hmmmm. I wonder. Did they enjoy my Pall Malls?

CLOSING THE CIRCLE -- THE QUESTIONS

The story of the 1995 climb continues. I returned home and a few days later sent a note to my friend, Greg, a climbing ranger in Canada who had climbed often in the Andes. I told him about the strange feelings on the snow plateau and my difficulty in comprehending them. Two weeks later, he sent a letter in return, with a page from a Canadian mining magazine included. It showed the picture of a mining company employee who had worked several years before at Mina Escondida, the mine near Llullaillaco. He had been reassigned back home to Canada to work at a mine there. The article went on to say that even though he lacked climbing experience, he wanted to return to Chile to climb Llullaillaco, and to do it solo. It turns out he rented a 4x4 truck in Antofagasta. He never returned it. And nothing had been heard from him since. The article said this happened in March, 1995, several months before my climb.

This posed several questions. Did he make it to the mountain? If so, because he traveled from Antofagasta, he might have tried to climb on my route. And if he used my route, did he drop the apricot at Camp I? Was it "his" spirit I felt on the ice plateau? If he did succeed in reaching the peak, what happened to his truck? Of course, maybe he never reached the mountain at all. The questions kept coming, but with no clear answers. In his letter, my friend said it all seemed odd to him also. He didn't believe in the supernatural, he said, so it must have been an unexplained set of occurrences. So I put the matter away as a mystery never to be solved.

CLOSING THE CIRCLE -- FIVE YEARS LATER

In April, 2001, two retired friends, Al and Gene, accompanied me on a visit to Chile. They wanted to see the peaks of my dreams. We visited Llullaillaco, spending the first night at the abandoned borax mine at 12,000 feet.

Near sunset, I asked them to move outside.

"Hey, guys. I want you to see something. And bring your cameras."

In fifteen minutes, the mountain was on fire and my friends were snapping away with their cameras.

"Bob," yelled Al. "You never told us about this. I've traveled all over the world. But I've never seen an alpenglow like this one!"

The following day, we drove to 16,700 feet, on the northern slopes of the mountain. Below, at 15,000 feet, is the road skirting the northern and western flanks of the peak. It begins near Estacion Socompa, in the north, and winds around to a small mine tucked behind the mountain on its lower, southwestern flank.

As we sat in our trucks admiring the jagged northern skyline, a vehicle appeared on the road far below. In quick succession, another truck came into view, and then another. They seemed extremely small, like Lilliputian contrivances transporting Lilliputian occupants. They inched along until they were below us. Then they stopped, and figures exited each truck. They milled about and, with our binoculars, we saw them looking up in our direction. Who were they? Climbers, miners, tourists out on a lark? Who knew?

We counted eleven people altogether. After thirty minutes of looking and motioning in our direction, they drove towards us. Within twenty minutes, they joined us and we welcomed these newfound companions. They introduced themselves as part of the staff at Escondida and said they intended to climb the peak. They resembled, in national origin, a mini United Nations -- two from England, two from France, one from Canada, the rest from Chile.

One of my friends, born in France, struck up a conversation with the two French miners. The other chatted with the Chileans, who spoke excellent English. When I heard of their plans to climb, I asked after their leader. When we introduced ourselves, he seemed startled. He had heard of me from a friend, he said, and tried to make contact during the last year. He had led mining groups seven times to Llullaillaco over five years and still hadn't reached the summit. Seven attempts. That's gritty determination. As we discussed the terrain, possible routes, the weather, and those things important for success, I caught parts of the conversations taking place nearby. Hearing "Canadian miner" and "abandoned truck," my thoughts leapt instantly to 1995 and the presence I encountered on the plateau.

"Please tell me about this Canadian fellow," I said.

"Well," he replied, "there is little to tell. Several years ago, mining staff driving on the salar spotted a solitary truck sitting behind low rocks near the peak. They found it locked and empty, with a sticker in the window identifying it as a rental."

He continued. "They returned to the mine and called the company in Antofagasta. They sent employees out later to haul it back to town. One of them said it had been missing and they had written it off as a loss."

There was more. "Later, one of our guys called the rental company and asked who had rented the truck. They said they could only tell him he was a Canadian citizen and their records showed no indication of his plans or destination."

Our miner friends departed; they had a mountain to climb. Our brief encounter with them helped me understand some of what might have occurred years before. It all began with finding the apricot and then feeling the closeness of a specter on the ice field. The article from my friend in Canada caused me to interject the missing miner and his fate into the series of events because I linked him to the apricot at Camp I. Then, this conversation with the miners caused me to conclude that he may never have reached the peak, since they found his truck several miles from a possible Base Camp site. What became of him is a mystery. This "closed the circle," because finding the truck on the salar likely meant his body was not on the mountain. It also meant that whatever I encountered on the ice plateau came from something other than this poor fellow. But the larger question remained unanswered. What caused those strange sensations that made me think I had company with me?

As for the missing miner, is his body still out there somewhere? Most likely. Perhaps he became lost and, at the end of his strength, sank to the earth and cloaked himself in dreams and snow. An entire, unknown world died with him. Who could know his failures, his fears, his loves, his deepest thoughts, his triumphs? Was he any different from the rest of us, who leave this world and step into the next in similar fashion, our beings, our souls known but to us and only to us and all gone in an instant, our uniqueness never to find a similar expression amongst the trillions of beings to populate mankind's past or yet to populate mankind's future?

CLOSING THE CIRCLE -- TODAY'S REFLECTIONS

All these many years after it happened, I have sought in vain for an explanation of what transpired on the snow plateau, but it remains beyond me. Recently, I revisited what took place from the perspective of external and internal sensory knowledge, our common sense, imagination, cognitive sense, memory, the intellect, and phantasms. I believe we derive our knowledge from the senses. The intellect depends on the operation of the internal senses: common sense, imagination, the estimative and memorative senses, as well as the external senses of sight, smell, touch, hearing, and taste. The intellect understands the world by processing phantasms, images in the mind formed by the imagination and created by information from both the internal and external senses. Yet, on the ice plateau, nothing presented itself to my external senses. So, what accounts for my mind speculating about an invisible being or unseen specter?

A possible explanation is that my imagination conjured up phantasms for my intellect, which then created the occurrences. When I first saw and felt the apricot and concluded other climbers were above me, my imagination created mental images of those climbers. My intellect processed those imagined likenesses and my mind gave them life. I continued looking higher for the real images to confirm the imagined ones. Then, on the ice table, my imagination produced unseen images, these the urgent ones indicating a spirit nearby, as a corroboration of my intellect's conclusion that an entity resided there. This might serve as a partial explanation, but it begs the question why the sensation manifested itself only when I was crossing the plateau.

Another answer might be a manifestation of the companion phenomenon. As I mentioned in the story, it has happened that some who found themselves unexpectedly in isolated situations at altitude turned to an invisible friend for companionship. This provided an emotional calm until the circumstance resolved itself. But I hesitate to attribute my experience to the need for a friend close by. My desire has always been to climb alone in the mountains, for the solitude and the solemnity. It is the safest and most satisfying way for me to experience big mountains. So, with soloing as my climbing preference, why, on one solitary climb, would I need a companion nearby?

I accept that I may never know completely what came my way on those days long ago. Nevertheless, I treasure the vibrant memories. The puzzle remains, the questions unanswered, a mysterious testament to the unchanging truth that the mind, and life itself, is more than we can ever know.

GOOGLE TOUR: This Chapter's tour resides on the website.

PANORAMIO: Select the "Tres Cruces" tag on the site.

MOVIES: The April,1999; March, 2000; and Chapters 9 and 10 movies all contain footage of Tres Cruces.

I do not believe in miracles. Yet, my solo life in the mountains has been one extended miracle, for I have survived some dangerous moments among them. This is necessary bravado. I must believe fervently in myself or I shall perish amongst the high peaks.

I try again to make that first step forward. But my leg lacks life, and repeated attempts at movement meet repeated resistance. It is immovable, as a sturdy tree rooted in the earth is immovable. The summit is mine. The weather promises success. The moment is propitious. I try again. I order it to move! But my leg remains firmly in place. I'm unable to control the most basic of human functions.

--From the author's personal climbing journal

CHAPTER 5

Nevado Tres Cruces, Chile:
The Cracking of the Will[37]

November 18, 1996, is a fine day to climb, with an amiable sky and the wispy hint of a fair breeze. The mountain is Tres Cruces Central (21,743 feet, and the eleventh highest in the Andes). It sits across a col, or mountain saddle, from Tres Cruces Sur (22,133 feet, the fifth highest). Today is my fifth day on the mountain and this is my second carry to Camp I, at 16,850 feet. I feel like a well-tuned clock -- my mood, my motivation, my physical condition, all have come together in harmonious unity. After I pack the remaining equipment for continuing up the mountain (tent, stove, food, gas, and miscellaneous items), my pack's weight is well nigh insufferable.

PHOTO: Tres Cruces: Central on the left, Sur on the right. Shot from Base Camp. (Photo 5.13 on the website.)

I plod painstakingly, stoically, upwards over well-known ground. This is my sixth visit to Tres Cruces and landmarks nearby seem like old friends well met -- boulders remembered for their shapes and sizes or their juxtaposition to the surrounding land; shallow ravines that in winter carry melted snow from high on the mountain; the small field

---

[37] Please consult Photo 1.2 for the location of Tres Cruces.

of nieves penitentes shrouding the land halfway to camp; the jumbled rock field that threatens a stumble by the unwary.

As I forge ahead, I ask myself why I persist with my climbing obsession. I know that I do not wish to die just yet, but I know too that the risk of that makes high altitude climbing interesting to me. The feeling of the constant challenges to the limits of my mental, physical, and psychological boundaries gives me the satisfaction I desire. And if danger is a side product of this, then it is another problem to confront and a secondary one at that. Does one need courage to climb the high peaks? No more so than the courage needed to deal with the everyday problems of life we all face -- to lead a moral life, to propose to the right woman, to raise children, to find a satisfying job, to defend our Country, to confront the emotional and physical hardships of our daily lives.

My long trudge upwards is over ground not particularly steep. The use of the rest step moderates the strain and allows me to acclimate gradually -- at times thirty steps to two rest steps; at other times five steps to one if the ground is more difficult. My heart and lungs are adjusting to the thinner air and will continue to do so, as long as my intellect's servants, judgment and reason, rein in the will's impulse to arrive at Camp I faster than my body can adapt. At all times, the intellect must control the will. Otherwise, its desire for the "apparent" good may lead to an irrational striving for the top when the danger is greatest.

Halfway to camp, the terrain changes from soft, yielding sand and small pebbles to larger stones, rocks, and hard slabs. When I pause to rest, my mountain psyche lectures me about concentration. Boot placement is important over this type of ground. An awkward step upon a shifting stone or a clumsy body movement might cause a fall and a twisted ankle or leg. To counter this, my climbing poles provide essential aids to balance and stability.

Thirty minutes from Camp I, the steep couloir leading to the col between Central and Sur, the site of Camp II (18,600 feet), draws my attention. It's 1,750 feet from here to the gully's top and I know the challenge well -- an obdurate piece of ground to confront, especially on a daunting second haul. It's a heartbreaker, too. A client once gave up after an hour locked in its unforgiving embrace.

PHOTO: A look up the daunting couloir that leads to the col between the two peaks. (Photo 5.17 on the site.)

As I stand here reminiscing, a giant condor sweeps into view! She's an extraordinary sight. Furthermore, I think I know her! My thoughts drift back to seven months before and the climb with Don, my client.[38] I believe she is the apple-snatching condor we met on that trip. I remember it well.

> We were standing at Base Camp, reconnoitering the peak and remarking upon its features and the parts of our route in view. A condor suddenly appeared and rode the wind drafts immediately above the lower part of the route to Camp I. We watched as she retreated behind the high mound of rock and sand rubble near our camp. The excitement over, I withdrew to read while Don stayed outside to repair a piece of gear.
>
> Twenty minutes later, an immense shadow passed over my tent. One instant light, then fleeting darkness, then light again. It startled me because of its unexpectedness and mystery. What caused it?
>
> "Bob, get out here and see this!"
>
> "What is it?"
>
> Don pointed skyward. "Look."
>
> The condor we had seen while examining the peak an hour before was cruising away, gaining height, and banking left,

---

[38] Don was my first paying client. See Chapter 6 for more client stories.

like a jet lifting off the tarmac and turning to its destination course heading. Adult condors can weigh almost thirty pounds and have a wingspan of eleven feet, and this majestic beast must have been close to those dimensions.

"Ten minutes ago I threw a rotten apple on the sand. I'm sitting here playing with my stove when this thing swoops right over the tents, not twenty feet above us, glides down to the apple, grabs it with its left claw, and takes off!"

We continued to watch her. Now high in the sky, she flew towards Central, no doubt to her nest somewhere amongst the crags.

What memories! Now back in the present, I watch the huge bird slide around on the air currents above and decide she might be the same creature Don and I saw back in March. I wonder if I will meet her again. If I do, I'll be sure to hide my apples.

Here at Camp I, a spot I've used before, no one in the world knows my whereabouts. Patricio is familiar with the location of Base Camp, but knows nothing of the camp above it. This higher camp sits thirty feet from a forty-foot-high wall of ice that marks the western boundary of an ice field that covers the lower slopes of this side of the mountain. The ice wall offers protection from the wind. During the day, the sun melts enough snow so that a little stream provides my water needs. This is fortunate; it saves me the gas needed to melt snow.

Baby Blue demands uncharacteristic attention. The zippers fail to close the door completely shut. The left fly zips three quarters up, stops, and refuses to budge farther. The right fly reaches the top and then stops. This leaves a four-inch opening on the upper left side of the door. My high-altitude tents are the best in the world, from Integral Designs in Canada. This one has been my home on every climb. Her soft blue outside color is soothing and the light yellow of the inner walls comforting. She is my refuge in the wilderness, my protection against the vagaries of Mother Nature. The zipper is no more than an annoyance at this point, but I'll have to watch this in the days ahead and hope the problem doesn't worsen.

The sky is clear until, in late afternoon, ominous clouds begin cresting both peaks, conjured up from nothing. I stare upon the fast approaching masses with increasing interest. But nothing comes of the threat. Later, a golden sunset streams its stabs of light across the high desert plains below, like flows of molten gold, smothering all in an evanescence that cheers my mood. This is my sixth day out here, with nine more to go. I miss my wife and daughters and grandson. What I wouldn't give for a plate of my wife's Italian lasagna -- the rich tomato sauce, ricotta cheese, Italian sausage, ground beef . . . . I can't go on thinking about her home cooking. I smile. I shall go mad with hunger!

My night marred by fitful tossing, I'm awake at 5:30 a.m. The opening in the tent door caused the inside temperature to drop, but I've made the decision to live with it for the present. I can't determine the cause of the problem, even after closely examining the fly teeth. Sleep comes hard at altitude, and so I linger, serenely awaiting the dawn. And then I must be off. Every climb becomes a race to reach the top before loss of appetite and sleep render my body incapable of further effort. I need progress upwards every day or risk exhaustion. There are no idle days on a mountain, unless forced upon me by health or weather problems.

A brief storm during the night has left a shallow blanket of snow on the ground that will burn off quickly if this morning's weather holds. Forty-five minutes later, I'm in the gully and laboring toward the top of the col and a Camp II site. The thirty-five-degree angle is constant and unchanging and, if it were loose scree and talus, would require a Herculean physical effort. But I discovered a unique characteristic of this gully years ago. For millennia, snowmelt has coursed down its center and created a concrete-hard channel its entire length. This makes solid ground for boot placement and no backsliding. So despite its unforgiving gradient, I make good time and arrive at the col in three hours. My barometric altimeter reads out at 18,500 feet.

Though I used the rest step the entire way, three steps to one of rest, still I'm fatigued and wrung out. That's how it is out here. Most of the time, I have the commitment to continue. Sometimes I have to seek deep inside to summon the determination to go forward. When I live moments like this and feel the strain on heart and lungs and their struggle to adapt, it causes me to admire the magnificence of the human body. And here I feel the "rapture of the heights," that euphoria I know only at elevations this high. There is nothing at sea level that compares with it and I wish to know it many more times in the years left to me.

At my chosen place for camp, I drop the first load's gear -- food, gas, ice axe, and other items. Early in my climbing career, I devised a list of what to haul on a first and a second carry. I have it with me on each climb. That way I'm sure the right gear goes on the right carry. The second lift has the heaviest pieces -- Blue, sleeping bag, stove, and other gear. My campsite sits next to a rectangular boulder, one of the larger rocks on this part of the col and a spot I've used before. It will offer protection if a wind stirs up.

My survey of the area reveals it as an old friend and an exhilarating location for camp. The ramparts of two of the highest peaks in the Andes tower above me, Sur to the southwest and Central to the northeast. I examine Central in anticipation of my climb to the summit. A large ridge runs horizontally across the slopes, a feature I named "The Balustrade" on a previous trip. Its underbelly looks contorted from here, but I must find a way through it to gain the heights above. It may test my mountaineering skills to their limit and I relish the challenge. Although I can't see the entire summit area from here, I know its contours after having seen it on climbs of Sur. The top is a blasted-out volcanic crater with an imperfect rim partially crumpled and broken on its western side, the remainder of it is intact and filled with snow. The apex of the mountain appears to be, as seen from its sister peak, the rocks of the northern rim.

Three pools of water lie on the col's surface, the two smaller ones lazuli tinted, their variously colored rocks beneath the surface clearly in sight. The largest of the three is the most stunning and stretches forty feet across, its side and bottom rocks several different shades of green. Its depth seems at least twenty or thirty feet. It's reminiscent of the geyser pools in Yellowstone Park. But why aren't these ponds frozen at this altitude? Their warmth must spring from hot vents deep within the mountain. Water this high is a real treat. I won't have to melt snow, and that saves gas.

PHOTO: Laguna "Greenie" at the col. This was the home of the *Tres Cruces Shrimpus Altitudus*. (Photo 5.20 on the website.)

When I plunge my bare hands into the waters of "Greenie," its warmth soothes my skin. Tiny orange-colored creatures flit about in its pretty depths. Are they related to the tiny shrimp the flamingoes eat at Laguna Santa Rosa and other highland lakes throughout the Andes? I take an empty camera film canister and capture several for later examination. If I can get them to Copiapo, someone in town may be able to analyze them. Maybe they are an un-catalogued member of God's wonderful and varied kingdom. If they are, perhaps scientists will name them after the mountain, *Tres Cruces Shrimpus Altitudus!*

It's time to leave for Camp I. I enter the couloir, avoid the center route used on the way up, and descend to its right in deep sand that gives way two to three inches with each boot placement. In one and a half hours, I'm back at camp just as clouds sweep over the peaks in late afternoon. One front pushes over Central, the other above Sur, both threatening a rendezvous of forces at the col. I stare at this new threat impassively, as at an annoyance, and take its measure. Snow begins its inevitable downward cascade soon enough, as a peal of thunder unhinges my mood. I place one of my long-sleeve shirts in the tent door opening to keep the snow and cold out.

As I settle in for the night in the closeted wherry of my camp, a portion of freeze-dried spaghetti provides sustenance for the coming day of hard labor. Later, to prepare for the long, interminable night, I arrange my gear in the pattern I've used on every climb. My preference is to lie with the door at my feet. This permits a fast escape should the need arise. Everything has a place, everything has a use: eyeglasses and flashlight in the tent pocket at nine o'clock, Walkman at three, pee bottle at four, water bottles inside my sleeping bag. My bag has a rating of zero degrees. (A minus 30 degree bag is too bulky and heavy.)

Mine isn't warm enough at these heights, but I place the foot of the bag inside my zipped windsuit jacket and this provides the right amount of comfort.

The tender sapphire blue of morning cheers my mountain mood as I shuffle out of camp at 10 a.m. The recurring weather pattern played out during the night as the storm quit at 1 a.m. after flinging a thin blanket of white across the gully. It burns off within hours. It's a good day -- windless and cloudless. Yet appearances perpetually deceive on this mountain's western slopes. In this part of the Andes, storms sweep across central Argentina from the Atlantic, inexorable in their passage and impatient to get west. When I'm in the gully between Camps I and II, half the sky above me is blocked from view by the enormous mass of the mountain. Unseen and unheard storms can envelop a climber in minutes when they burst over the col from the east with no warning. The desert land resides in complete sunshine one minute and then snowstorms engulf it in thirty, the temperature plummeting twenty to thirty degrees within that brief span of time.

The altitude and unremitting slant of the couloir keep the pace slow as I labor with determination at my climbing craft. Also limiting my speed is the second haul's weight, a load that makes the journey wearisome in the extreme; one foot gained feels like many yards of effort. Yet it's easier to go forward than turn back, more fulfilling to focus on the next step than the next less one. Counting out the rest step is the antidote to pain messages that swarm my brain, and presently I feel nothing. At one point, it seems as though I have labored only a short hour when, in fact, it has been three times that. I long ago trained myself to accept physical discomfort. This is a warped kind of idealistic pursuit to some, but it has deep meaning for me.

At the top of the gully, I pause and steal a glance to the west at the brightened white expanse of the Maricunga Salar. What a jewel it is. As I approach my campsite, I pray for the weather to hold. And where is my condor friend? Her nest is somewhere on the north walls that border the couloir. I have yet to see her since she appeared at Camp I.

Once more, I look to the flanks of Central to plan my route and notice that the first 700 feet are steep, with loose scree and talus to complicate the situation. When I prepared for this climb at home, the pictures I had taken on prior trips to Sur helped me design a strategy to tackle this part of the slope. I also recall the times I often looked over at the Central summit. Those pictures and memories helped me to create a possible route to the top. The huge, bulging ridge, the Balustrade, slanting horizontally across the route from right to left, will serve as a Camp III site. The top of its gently sloping mass promises a suitable place. From there, the summit will be only 1,700 feet away.

PHOTO: View from the col at a full moon next to the Central summit. The southern portion of the Balustrade is on the left. (Photo 5.19 on the site.)

My pulse, at 80 beats a minute, will drop to the sixties in an hour. Vigilance is necessary on a big peak as to the effects of high elevation on the mind and body. At altitude, the mind does not operate optimally. Decisions required down below use the entire ability of the intellect. At altitude, the thinness of the air deprives the intellect of its full capabilities and distorts rational decision-making. As an antidote, if the situation doesn't demand instant action, my decisions benefit from my taking extra time to examine and consider things before making a judgment. I demand of myself extra caution in everything I do, and this accounts for my slow, determined progress on a mountain. If I push myself to go faster without the need to do so, I risk altitude sickness or the edemas. The first is uncomfortable; the second are deadly.

Near the large rectangular rock, I secure Blue with parachute cord to stout rocks I've used on other trips. After throwing all my gear inside my home, I hesitate a moment before zipping the door. It must fasten up here. The left slide stops at the same point it did at Camp I. The right one rises towards the top and, in the last several inches, fails to bring the two teeth strands together. Movement back and forth proves useless; the teeth continue their steadfast refusal to lock and hold. Sometimes things in the mountains happen so fast that only instinct and experience determine a response. Sometimes events unfold so slowly that the ultimate danger isn't apparent. Insignificant incidents often don't provoke suspicion or alarm. It's when things culminate in an unfortunate climax that one recognizes that those innumerable smaller events flashed bright warning lights. Is this one of these slowly evolving episodes? Circumstances now have taken a more sinister form. There's an opening eight inches wide where the zippers have failed to come together. What might be an innocent state of affairs in everyday life becomes one of real concern up here. A yawning, gaping space like this one violates Baby Blue's integrity and invites possible disaster. If a violent windstorm stirs up, the wind gusts that will fill the tent will pressure the anchors. And if those fail . . . .

I've been developing a plan to confront this situation since the problem first arose. The surest way to combat strong gusts is to first flatten the tent; this will lower its profile and forestall a windy ride into Argentina. My plan:

1. If it's night, turn my headlamp to "On."
2. Unzip the tent door's screen lining.
3. Face the rear of the tent. (When it falls around me, the door will be above my head and chest.)
4. Grip the intersection point of the poles with the left hand before uncoupling the Velcro fasteners.
5. Detach the pole fasteners while gripping the pole intersection point.
6. Pull the "under" pole from the front corner pocket with the right hand.
7. Release both poles with the left hand at the intersection point and pull the tent inward as it collapses.

Plots, designs, strategies. I'm like a mad monk accountant trying to divine the different ways to cadge a pass through the Gates, with a fallback plan for the fallback plan. When I'm alone out here, nothing occurs without a kind of existential implication, an existential meaning. My ideas inventory even includes a plan for if I happen to peel off a slope and drift downwards in a freefall, detached from the earth, away from the mountain, soaring through the air, plummeting towards who knows where: extend arms and legs outwards and hold them there. Upon impact, my body won't roll but pancake, and that will slow a tumble farther down the mountain. It isn't much, this plan. But out here, alone, I must hold on to something or risk losing my grip and finding myself outside looking in, a witness to my own undoing.

My thoughts again return to the climb with Don back in March and the problems we had with the wind.

As we acclimated at the Refugio of Laguna Santa Rosa the first day, the unsettled weather gave an indication of trouble to come. Strong wind gusts continued the two days we stayed there. When we looked east to Tres Cruces fifteen miles distant, things seemed troubled there also, with afternoon clouds forming over the two summits. There seemed little wind on the mountain, but great distances often obscure the real conditions.

Patricio returned and drove us to our Base Camp site. Stiff wind gusts buffeted the truck at 14,000 feet. At 15,000 feet, he dropped us off, to return in twelve days. We wrestled with our tents to get them up and anchored. The wind kept blowing, not in a sustained manner, but in frequent gusts. High winds are common here, but usually higher on the peak, in my experience. There were no clouds over the summits in the afternoon, yet the winds persisted throughout the night.

PHOTO: Don poses next to a nieves penitentes field near Camp I. (Photo 6.10 on the website.)

During the following days, we acclimated at Base Camp (and experienced our "Day of the Condor"), made the double carries to Camp I, and the first carry to Camp II at the col between Sur and Central. The wind remained absent those days. This changed, and abruptly. On our second lift to Camp II, we worked away in the couloir. Three quarters of the way up the slope, we rested, looking out over the vast expanse below and enjoying the view. Then Don remarked upon a loud clamoring sound above us.

"What's that? That noise."

"It sounds like wind at the col."

"Are we still going up?"

I decided to keep going higher; after all, the sky was still clear and this windstorm might die out soon. We continued upwards towards the top of the gully; the uproar became louder the higher we went. The omen meant little at the time. It was one I should have recognized and acted upon but didn't.

Then, a sharp wind caught us from behind. It wasn't strong enough to knock us off stride, but its force gave me an uncomfortable feeling. Then another hit, this one with more insistence and heaviness.

"Hey, Bob," Don yelled. "I think we're climbing into it!"

"Yeah, we are. We're going to catch it with this one. Our gear is at the col so we need to retrieve it. We'll get there and decide what to do. All this could blow over when the sun goes down."

"Okay. Let's go."

Don was a good man. Twenty-eight. Six foot two. Thin and wiry. Hard attitude. Intelligent, with a solid moral compass. I have not often found these traits in other men.

The gusts had the force of a hurricane when we reached the col. It blasted in from all directions as we lurched forward like punch-drunk fighters, determined to reach the campsite. From the top of the couloir to camp requires twenty minutes on a calm day. It took twice that as the wind forced us to stop often to catch our breath.

We approached our gear stash utterly spent in strength. When we reached it and Don bent over to wrestle his pack off his shoulders, as soon as he did so a mighty whoosh of wind actually lifted him off the ground for almost three seconds! I could not believe what I saw. When he fell to earth, we immediately took cover next to a large rock.

The struggle to set up and anchor Baby Blue proved staggering. Once inside, there was no time to rest and recover as we tried to wait out the wretched situation in the hope that the frenzy outside would eventually subside. To lessen the strain on the tent anchors, we leaned against Blue's sides receiving the hardest blasts. I rejected any attempt to light the stove. We didn't possess the coordination to do it, what with trying to keep our home in place. And if we did manage to light it and the wind popped an anchor and collapsed our shelter, a horrible conflagration would prove a cruel reward. Instead, we ate candy bars and dried fruit. Hours passed with no letup in the howling maelstrom. It continued throughout the night, the spindrift and sand hissing and hurrying past, over, and around Blue, her sturdy frame shuddering, full of convulsive murmurs, the wind probing and probing, trying to find a weakness, a weakness into the very heart of our existences. Was this climb an inglorious attempt at glory, one risk too many? I didn't think so. Despite the abominable winds, my sanguine personality predicted eventual success.

Back in the present, I'm fully aware that revisiting those events with Don months ago will eat at my will to continue. If a storm like that one were to strike now with Blue's tent door in the shape it is, I would be in for a tough time. I emphasize the positives. There has been little wind since I arrived on the mountain. I'm acclimating well. And all that I need is one more day to reach Camp III, another to go to the summit and return to II, and then a day for the descent back to Base Camp. Three days is all I require.

My personality views the situation in an optimistic light. I always see endless possibilities and those are usually bright. The future is more attractive than the present or past, and my thoughts frequently operate in that future time. The high hopes and endless vitality of youth have never left me, though at 52 I'm now deep in middle age. There are no warnings from my mountaineer's intuition. But is the danger too large with a malfunctioning door zipper?

I examine again Central's slopes and tomorrow's route and note another dominating characteristic: the half-clamshell feature I christened "The Amphitheater" on a previous trip. Its wide base rests right here on the col floor. Its shell curves into the mountain's flank and its apex stretches 200 feet above its base. The far left extension of the Balustrade is above this high point. My route will pass briefly above the Amphitheater. At one point, a traverse to the left will bypass the steepest portions of the Balustrade and allow me to pass through its less protruding part and to a spot on top of it for Camp III. This part of the route looks difficult from here. It's important, and I commit it to memory, that I exercise extreme care when I climb anywhere directly above the Amphitheater. There is a patchy snowfield between its top and the underside of the Balustrade. If I slip or fall there, I'll careen over the Amphitheater's top and freefall to its base, like a modern day Icarus punished for his hubris in seeking to master heaven's heights.

A pulse of 60 and clear urine tell me my body has acclimated to this elevation. After nine days out here, my physical condition is excellent. A test of Blue's zippers, however, finds them continuing to malfunction. I remain positive despite the possible risks. I stare at Blue's slightly open door. It hangs there limply and flutters in the occasional breeze. It will be cold tonight and that open door will make things uncomfortable. But as long as the wind keeps its distance, I should be able to see this climb out.

A fleeting, silent storm slips over the col during the night, the soft drumming of flakes upon the walls announcing its presence, its peculiar whisperings entering my deepest psyche. The small snow hood above the tent door and my pack stuffed into the door opening keep unwanted snow out. There's no wind to accompany the stealthy visitor, and that spares me a night of discomfort. As the soft whiteness caresses Blue and me, I again ponder my chosen vocation. Early in my career, I wondered if climbing a very high mountain might confer special riches, like becoming a better person or bestowing strength in other parts of my life. But I found only too soon that the physical properties of a summit are just a collection of rocks and stones. That is what it is and all that it is. To stand upon a summit does not make me a better man or confer strength. But the challenges and risks of the entire journey provide deep satisfaction, and that satisfaction remains with me whether I reach a summit or not.

Next morning, my workday begins as dawn ushers in the newest of days. My tent, stove, gas, sleeping bag, air mattress, liter of water, ice axe, and food are ready for the single carry to Camp III. It will be one punishing lift to the heights above. When I don my windsuit, its bright red color animates me and imparts a sense of power and invincibility. It's amazing how color can accomplish this. A climber also needs the intensity of high energy, and adrenaline provides it in abundance at moments like this.

With mirrored sunglasses in place and my balaclava pulled tightly about my head, I'm prepared for another day on the slopes. Sand and scree are underfoot as the feeble warmth of the rising sun in the east chases the chill of the night away to the west. I work with tempered exuberance into my landscape. A light dusting of snow covers the terrain, but it will soon pass with the warming of the sun. The carry to any Camp III is a difficult effort. At these heights, where minimum exertion requires maximum fortitude, I feel bent beneath my burdens. Still I labor on, for although the pack is heavy, there is no alternative to this dull agony. It's tiring in the extreme, my legs barely withstanding the strain as I seek to pinch a few precious yards upwards from the mountain. I accept it all, my stoical nature actually welcoming and even enjoying it. A journalist once asked Hillary of Everest how he had reached the summit. "One step at a time," he replied. That is the penetrating essence of it all. It's sublime in its simplicity. It's placing one boot in front of the other, over and over and over again. There's nothing magical or mysterious about it.

I climb well to the right of the Amphitheater over ground composed of loose rocks and sand that shift with the slightest invitation; even a glance in their direction seems to provoke their movement. After 200 feet, the ground becomes steeper and it requires my ice axe instead of poles. It provides stability and strength in the labored progress upwards, its cold steel an extension of either hand and arm. Should I slip or fall, a thrust of its curved pick into the ground will create an anchor to stop me from falling farther. Terrain such as this can break a climber's heart. I concentrate on counting steps, and this blocks the pain and discomfort messages. Indefatigability. One must possess it in abundance or success is in doubt. I stop often, closeted in a closed and private world, suspicious of my intelligent faculties with the air now thinner. It is as though my mental abilities have atrophied. My brain processes things slowly and I'm vaguely aware of my diminished capacity. It is easier to be without a thought at times, and safer too, since the cold reaches through my windsuit whenever I halt. Despite its warmth, I sometimes feel as though I have little on.

Three quarters of the way to the Balustrade, its underbelly now looms above me as an overhanging bulge of massive rock. It thrusts outward from the mountain slope and forms a huge roof. I stare up at the fissures and the clefts and ask myself why these tons of rock and ice don't come tumbling down. They must remain in place if I am to remain intact, and that is my fervent prayer. I see no way through it from my present position. But from my vantage point at the col yesterday, I saw that the roof recedes towards the slope somewhere to my left, and that place will be the way past and over it. The stones and ice continue to hang together above me as I continue underneath the barrier with trepidation.

Stiff breezes blow across the slope. Two steps cause me to gasp for air. I then resume the assault. I use my axe to support my efforts as I struggle over the unrelenting steepness of the incline. I know it will lessen at some point. After an age, it does, and I continue traversing to the left in order to maintain progress. Of course, I must beware the yawning opening of the dreaded Amphitheater below me. I scramble across a patchy snowfield knowing I must take care here. At this fragile moment, at this fragile instant, with hopeless depths below, a slip or misstep will send me on a fatal ride all the way down to the col.

As I continue my movement to the left, the roof of the Balustrade gradually recedes towards the mountain. Presently, at a place where the rocks no longer form an overhang, I move up and past a large stone. Here lies the passage through! A rock wall presents a problem. But I am prepared to risk what I may and risk what I must. I thrust my boots and gloved hands into several crevices and presently work my way through. A few more labored moves and I am once again on scree and talus on the gently sloping back of the Balustrade. It's an exhilarating place to be, and it falls to my rapturous imagination. Occasionally I have found these silent places, unknown to all but me. This is its own trusting refuge, a welcoming point on my journey, and it offers peace and solace after a grueling day. It's thirty feet across and narrows slightly as it ascends to the right, or south, for almost 100 feet. At its high point, a spot near a car-sized rock becomes my latest home site. Less than 2,000 feet away, the summit looms above me, although an intervening ridge blocks its full view. There is no wind here, although I hear its noise somewhere below. I have found my own version of the fabled Shangri-La. My altimeter reads 19,950 feet.

Before I set Blue in place, I wish to see from this height an old friend, the majestic outline of Sur. Large rocks and boulders of the Balustrade block a complete view, but after I maneuver through them, the powerful presence of the southern summit fills the skyline. I see clearly the stone stalagmites that dominate the summit block and make it one of the most dangerous summits I have visited. Visible from here is the jagged, vertical stone gendarme I named the "Obelisk" years ago, since its distinctive outline pierces the sky like, well, an Egyptian obelisk.

PHOTO: A look at Sur from below Camp III on Central. The Obelisk is faintly discernible. (Photo 5.10 on the site.)

As I admire the scene, my mind drifts back to the summit climb in March, 1992, my first visit to Sur and my first solo climb in the Andes.

I went to Tres Cruces with complete naiveté and lack of information, as though I were the first to have visited the peak. My initial sight of it was on the drive to Ojos del Salado in November, 1991. We passed Cruces to the south and it tugged at my imagination like a light breeze, like a winged dream. I vowed to capture some day both Cruces summits. And here I was on the mountain to attempt the southern peak in fulfillment of my pledge. I chose my camps and the route as though it were a first ascent; after all, I had no maps, no pictures, no route description. From the col between the two summits, the route higher led over loose ground and eventually to a slightly canted area suitable for a Camp III at 20,500 feet. This was directly below the summit block, which was a rounded mass of stones that prickled with strange, jutting rock formations. These outcroppings extended around the outside of the western, northern, and eastern sides and were distinct in color and composition from the stones below, making them in appearance like Christ's "Crown of Thorns."

PHOTO: Underneath Sur's "Crown of Thorns." The author had not yet spotted the "magical staircase." It's entrance is out of the picture to the left. (Photo 5.26 on the site.)

At dawn, I continued the fight for the summit. The loose sand and scree below the Crown proved a tormentor's delight, as every several steps forward resulted in sliding several steps back. I clawed my way to the bottom of the Crown, all the time looking for an entry point through the bizarrely shaped rock forms. When I moved to the left to probe for a passage, a casual glance to the right revealed a magical staircase, mysterious in appearance -- a narrow chute of stair-stepped rock leading to the summit plateau, protected on left and right by overhanging rock banisters. Once I entered its lower reaches, the rocks and stones provided a rocky stairway to the heights above. I worked my way up, pausing once, I recall, to recuperate. Then I continued. A steep, but final, step soon loomed ahead, and as I came upon it, I prayed for the strength to surmount it. I got the last few feet up and, with my last effort, pulled my body up and over the top. There I stopped, panting and heaving from my effort. An otherworldly terrain lay before me. The summit stones were clearly in sight, the intervening ground littered with fantastically formed rocks that seemed to gesticulate and point skyward. Truly, it resembled a phantasmagorical garden of exotic plants and trees, but one completely rendered in stone. And, similar to a garden of flowers and plants, these formations also "lived," as the daily scouring action of sand, snow, and wind altered their contours and silhouettes over the centuries. This place demanded my complete and total concentration. A busted knee, a twisted leg, any injury would have held me there forever.

After twenty minutes of climbing through this wonderland, I realized I had not marked my path. How would I identify the return route? Already I had covered a good deal of ground. Aware of the future danger, I stacked three stones at intervals in line of sight to mark the way back. I picked my way carefully through the jumbled terrain and the "Obelisk" came into view in the near distance, 100 feet away. After I passed it, I gained the summit just as clouds began to form to the south. I stayed only a moment and then began the descent as the clouds continued to build and threaten directly above me. Despite the rising storm, I could not move too quickly over the dangerous rock forms. The risk of losing my balance amongst them was too great.

PHOTO: View of Central from underneath the summit of Sur. The Balustrade is the horizontal slant of rock above the base of the photo. (Photo 5.31 on the site.)

I followed my carefully stacked little stone beacons, but their late placement caused a yawning gap of space between my first marker and the precious trough leading off the top. My view of Central across the col gave me a vague sense of direction, but I had to find that little gully; it was the lone, sure path through the Crown of Thorns and back to safety. At the point where it should have been and wasn't, a sense of unease gripped my inner stomach. I backtracked thirty feet, thinking the way might lie to the right, but that led to nothing but increased exasperation and annoyance. A search to the left produced the same thing. Clouds continued to build and were now an ominous color of dark grey.

Desperation. I felt it beginning to well up inside me and knew I had to tamp it down or else run the risk of pure panic taking hold. If I forsook the stairwell, what were my options? I remembered the lip of the Crown and its dangers. There was a sheer drop of forty feet to loose sand below. I might first fling my pack over the edge and then follow it with my own desperate jump. But the sand slope underneath was canted at forty degrees and, when I hit it, I would tumble until I struck the rocks another hundred feet below. A cloying, clammy sweat ran down my face and dampened my balaclava. In the event, I valued a priest for the sacrament of Extreme Unction, to ease me on my journey. For if I jumped and broke my body, I might never get off the mountain. Then I would confront that question some ultimately must answer in this life: at what point does it become more difficult to live than it is to die?

I climbed back forty feet so I could focus on the rim of the Crown and seek again the opening at the top of the staircase. Trying to remember the rock features there, my oxygen-deprived brain struggled to process memories in anything other than a serial manner. Then, a refrigerator-sized rock came to mind. It sat at the top of the chute, on the left at its exit, and had alternating streaks of white and black, like Siena marble. Two protruding "nubs" on its surface projected out several inches, making it distinctive. My entire attention turned to locating that rock.

The urge to flee became more pressing. It took all my composure to remain calm. I knew I must hold firm at this moment or else all would be lost. Slowly and purposefully, I examined each rock with growing anxiety thumping in my chest. There! The marble stone with the two nubs stood not 150 feet away. It arrested my eye as a sudden shout arrests the ear. Escape! Salvation! This was not the time for celebration but the time for attentiveness and measured steps towards the enchanted stairway to safety and life. Once I reached it, I was on the sand slope below the Crown in twenty minutes. This was still not the time for thanksgiving. A close clap of thunder arose, the suddenness piercing the quiet with its forecast of impending danger. I moved determinedly towards my Camp III and entered the safe confines of Baby Blue just as white dust began to drift from the sky. Only then did I give thanks for my deliverance.

As I reflect upon that climb now back in the present on Central, I see it was a close thing. If I had not found the top of the chute and instead decided to jump to the steep sand incline below the Crown, the resulting injuries might have kept me on the mountain. How do you "die well" on a mountain, when no person in the world knows where you are and, even if he did, couldn't find you before the end?

I leave off my musings and return to the task at hand here at Camp III. When I place and anchor Blue, I hesitate a moment before I pull the zippers. They "must" work up here. But the door is in worse condition than it was down below. Less than one-third of it now zips shut. Working both slides back and forth produces nothing but my curses and epithets. The situation at this point is a precarious one. It seems fortune has abandoned me. My large pack plugs most of the gaping hole, but that won't offer much protection in high winds and snow. I begin melting ice for some broth and contemplate the risk dynamic, now raised to a much higher level.

My thoughts return to the climb with Don back in March, despite my attempts to keep them buried.

> The first night on the col. No sleep. The continuous howling of the wind. Don's cool demeanor. It still amazes me that on his first climb at altitude he never became flustered, never lost his head, never became a burden to me.

> The next morning, the tempest still raged at full force. The wind, mixed with snow, jostled Blue's walls continually. I decided we should remain at camp, since a retreat back down the mountain seemed too dangerous and desperate. Besides, this entire thing might soon blow itself out. In the early afternoon, darker clouds joined the fray, gyrating and contorting like Chinese dragons at a New Year's parade, turning and spinning, seemingly upon capricious orders from the mountain gods. We were now out of water and needed to drink to stay acclimated.

> "You stay to keep the tent weighted and I'll try to reach the pond," I yelled over the screeching of the wind.

With two one-liter bottles tucked beneath my windsuit jacket, I entered the tempest. The wind was so strong I couldn't stand upright. I crawled on all fours around Baby Blue, using my "col crawl," and found the four anchors solid and strong. The journey to the pond thirty feet away proved harrowing, since I felt as though a giant hand were about to lift me from the col's surface and deposit me I knew not where. When I unscrewed the top of the second bottle, a ferocious gust almost ripped it from my grasp. On the return, I raised my bent upper torso and the wind forced me back on my haunches as it tried to flip me from the mountain. I lay there, believing the fiend might actually have its way with me. What implacable insanity! Back in my crawl position, I murmured a silent prayer of thanksgiving as I re-entered the protective confines of Baby Blue. I said not a word to Don about my experience for fear it might disturb his equanimity.

That night we endured another wretched existence in our turbulent hell as we leaned against the tent walls to reduce the pressure on the anchors, as the wind exulted in its mastery over us. It hummed, it screamed, it whistled in endless vehemence. This all seemed unreal. My stoical nature endures physical and emotional hardships, but stoicism carries its own predicament, for the man who is too long-suffering may wind up doing nothing when a situation requires quick action.

The next morning I decided we must retreat. At 9 a.m., we packed all our gear and readied ourselves for the demanding task of collapsing Blue and stuffing her in my pack. At one point, a wind gust succeeded in pulling her from my gloved hands. But Don's firm grasp kept her from sailing into Argentina. We fought our way off the col. We couldn't stand. The wind was too strong and vicious and still blew from all angles. We crawled instead and dragged our packs behind us to the top of the couloir. Only when we were 150 feet lower in the gully were we separated from the fury, for the couloir's contours put us outside the reach of the winds, although they raged only feet away. It was a surreal place, for we resided in relative calm, as in a distant land. Had I not witnessed this with my own eyes, I should have found it hard to believe. We were able to stand once again and retreated all the way back to the security and safety of Base Camp.

I force my thoughts back to the present. I know the climb with Don might have become a disaster in the end. And it all happened down there at the col. If those winds were to return here now, with Blue's tent door open and compromised, the gales would sweep us off the mountain and into eternity. My intuition now grasps the seriousness of the situation. Rather than conjuring up hopeful images, it now sees the accompanying dangers. As a result, my will wavers. Reason is now convinced that to remain here is foolhardy. Yet, my intellect remains indecisive.

During the endless night, I play the alternatives back and forth. On the one hand, I see myself collapsing Blue, dashing to the summit, returning here, and hurrying down to Camp I, where there is safety from a death wind. As long as it's calm at daybreak, I can do it. Then the doubts come. What if vicious winds arise on my way to the summit and force a retreat back to Camp III? It's impossible to camp here with a damaged tent door. I would have to reach Camp II at least. And a descent from III to II over steep, dangerous ground in high winds, especially the slopes above the Amphitheater, would be akin to signing my own death warrant. And what if at Camp II my exhaustion, the lateness of the day, or something else prevents farther progress? This would mean another night in a hurricane with an open tent door. I would have to keep the tent collapsed and draw it about me like a death shroud. I'm anxious about the unknown, and the unknowns on this day are infinitely insidious and numerous. A brief time is granted us on life's journey and I wish to hold and live my life another day.

Back and forth the inner raging goes all night. I stare into the heartless gloom and see myself staring back. Am I a witness to reality? Or am I, like the chained men in Plato's parable of the cave, watching false images play across cave walls while the truth exists outside, beyond their observation? Have I gone so far I might never return? I must be careful. These thoughts may lead to my psychological undoing.

At last, the long night ends. A clear sky awaits the sun's warming rays. A breath of a breeze rustles Blue's door; its frigid breath causes a momentary start. I lift my head as one mourning amongst ruins, as a languid torpidity makes my summit preparations slower than usual. Everything I do is in slow motion and lacks the hopeful anticipation I usually feel. Finally, I'm ready. But it's taken twice the usual time to prepare, probably caused by self-imposed mental stress. I carry out my activities without a firm commitment to do anything and go through the motions like one committed to an inconvenient inevitability, with no heart, no passion, no focused movements.

In a desultory manner, I collapse Blue and weight her with several stones to guard against a sudden gust of wind. I stand to go and glance to the summit. It's so close I might touch it. I lean forward on my poles and raise my right leg for the first step towards the heights. Yet it refuses to move and remains motionless, an immobile pillar supporting an unwilling burden. I try again to make that first step forward. But my leg lacks life, and repeated attempts at movement meet repeated resistance. It is immovable, as a sturdy tree rooted in the earth is immovable. The summit is mine. The weather promises success. The moment is propitious. I try again. I order it to move! But my leg remains firmly in place. I am unable to control the most basic of human functions.

After several minutes of silent reflection, I see everything in a pure light of complete understanding. My intellect finally has concluded, after consulting with judgment and reason, that to continue is to risk the whole lot. My will, too, is convinced the danger of proceeding upwards is too great and has cracked beneath the strain. My body won't perform against the intellect's decision and has locked my leg muscles in place as though in a brace.

I turn about, towards Baby Blue, and manage a hesitant step forward. The next is more purposeful. Only now does my body obey. It agrees with my mind that life is down; safety is down; family is down.

As I pack Blue and all my gear, I find that I can move again normally. I'm off the Balustrade and proceeding downslope, angling away from the Amphitheater and climbing confidently, assuredly. I commit mind and soul to a descent I know to be more dangerous technically than the ascent had been. Within an hour, I am past the treacherous upper reaches of the route. My diligence has been rewarded.

I stop and ponder what transpired, an immense weight now lifted from my shoulders. I realize that my acceptance of the malfunctioning tent door pushed the risk factor beyond the acceptable. At the end, this climb was about the occasional futility of high altitude mountaineering and has proven an instance of utter disenchantment. Have my efforts been for something completely without substance?

Still, I must own that the most man may hope to know is to fulfill Plato's admonition, "Know thyself." Men go abroad to wonder at the heights of mountains, yet they pass their daily lives without wondering in the least about themselves. I'm happy to say this did not happen to me, because I learned much about myself on my innumerable forays into the unknown, and this climb was no different.

I pass through Camp II, pick up the garbage stash, and press down towards Camp I and its relative safety from the wind. And where is my condor friend? It's been a week and a half since I saw her last. At night, even with the tent door almost completely open, there is peace and tranquility. With tomorrow's return to Base and Patricio's arrival the following day, this journey will be over, the end of another grand adventure. I dislike these times. After thirteen days, I do not wish to leave my mountain. A further sadness is that the lid of the film canister with the *Tres Cruces Shrimpus Altitudus* inside has come off, and their broken little bodies reside somewhere inside my pack. I resolve to capture another batch upon returning to this mountain, which has become so much a part of my being and existence.

PHOTO: An alpenglow moment on the western walls. (Photo 5.32 on the website.)

On the way home, the big LanChile 767 lands in Lima, Peru, to refuel and take on passengers. I recall my daughter's request when I left home several weeks before.

"Dad."

"Yes, Maria."[39]

"Will you buy me and Sarah gold rings in Lima like the ones you buy Mom? We'll pay you for them."

"Let me see what I can find. I'm sure I can locate something within your budget."

Well, not exactly. The small rings I choose have Incaic markings that befit my daughters' Inca heritage. And they certainly don't match their allowance limits. But the women in my family deserve the best.

---

[39] Maria is Alex's mother.

GOOGLE TOUR: The Tour for this Chapter is on the website.

PANORAMIO: In the Panoramio section, choose the "Tres Cruces" tag.

MOVIES: The April, 1999, and the Chapter 9 and 10 movies are appropriate for this Chapter.

Today I believe he was the luckiest of men that day. This incident closed out my guiding career. I found leading others on a big mountain too stressful. And who needs that kind of tension at 57 years of age?

--From the author's personal climbing journal

CHAPTER 6

Interlude: Clients

*T*he majority of my climbs were solo. Several were with paying clients, however. In 1995, I decided to offer other climbers my services as a climbing guide. I had sixteen climbs to my credit at that point, three with the guiding company American Alpine Institute (AAI), two with friends I had corresponded with over the years about the Andes, and the rest on my own. I had the skills to teach others about climbing at altitude and I wanted to assist beginning climbers to live out their high altitude dreams. In this chapter, I tell of my experiences with four clients on three separate visits to Tres Cruces. I always chose Tres Cruces Central or Sur for these climbs, since the Chile-Argentine road is only two miles from the foot of the peak.

A DISAPPOINTING RETREAT

The Maricunga Customs Station on the northern limits of the Maricunga Salar saw me several times over the years. This climb took place in March, 1998, when the Station served as a refuge during a stormy night of lightning, thunder, rain, and snow. That's where the trip ended. It began more than a week earlier with my arrival at the Laguna Santa Rosa Refugio (12,000 feet) with two clients, Frank and Bill, both in their late twenties. I'm very fortunate. Although 54, I am still able to live out my high altitude dreams. Our goal: the summit of Tres Cruces Central. Frank, who graduated the year before from the

National Outdoor Leadership School (NOLS), had climbing experience, but not at high altitude. Bill had the absolute barest of resumes, with only strenuous hiking as preparation. Yet, at Frank's request, I agreed reluctantly to let him join us.

Patricio dropped us off at Laguna Santa Rosa for acclimation and planned to return in two days. Both men endured the usual headaches but nothing more serious. Clouds covered Central and Sur during the two days at the Laguna, a Cassandra-like warning foretelling troubles ahead. Pat returned on the appointed day and deposited us at our 15,100-foot Base Camp site late in the morning. Within the hour, Bill felt the altitude with painful headaches that drove him to his bag. Later, after hot tea, he improved, although he still felt uncomfortable. Frank and I had only slight headaches.

PHOTO: Frank and Bill at Base Camp. (Photo 6.1 on the site.)

During the next days, I watched them closely and insisted they stay hydrated and share with me their heart rates and the color of their urine. A guide's categorical imperative is to see to the safety of his clients; there is no greater responsibility than this, and no greater burden. This absolute, unconditional requirement asserts its authority in all circumstances. So this monitoring was to satisfy me, before we set out, that they were fit to go higher. Should tragedy strike, I could be subject to lawsuits from the victims' families. Even though I required clients to sign legal documents absolving me of all responsibility, one can never be too careful in such matters.

In the meantime, both summits remained covered in clouds. They came into sight on the second day and then disappeared again two hours later. Might the peaks be part of an Andean imaginary paradise, a mysterious and remote utopia isolated from the outside world and inhabited by a permanently happy people?

After three nights at Base, we all felt fit enough to make the first haul to Camp I. As on previous days, the summits remained hidden, like demure young women hesitant to reveal their beauty to the prying eyes of inquisitive young men. Frank did well, yet Bill often lagged behind, though we moved with a slow, unhurried rest step. It took us five hours to reach the Camp I site. With the light load of a first carry, it should have taken us three and a half. On the descent to Base Camp, Bill again failed to keep the easiest of paces. I began to wonder. Had I been mistaken in granting Frank's request?

In the evening, the ever-present wind, now freighted with light snow, bore down upon our tiny camp and buffeted us for an hour before it departed in the early morning hours. Baby Blue and I were used to the storms; it was a unique experience, however, for my two friends. A warming sun greeted us next morning as we set off late with our crushing second loads, much of the snow already melted and evaporated. Bill was slow once more. The loads we carried were heavy. Still, it took us over six hours to arrive at Camp I. Now I realized the truth of the problem: Bill not only had difficulty with the altitude but was also out of shape.

That afternoon, I sought to motivate them for the next day's climb by explaining the route's characteristics so they could prepare mentally for the challenge. The gully to Camp II was an unremitting thirty-five degrees that required a two-step rest step most of the way. The first day would be difficult and the second more so because of the extra weight on our backs. Bill's response was a mild surprise to me.

"I'm not cut out for this, Bob. You guys go ahead without me." The shrug of his shoulders implied surrender. His tone of voice suggested defeat.

I thought he had been unraveling over the previous days, and here was proof of it. But I tried to coax him forward.

I put my hand on his shoulder. "It takes a truthful man to share that, and I admire you. But let's see how we fare tomorrow in the couloir. You've traveled a long distance and spent a lot of money to get here. Give yourself one more chance."

As he mulled this over, I made clear to both men the consequences if Bill did not continue, at either his decision or mine.

"If I decide to end the climb, we all go back to Base, walk downslope to the highway, hitch a ride to the Customs Station, and I'll call Patricio."

"Why can't I go back to Base and wait for you and Frank to finish? I can take care of myself. I've done it all my life."

119

"I can't do that. I can't leave a client alone. A climbing party should never separate in the mountains. It's vital we stay together." I had to make this point completely understood. Tragedy often strikes when teams break apart on a big mountain.

Bill didn't like being the one to end the climb for all of us, should it turn to that. I was empathetic, yet firm in my resolve. After my further attempts at motivation, I was pleasantly surprised when he agreed to try the gully next day.

"Remember, I'll be right there, reminding you to drink and stay at the proper pace. We'll see it through. Stay positive!" I wished fervently for Bill's success; nonetheless, we could not continue unless he showed definite improvement.

Later in the afternoon, clouds from the east crept up out of our sight and stole the summits from our view, bringing with them a desultory, timid storm with light snow. It ceased in an hour.

We rose early to a welcoming sky. When we reached the bottom of the couloir, I took the opportunity to rally our efforts.

"Frank, why don't you lead. Stay to the center where the ground's good and hard, and stay out of the loose stuff to either side. I'll climb with Bill."

Bill kept a good pace, at least until halfway up the incline, where things came apart rapidly. He was unable to manage more than one step before stopping to gasp for air.

In moments, he was finished.

"It's over for me. I can't keep going," he said as he sank to his knees in the unmistakable gesture of defeat.

We sat and rested while I took stock of the situation. He didn't have a headache or any symptoms of serious altitude sickness, yet the elevation and his physical weaknesses had taken their toll. Just as important, he had lost his will to continue, and when the will retreats, the body follows in close order.

"Okay, the climb to the summit's over. You gave all you had, and I'm proud of you for having the courage to make the effort." I shook his gloved hand in a gesture of understanding and acknowledgment.

I yelled to Frank the climb was at an end but to stay in place.

"Bill, please listen to me. I want you to make the col, at 18,600 feet. It will be the highest you'll reach the rest of your life. And the view is unforgettable." I paused a moment to let that sink in. "We'll leave our packs here and go the rest of the way with just your water bottle and camera. I know you can do it."

He remained silent.

"Dig down deep for something extra. Think of successes in your life. How did you feel? Bring those feelings here, right now, to this mountain. If you get to the col, it will be another one of those times for you."

After we rested several minutes, it seemed that my admonitions had made their mark. He agreed to continue. We abandoned our packs and stepped off, now at a good pace. I waved to Frank to continue, and our little procession plodded along on its determined course.

PHOTO: The author and Bill halfway up the couloir. (Photo 6.2 on the website.)

Bill waged a gritty performance during two grueling hours. Eventually, the incline lessened and we were at the col. I congratulated them both, but especially Bill. He had pushed himself to a place he hadn't been before, and he thanked me for motivating him to do so.

After briefly enjoying the views to the northwest, we began the descent. The usual late afternoon storm formed above us, and it began snowing in earnest when we arrived at Camp I. It continued for an hour and then left to torment some other part of the Andean landscape. As I listened to the quiet patter of flakes against Baby Blue's enduring skin, I pondered what happened in the couloir. Since Bill made the decision to quit himself, it made it easy for me to call an end to the climb. Moreover, as we were soon to learn, our team was better off for this turn of events.

We left late the following morning to return to Base Camp with the usual punishing loads on our backs. Should things have gone differently, this would have been the day for the second carry to Camp II at the col, followed the next day by the single carry to a Camp III. Three hours later, when Base came into sight, things seemed amiss. The distant view was askew, in disarray, and the cause wasn't apparent. As we moved closer, things became clearer. My bag had been unzipped and clothes, food, and gear strewn about the slope. There were no scratch marks on the bag near the zipper's teeth. That suggested that whatever it was either had done this before or was intelligent enough to figure out the means of entry. A condor? Perhaps. But we hadn't seen one flying around. Foxes? In November, 1995, on Llullaillaco, I suspected foxes as the culprits in tearing apart that Base Camp. In the end, we never determined the cause of this latest incident, one more humorous than anything else. At least I still had my wallet with my money and credit card!

The next day dawned as we made plans to hike down and reach the highway. From there, we would hitch a ride to the Customs Station. We took what we needed, food, gas, sleeping bags, and stove, and buried our two garbage bags beneath the soft surface of the sand and under several rocks to prevent the wind from setting them adrift.

"Hey," said Bill, "today the plan was to make the single haul to a Camp III. Right?"

Yes, that had been the plan. Fate, however, had chosen a different path for us, one that would soon prove providential. We reached the Argentina road in two hours and struck out towards the Station. In twenty minutes, a small SUV approached. We were in luck, thanks to the generosity of those inside. The passenger was a geologist working at a small mine several miles to the east, the other fellow his driver.

"I'll send my man back for you after he drops me off. He'll drive you to Customs." He offered his hand to seal the deal. Perfect English. Perfect courtesy. Indeed, the driver returned in an hour and off we flew, on a straight stretch hitting 140 km/h (86 mph).

I glanced at Frank. I knew what we were both thinking: this guy is more dangerous than the cold and high altitude back on the mountain.

At the Station, I asked the driver to wait, wrote a thank you note to our geologist friend, and pressed it into the chauffeur's hand. "For your *jefe*, señor."

Of course, the Station Colonel received us cordially and showed us to a multi-room storage shed, our room for the night. I called Patricio, who assured me he would pick us up the next morning. We settled in for the night and looked forward to a restful sleep.

At 10 p.m., a distant rumbling disturbed the night. Soon, the booming was directly above us and, for everlasting minutes, brightened bolts of white-hot light cracked across the darkened land, so bright it were as though the heavens had quickened their usual course of turning and unleashed the full light of day. Down they came, Zeus-hurtled sparks of phosphorescent beams filled with airborne fire that exploded upon the Maricunga Salar. We looked south over the flat, brooding spaces, spellbound by the light show that played before us. When stiletto-like stabs hit a mile off, a crackling noise like splintering wood detonated above us. The flashes brought to life each stone and speck of sand, leaving each luminous in the desert night. Presently, the lightning passed, followed by a watery deluge, heavy, like that in jungle lands, and it beat against the roof of our shelter so thunderously it might have been the loudest sound heard for 100 miles. Water poured from the sky like a giant river over a falls and cascaded downwards to burst in all directions upon the rocks and sand below. This created a shallow, temporary lake that surrounded the Station, revealed luridly by the buildings' arc lights that proclaimed its lonely, singular existence in this lonely, singular land.

"I have never seen anything . . . ." Bill's voice trailed off, lost in the clamorous noise of the torrential downpour. I agreed. Mother Nature was outdoing herself this night.

The rain slackened and a sudden cold settled over the gloomy, murky night. Then, a cascade of snowflakes tumbled from the heavens, sometimes so thick the Station buildings were lost to sight and, lost, after a while, even to thought. Never had I witnessed such a magical display. After an hour, the storm lessened and finally ceased at 4 a.m. Several cars and trucks stood in line outside the Station, all travel across the Great Plateau to Argentina halted by the Station carabineros. At daybreak, an immense white sheet covered the Salar, a sight I'd never seen there before.[40]

---

[40] The Station Colonel later told me that during his two years of duty here, now in his third year, this was the fourth such storm to hit this area during his service.

The golden disk of brightened light rose above the eastern horizon, and a small measure of welcome warmth embraced the forlorn land. When Patricio arrived at mid-day, vehicles in both directions had been released and most of the snow across the Salar had evaporated, proof that this desert is one of the most dry and most arid amongst all the world's dry and arid deserts. I worried that the storm had dumped so much snow on the mountain that it might prevent us from retrieving our equipment.

Pat was eager to return to Base Camp for our gear.

"We try. I feel lucky. Tomorrow my birthday." That's right. Patricio was due a birthday dinner when we returned to town. After a hasty farewell to the Colonel, with a pack of Camels as thanks for his kindness, we set off for the peak.

When the mountain came into full view, the lower slopes upon which our camp rested presented a mixed picture of bare gravel and rock expanses with occasional patches of snow. Patricio, a skilled off-road driver, stopped at the bottom of the incline and surveyed the route as his right hand gripped the shift knob.

"Bob. This difficult. Is possible go back to town and come back tomorrow?"

"Well, if we do it now we save a trip." Besides, I didn't want to pay for gas for another day.

With Pat's deft skill at finding a route, our tents and bags soon came in sight. The topmost half of Baby Blue stood out; the other half was buried under two feet of snow. I marveled at this; I had never seen so much snow at this elevation. But we didn't find everything. We searched the camp and failed to locate my ice axe, which had been resting on the sand near Blue, or our two garbage bags. I wished especially to locate the garbage; the wind might one day rip the bags open and spew their contents over the mountain. Even with all four of us tramping back and forth through the snow, we did not find either the axe or the bags. I felt the loss of my ice axe keenly. No doubt only one who has lived and labored on high peaks can understand this attachment to a lifeless piece of metal.

"Pat, we'll return one day, mark my words," I said, with a measure of determination in my voice. I wanted to find my axe and that garbage.

Before we headed back down, we looked again to the col between Central and Sur, now plastered with snow.

Frank let out a low whistle. "You know, we were supposed to be at Camp III when the storm hit last night, according to your schedule. I'm going to remember our luck for a long time."

"Yeah. In a storm like that one, we might have been in a fight for our lives coming down through those snowdrifts. And that would have been today. There's no telling from here how deep that stuff is. We're fortunate to be here rather than there finding out."

Bill saw fortune in his problems on the climb. "I don't feel so bad now. I saved us all!" He slapped the back seat several times for emphasis.

One thing is certain. Had we continued higher, it could have been a disaster, because the storm was one of the more punishing I had ever seen. And trying to lead clients through the mess would have tested my guiding abilities to the fullest. There, at over 20,000 feet with two complete novices, trying to survive a fearsome storm and attempting to retreat with them down slopes covered in snow would have proved a nightmare.

"Pat, it's time for your birthday dinner. Let's get back to town."

Even today, years later, this climb plays in my mind and causes a faint shudder as I think about what might have happened. It's an incontrovertible truth that there are myriad ways to wonder at circumstance, and this offered one of those, for Fate forsook moving Her hand one more time.[41]

THE SEQUEL

In March, 2000, I found myself in Copiapo for a new attempt on Pissis. My goal was the ascent of three of its five summits. In March, 1997, I made the first solo ascent of one of the five, the subsidiary summit that sits on the western side of the Pissis massif.[42] On this climb, my plan was to make a solo attempt of the three subsidiary

---

[41]   I've lost track of Frank and Bill over the years.

[42]   See Chapter 7, "Pissis: The Hand of God."

peaks residing on the eastern side of the mountain. I intended to climb the southern peak first and spend the night at the shallow col between it and the second summit to the north. The next day, I would climb that middle peak, descend into another col, and then climb the third summit. From there, I would descend to Base Camp. These peaks had dominated my thoughts ever since I first saw them years before. If I succeeded and climbed the three, in November I would attempt the main summit and celebrate the accomplishment of having ascended all five peaks, solo. Instead, this trip was destined to become a rescue mission of sorts that had nothing to do with Pissis.

My physical condition was poor, since I had contracted a cold the day before leaving home. It was in my lungs upon landing in Copiapo, complete with bouts of heavy coughing. It wasn't as onerous as it could have been; still, it was discomforting and distracting and caused a bad start to the trip, because I was physically out of sorts. That wasn't all that was affecting me. Pissis is a precarious undertaking. Ever since my first visit to the mountain in March, 1994,[43] I approached it with deep respect. The nearest mine is forty miles away, the entire distance off-road. And, should it snow before Patricio returned, that could prevent him from reaching me for days. I had to steel myself for every visit to the monster. It was the embodiment of all to dread in this life, a dread that demanded the utmost in motivation to set off alone with its summit as the goal.

At the pass overlooking Laguna Santa Rosa, 2,000 feet below, Pat and I looked across the Maricunga Salar to Tres Cruces fifteen miles away. We stared in astonishment at the great expanse of snow on its slopes. White covered the two summits, down to just above where I usually placed my base camps. It had been a stormy summer.

"They close Plateau two weeks in January. This is what I hear."

Vicious summer storms had dumped record amounts of snow in this part of the Andes. That was evident not only from the heavy snow on Tres Cruces, but also from the lower snow lines on all the peaks in the neighborhood. The Chilean police close the highway for three to

---

[43] See Chapter 2, "Pissis: High Winds from Tartarus."

four weeks during the winter, usually in August. It is rare for them to do so in the summer.

We spent the first night at several abandoned mining buildings at 13,600 feet, eighteen miles south of the shuttered Mina Marte and due west from Paso Valle Ancho Sur (15,055 feet), our entry point into Argentina. That is too high for an initial night at altitude, and we paid for it with painful headaches. They left off in the morning as we drove to the peak.

At the crest of Valle Ancho, we paused for pictures at the thirty-foot-tall Eiffel Tower-like metal marker. (These structures mark all the significant passes through this part of the Andes.) I gazed fixedly to the south upon the immense mountain, Pissis. Unfortunately, seen from this angle and at a distance of twenty-five miles, the conditions on the three subsidiary summits were unclear. An alternate route, the one I used for the first solo ascent of the western subsidiary summit, lay under a white shroud and was thus out of the question. And the normal route, below the eastern glacier's face, I ruled out for the same reason.

We drove south towards the peak and stopped to enjoy one of our favorite natural phenomena, an ojo, a burbling artesian well. A small stream flowed from it and nourished hardy plant life on its banks. These gurgling fountains were exciting and wonderful to encounter because of their sheer novelty, and I never tired of watching the bubbling water flow from them.

Patricio maneuvered the truck through shallow ravines and over slight ridges as the mountain gradually loomed larger in our front window. An hour later, we could see enough of the vast eastern slopes for me to render a verdict. Snow completely covered the two possible routes to the subsidiary summits, making a solo attempt very risky. This was a disappointment, as I was quite keen to capture those three peaks.

"It will have to wait for another trip," I said. Though I was reluctant to leave, the only option for me was to abandon the quest.

"I think it still be here next time. What now? Different mountain?"

In fact, I had another mountain as an alternative -- Tres Cruces, and a climb to the summit of Central over the northern or northeastern slopes. I had no information about a route, which made it perfect as an adventure. Pat agreed to this and we set off towards Valle Ancho. Once we were over the Pass and back at the road connecting Mina Marte with Laguna Negro Francisco, I asked Pat a favor.

"Can we visit Laguna Negro Francisco to say a prayer at Giancarlo's cross?" I wished to pay tribute to our friend.

"I just realize. We don't have gas to go there and Tres Cruces and back to Copiapo."

We had already used the extra ten gallons Pat brought along for added range. Rugged off-road driving is tough on gas mileage.

The sole choice was to go back to Copiapo and return the following day, so we did. The next day at noon, we arrived at Tres Cruces in position to gauge whether a route from the north was possible. The most appealing passage upwards appeared to be over the northeastern slopes.

Yet, as on Pissis, the inclines were choked with snow, just as they were on the western and southern sides of Cruces, in yet further testimony to the rough summer. The trip was at an end. I'd have to return to town and book an early flight home. This disturbed my normal mountain equanimity.

"Okay," I said. "Let's go back to town. There's little left to do out here." This would be only the second time I left the Andes without attempting a climb. It was an unsatisfying experience, but at least I was alive and well.

When we regained the highway, I had an idea.

"Wait a minute. We have some time. Do you think we can rescue my ice axe and the garbage bags we left last year on the western slopes?"

"Sure."

In twenty minutes, we arrived at that side of the peak. Together, we stared at the slope where I had placed so many base camps over the years. It looked impassable in places because of patches of snow. But Pat had a practiced eye for this sort of affair and agreed to try it, although he cautioned it might be impossible. If we located the axe and garbage, however, that would provide a measure of accomplishment for this disappointing journey.

Somehow, Pat worked through and around snow banks and drifts in a valiant effort to find the camp. We soon came upon a large, snow-free area we both recognized at the same moment as the site.

"There's the axe!" I shouted. It lay on the sand as though recently dropped. Close by we found the half-buried, undisturbed garbage bags, still positioned underneath their coverings of small stones. This fortunate turn of events brightened what until now had been a rather forlorn exercise in continual disappointment.

"Remember, Pat? I said we'd return for this stuff. I'm happy we did."

He looked aside and smiled in satisfaction. My mountains were also his mountains.

THE FEAR FACTOR

In March, 1999, my client was Richard, a British citizen in his early thirties with several climbs in the Alps on his resume, yet no experience above 14,800 feet. He seemed motivated to attempt a big mountain, had read the preparation materials, and one day called from Liverpool to say how excited he was about the climb. My choice for a mountain was the usual one: Tres Cruces -- on this occasion, Central.

Patricio dropped us off at the Refugio Laguna Santa Rosa to acclimate for two days. Richard adapted well at 12,000 feet and that gave me a quiet optimism that he could handle higher elevations. He talked easily and often of life in England, his job as a software developer, and his days as a young man growing up in South Africa as the son of a British mining executive. There wasn't anything in his overall manner to worry me. But he did mention that his girlfriend wanted him to reach the summit and had bragged often to her friends of his climb. His throat tightened when he told me this, as though it were something of some emotion for him. Why? I didn't wish to know more than what he told me. It was none of my business. However it did cross my mind that if he were out there only to impress a woman, then that might affect his motivation to brave the hardships to come.

PHOTO: Richard attends to his gear on the porch of the Refugio. (Photo 6.5 on the site.)

Two days later, we waved to Patricio as he left us at our Base Camp at 15,200 feet. It was a large jump in elevation in one day for anyone, especially someone like Richard who had never been at that altitude before. Still, he was doing well, although he had become very quiet and withdrawn. We both had minor headaches, although of the ordinary kind. The plan was to spend three nights at Base and then begin the double hauls up the mountain.

The next day, to counter the boredom of sitting in camp, I showed Richard how to pan for gold. On my second visit to the peak in November, 1992, as I sat in the sand outside Blue enjoying a rare day of warmth, a golden glint at my feet hinted at something of value. I used a pan lid, water, sand, and my best panning technique; several golden flakes were my reward. On each succeeding trip to this mountain, I found the opportunity at base to continue the tradition. Finding gold wasn't really a surprise. Mina Marte lay only twelve miles away as the condor flies.

We whiled away the afternoon panning for flakes, until Richard stopped abruptly and stared towards Laguna Santa Rosa in the distance. I caught his movements out of the corner of my eye.

"No one knows where we are."

"What? What are you talking about?"

"No one knows where we are."

"Patricio knows."

"What if something happens to him?" His raised voice alerted me to the tension he felt.

"Don't worry. He'll come back."

"What if he doesn't?"

"He has never failed me."

"This may be the first time."

"See the road over there? It's less than four miles away. We walk to it, wait for a vehicle, hitch a ride to the Customs Station, call him from there. Remember? We talked about escape."

He neither moved nor spoke for long moments and remained motionless the entire time. I watched him closely.

"What's the matter?"

"I don't know. I just don't feel safe out here."

"Why don't you feel safe?"

"There's no one within forty miles."

"I made it clear all along we would be alone."

"I guess I didn't understand what it meant."

"And now you understand?"

"Yes."

"And?"

"I want to leave. I don't want to stay here."

I moved over to where he sat and placed a hand on his shoulder.

"Let's see what you feel in the morning."

"I know what I'll feel."

"What will you feel?"

"I won't want to stay here."

He raised his pan lid and flipped it the way one flips a Frisbee. The climb was over.

You can read fear in a man's face, as if writ in a book, there deep within, the enigmatic stare, the vacant eyes. Richard seemed vanquished, a beaten man. There was no indignity in reaching his limits. Robert, my Angel, knew I felt gripping fear once, the deep, visceral kind that caused me to empty my bladder. Not on a mountain. Robert knows when and where.

"It's too late in the day to leave. We only have two more days out here before Pat arrives. Can you hold on? If not, we can walk out and try to hitch a ride to the Customs Station. But Patricio comes for us the day after tomorrow, so if we walk out now he will still pick us up on the same day."

"We can stay. But I just don't feel safe. You know?"

"I understand. Don't worry about it. We'll be out of here soon enough."

Back in Copiapo two days later, we were able to obtain early flights home. Truly I must say, never did a climb end so quickly. It left me wondering what Richard's girlfriend had to say about it. I lost all contact with him after the climb. I hope she was an understanding woman.

I had a pleasant surprise the night before I left. At dinner, Pat introduced me to his new girlfriend, Elise, a delightful and beautiful woman.

Next day on the drive to the airport, he told me more. "This serious, Bob. I let you know in months what happen!" [44]

A NEAR TRAGEDY

In March, 2001, another client accompanied me to Tres Cruces. Sam was in his mid-thirties and eager to experience high altitude. He had climbed Mt. Whitney (14,495 feet) in California twice, and he planned to climb Aconcagua one day. Prior to taking on the Argentine giant, he wanted to test himself on a peak of Tres Cruces' elevation. I advised him to try Ecuador first, because of the moderate heights of the peaks there, and then move to the higher ones in Bolivia. Yet, he persisted, and his motivation convinced me to take him on as a client. In our correspondence before the climb, Sam seemed possessed by the dream of climbing Aconcagua.

At dinner on the first night in Copiapo, he talked more of his dreams. "Sometimes I think about Aconcagua to the exclusion of all else." He said this with some emotion, slowly enunciating each word to give it meaning.

I like passion in any human being I meet, as long as it is a reasonable passion. And his passion for climbing was reasonable. Besides, without hopes and dreams life would be a dull thing, so I admired him and his aspirations.

PHOTO: The author, Sam, and Patricio at Refugio Santa Rosa. (Photo 6.8 on the website.)

Patricio drove us to the Refugio at Laguna Santa Rosa and left, planning to return in two days. Sam suffered headaches the first afternoon and early evening and then improved over the following days. The weather also was favorable, with occasional breezes during our stay

---

[44] Patricio and Elise soon married. In December, 2010, the twins, Tomas and Victoria, were born, a double blessing for two wonderful people.

and no clouds on or near our mountain. The signs were positive and indicated a chance at success. In truth, they masked the near tragedy soon to befall us.

Two days later, we were on the way to base camp with Patricio, cruising over the flat sand and earth of the Maricunga Salar beneath clear skies. We intersected the Chile-Argentina road and began to rise as we drove towards the Great Plateau stretching from Tres Cruces in the west to the Carabinero Station at Laguna Verde in the east, almost forty miles at a near constant elevation of 14,300 feet.

We passed through 13,000 feet, then 14,000 feet, and stopped at the waterfalls of Rio Lamas. The base of the huge peak stood two miles to the south, its bulk blocking out a quarter of the sky. I remarked upon the beauty of the scene, and Sam answered with a faint "beautiful." His voice didn't sound right, for some reason, but didn't cause me alarm. I thought the sight and surroundings overwhelmed him. At that moment, I should have turned and spoken directly to him.

At the foot of the mountain, we began the drive to base camp over ground bearing the imprint of tires most surely ours from our many trips. Patricio and I exchanged few words; while he concentrated on the best route, I concentrated on the intense beauty of this never-changing land.

"There, there it is." I knew this place like the ground around my California home. When we stopped, I turned to the back seat.

"Here we are, Sam. Let's make camp."

The words no sooner passed my lips than I knew the horror.

"Sam! Sam! My God, what's the matter?"

I bolted from the truck, jerked open the back door, and was at his side in seconds. His head lolled back. His eyes stared blankly.

"Talk to me, man! Talk to me!"

All he managed were barely coherent words sounding like "where a . . . ." and "wha . . . ." They were accompanied by a low gurgling sound in his throat.

"Pat! It's cerebral edema! We have to get down to the Salar!"

Patricio was away in seconds, Sam's head firmly in my grasp to protect it from the inside door jamb as we bounced along.

"Hang on, Sam! Hang on!

"Pat, don't rush it! If anything happens to the truck, we won't be able to drag him down lower. I think we caught it in time. We'll know for sure when we're down at least 1,000 feet."

My thoughts raced ahead. He must come out of it! He can't die out here. In thirty minutes, we were at the bottom of the mountain at 14,200 feet and Pat angled across the sands to the highway. Sam had regained partial control of his neck and head; I felt it in my hands. Now must come coherence, lucidity, responsiveness to the surroundings -- anything to indicate he was recovering.

At the highway, we were on the descent in minutes. 13,800 feet. Sam blinked his eyes and looked at me with a steady gaze. He had gained control of his neck muscles and I no longer had to hold his head. His eyes followed my hand moving up and down and side to side. I thanked God for that.

"You're going to be okay. Don't worry!" I heard the emotion in my own voice.

13,500 feet. 13,200 feet. Finally, at 13,000 feet, he was in control of his arms and legs.

"Do you want to talk? Tell me what you feel."

"Yeah, I feel okay. I don't have a headache. My vision is clear."

"Don't strain yourself. Take it easy."

After a short pause, he went on.

"I think it all started when we entered the highway and began going higher. At some point, my head really began to ache. I didn't want to tell you, though."

"You should have. What happened next?"

"I lost focus and things were blurry. I remember we stopped and I heard you say 'beautiful' and I tried to say it."

"Yes, you did. It was faint. I should have turned to look at you. But I thought your tone was caused by the wonder of it all."

He continued. "Things became more clouded when we got going again. I heard the truck engine. Beyond that, I didn't know what was happening. I lost control of my neck and realized I was in trouble. I was too weak to do anything about it. And the headaches. I felt the headaches."

We arrived at the Salar, now safely down to 12,000 feet, and Patricio headed towards the Laguna over the dry lake bed.

"We're back on the Salar, more than 3,000 feet lower. I have to say, you look and talk as if completely normal. When we get back to Copiapo we'll have you checked at the hospital. Patricio, can you take us to a doctor?"

"Sure, no problem."

"Sam, do you recall what happened when we stopped?"

"There was no engine noise. I heard you shout, but it wasn't clear what you said. I felt your hands holding my head and that made me believe I was all right."

"I think you know you had cerebral edema. And you've responded exactly as the textbooks say. The body recovers after going down at least 1,000 feet. You seem all right now."

"I feel fine."

"I still think you need to see a doctor."

"Yeah, I want to take that precaution."

Back at the Refugio, we got out to stretch. Sam's movements were back to normal. He even said he felt good enough to go back up! As if that were going to happen. It was a pleasant surprise when he put his arms around me in a warm hug.

"Bob, you saved my life. I can never repay you and I'll remember today until the day I die."

Postscript: This climb was one of my most dangerous. On the retreat with Sam down the mountain, fortunately we had the truck. But what if the edema had occurred after Patricio left? Would Sam have been able to walk? I don't think so. He wasn't in control of his legs at Base Camp. Today I believe he was the luckiest of men that day.

This incident closed out my guiding career. I found leading others on a big mountain too stressful. And who needs that kind of stress at my age? I witnessed the work of Divine Providence several times during my long mountain career. On this occasion, one near me witnessed it also.

Sam and I still stay in touch by e-mail. He never returned to the mountains, but he found other dreams and passions. He is a successful real estate developer in the Midwest.

GOOGLE TOUR: The Chapter 7 Tour is on the site.

PANORAMIO: Choose the "Pissis" tag for peak photos.

MOVIES: The March, 2000 movie has several Pissis scenes.

Perhaps this is not the place for me, a place
where I shall have to pay for the things I've
done as well as for the things I haven't done,
a crazy kind of place turned upside down where
they kill you as a criminal or they kill you as a saint.

It's a whiteout! The word itself is enough to
strike sheer, unadulterated terror in the
heart and soul of any high altitude climber.
Of all the words in all the dictionaries in all
the libraries in all the world, this is the most
dreaded, the most feared, the most frightening
for me, and I suppress a momentary urge to
pass water.

It remains for me to marvel that I still breathe.
And I reflect that we either live and die by accident
or we live and die by plan. Some say that we shall never
know and that we are like small bugs that children kill
on a summer afternoon. But some say, to the contrary, that
even the sparrow does not fly without a gentle push
from the Hand of God.

--From the author's personal climbing journal

CHAPTER 7

Monte Pissis, Argentina:
The Hand of God

April, 1995. The weeping and sobbing on the telephone were uncontrollable. It took several moments before I understood that the person on the other end of the line was Maria Ester. She was calling about her husband, Giancarlo Fiocco, who had been my driver to Chilean and Argentine peaks.

"Maria Ester. What is the problem?"

"He's missing, Bob."

"Who is missing?"

"Giancarlo is missing."

It was an answer as outlandish and astonishing as I might expect in an exchange with a deranged person.

"He's missing? What do you mean he's missing?"

After a minute, her story became clear. Two days before, Giancarlo failed to return to his part-time job at the Maricunga gold mine, east of Copiapo and south of Cerro Copiapo, where he worked as an adviser on food menus and food preparation.

"Bob, you know the mountains where he is. You must come to help find him!"

How could I forget such a call? It's a moment frozen in time, unfading, and coming over a wire that never stops sending the same anguished plea for help. Within days, I was on a flight out of San Francisco, though by that time I knew rescuers had found my friend, frozen to death in the high mountains. Instead of going to find him, I was going to honor him and help console his family to the extent that I could.

Later, after speaking to friends and miners in Copiapo, I learned he left his job at the mine at lunchtime on April 21 and failed to return as expected two hours later. The mining company and the carabineros at the Customs Station organized a search the next day. On April 23, Patricio found his empty truck, stuck in a shallow snow bank with the doors unlocked. It was located on the southern slopes of Cerro Copiapo at an elevation of 14,700 feet, fifteen miles from the Refugio at Laguna Negro Francisco. They used a plane to widen the search.

PHOTO: Giancarlo's cross on Laguna Negro Francisco where his body was found. (Photo 7.1 on the website.)

They located his body on the 24th, frozen to death. He had reached the northernmost edge of the Laguna and walked out upon the mud flat on the lake's perimeter towards the light of a backhoe, which was working around the clock to dig a trench for water pipes to supply the mine. He was confused in the darkness and, affected by the cold and his exertion, fell face forward into the mud and shallow water. He tried to go forward. They could still see in the mud the impressions of his outstretched arms as he tried to "swim" towards the backhoe. He continued for forty feet and there expired, a quarter of a mile from his goal.

Now, in March, 1997, I am at Base Camp ready to climb Pissis, Argentina, at 22,293 feet the third highest mountain in the Andes. My memories return to those unhappy events of many months ago. I have made three trips to other peaks since his death and have stayed at La Casona and seen Maria Ester each time. Yet, Giancarlo died only fifteen miles to the west of Pissis, and the nearness to the scene of that tragedy disturbs me. What a wonderful friend he was. He drove me to six peaks, and there's a need to mark his passage in thought and word, because when he died it occurred to me it could have been me and not him, and then there would be no one to record things.

It has been almost two years since his passing and Maria Ester, his widow, has been able to move forward, despite the suddenness of his departure. She told me the other night that it took her six months to get over the shock that he was dead, that it was definitive, and that the kids, Catarina and Giancarlito, would never see their father again. The children took it especially hard. When she remembers him now, it is with a deep pain in her heart. But she has tried to move on with her life by devoting time to the children and to the hotel. The children still miss their father. She has not remarried.

PHOTO: At La Casona, waiting for Patricio. Of course, the author had no idea what was about to take place on Pissis. Maria Ester is behind the camera. (Photo 7.2 on the site.)

My memories float away. My concentration upon this living monster of a mountain reclining beneath me is all that matters now. It's alive. I feel its force, its power, its overwhelming presence. Pissis is more than a mountain to me. It's an emotion; one that pervades my entire being. It reminds me of Moby Dick, and I pray that it doesn't drag me under as the whale did Ahab. The first visit here seared its memory upon my soul like the holy chrism of a sacrament, imprinted there for all eternity. And when a mountain becomes like that, it's more than a high peak; it's an element of your very being, an integral part of your soul that never drifts out of sight or out of mind.

I have returned to this five-peaked massif for another attempt at the main summit. Of those five, the highest one sits in the north. As Patricio Rios, my driver since Giancarlo's death, and I motor towards a base camp site, the favoring terrain lures us on as the truck takes to it with ease. But large rocks and boulders soon bar farther progress, right at a perfect spot to make camp. I have a new home. Its address: 15,500 feet, - 27.7693 latitude, - 68.8151 longitude, Northern Slopes, Monte Pissis, Argentina, SA. It sits below the major summit and is one of my higher base camp sites.

A wonderful spectacle greets me as I stare upwards and blink in the sun's glare. Pissis is beginning to reveal her secrets as a mountain that overwhelms me with its proportions, an ethereal world that is dazzling and threatening. I'm very excited, for the northern side is in full view and the first leg of a clear path higher sparkles in the light. It proceeds upslope and then traverses over to the western side (out of sight from here). Though I can't see that part of the mountain, I know a possible route wends south and eventually turns due east as it rises to a ridgeline to the right of the main summit. I don't know if anyone has tried this way before. But I wish to avoid the normal route. It's on the eastern side and is perfectly uninteresting. My new route on the western side will be perfectly interesting. I planned it in 1994 when I first tried to climb the mountain from the west. I studied the walls several times and thought that, should I ever find myself here again, a traverse around the northern side would put me high enough on the western slopes to make a summit attempt possible. This will be pure, unadulterated high adventure, and I will need all my imagination, route-finding skills, and luck to achieve success.

"Okay, Bob, see you in twelve days." Patricio heads back down the slope and then turns north towards the pass we came through, Valle Ancho. He soon disappears behind a massive promontory of rock and earth. Now, I'm almost off the map. Pat is the sole being who knows my whereabouts. Once I start higher, I'll be utterly "lost to headquarters." "Where is he?" "No one knows. They say he went in one day and never came out." "What's he doing up there?" "Hard to tell. Perhaps he's alive. Perhaps he's dead. Don't know for sure."

The nearest human being is forty-five miles north at the Mina Marte gold mine. The mountain is encircled by isolated, tortured ground. I feel exposed and vulnerable. But my mountain attitude is coursing through my psyche like an electric current through a grid, lighting up and powering everything in reach and sight and it snuffs out all reasons for anxiety. At times like this, I understand that I'm employed in something of very great meaning -- the climbing of a very great mountain.

Pissis moonscape! You could pluck this place up, the mountain and its surroundings, and put it on the moon, say, at the Sea of the New Religion, or wherever, and no one there or here would even bother to notice. As I stare languidly out the tent door at the dry lakebeds, the shallow lakes, and the nearby peaks over which this monster of a mountain reigns, I imagine Neil Armstrong and Buzz Aldrin sauntering by. They want to know if there are moon rocks for sale. "Sure, fifty cents apiece; three for a buck." They amble off, their bags full. "When you return, don't tell them you saw me here," I shout after them. "My wife and kids will worry sure."

PHOTO: Base Camp tent at 15,500' on the northern slopes. The main summit is on the right skyline. (Photo 7.10 on the website.)

My Base Camp tent! Beautiful. The best high altitude tent makers in the world, Integral Designs of Canada, manufactured a work of illuminated mastery struck by pure artists, this specially designed one made to my specifications. I asked them to use a rainbow theme and they delivered. They cobbled together spare Gore-Tex swaths from finished tents in a magnificent color array of red, blue, and yellow. From the outside, it's reminiscent of a sheik's shelter on one of those camel caravans out of Samarkand. It's large enough to store my five-liter water jugs, all my food and equipment, and even has space for a legless chair. It's too heavy and bulky, however, to take above Base. This isn't Everest, where Sherpas haul everything, even climbers, to the top. Here in the Andes, I'm my own porter and must hump the loads up and down the mountain all by myself.

I take the measure of my new home and know this is a good place. This is the right place. There's no snow here at Base Camp but, with my water jugs from town, I have enough water, and the few lacy fingerlings of ice around 17,500 feet, a good spot for Camp I, should satisfy my needs up there.

As I look upon the vastness that surrounds this peak, a snow-bound peacefulness invests this part of the Great Andes; the summer snows rest comfortably upon the brows of the nearby mountains. For miles and miles around there is no human existence, no motion, and no semblance of life, only high majestic mountains and broad desert plains.

The second afternoon at Base Camp proves jarring. An impending storm to the east heralds its approach by the silence of the clouded sky and the windless air. A crooked shaft of flaming fire breaks the black of the distant horizon and illuminates the sky with glittering flame, heightened by alternating bursts of silvered splinters of palpitating radiance. In quick succession another tortured spurt of light -- ephemeral, menacing, violent -- tosses upon the land a raucous, isolated clap of thunder. It's all astoundingly eerie and all captivatingly wondrous.

In the several days I spend at Base before beginning a climb, sometimes I have too much time to think. Perhaps this is one of those times, for I ponder whether to leave a note here as to my plans -- my attempt to climb up the north slope, traverse around to the western inclines, and from there try an ascent of the main summit. Should I fail to return, Pat can provide this information to rescuers. But who am I kidding? Should calamity befall me, no one might possibly locate me and, should they, do no more than leave me where they find me. I decide not to leave a letter.

Mornings are special out here, for first light is a sudden moment lacking beauty. One instant it is dark, the next barely light, as though the deadened Lazarus has been given life. In minutes, the dawn brings color and warmth to the vacantness of my icy world and strikes the spark of life. The Inca Nation knew well the haunting beauty of sunrise in the Andes, when peaks blush crimson at morning's first blush, and the snows above glow with a magnificent rust.

After the three nights at Base Camp, I strike out for Camp I. When I do, my body handles the elevation gain, except for the dry, hacking cough always caused by altitude. A spot for the next camp proves less than ideal. The altitude is within the proper range, but the ground lies at an annoying angle. After the second carry with a backbreaking load the next day, I use my ice axe to chop out a level platform for my home. The work is tiring, as just three swings of the axe cause me to gasp for air here at 17,600 feet. With the tent up, my Baby Blue, my first task is to gather ice from the nearby patch for snow to melt. Later, clouds begin to form and encircle the summit. A spark of dulled lightning breaks through the darkened cloud mass, but it proves to be a singular, isolated event.

This is my first trip back since March, 1994, the climb I will never forget. Since then, each November and March, other peaks in northern Chile and Argentina have been my focus. I have avoided this mountain until now. Snowstorms out here are menacing. If it snows prior to Patricio returning, he will be unable to reach me. In 1994, it began to snow the evening after Giancarlo dropped me off at Base Camp. All night flakes fluttered to earth, lightly at camp, heavily away from the mountain. The next day, a solid sheet of white covered the entire distance to Valle Ancho Pass and remained for three days, an intimidating sight. It was twenty-five miles no 4x4 vehicle could ever hope to negotiate. Possibilities of another snow dump like that one have haunted me over the years, and I delayed a return to Pissis for that very reason.

Next morning dawns clear and bright. Soon after I leave for Camp II, the incline steepens. I shift from climbing poles to my ice axe and revert to a two-step rest step -- two steps up, a brief rest, and then on again. I traverse the slope, first to the right, then to the left. While this lessens the strain, the grade is still so steep I pause often, heaving, heaving, heaving. High altitude sucks the breath straight from the lungs like a vacuum. My look right and due west reveals an out-thrusting of mangled gendarmes. My intuition tells me there could be a place to make camp behind its menacing face. When the slope underneath my boots becomes intolerable, I turn west to forge a route to the rocky projections. On my traverse to the right, I encounter the broad expanse of a northern-facing incline, angled at thirty-five degrees. I must cross this to reach a possible campsite. At its foot, 400 feet below, is an extended glacier stretching east to west. It resembles a banana from this height, so I name it the Banana Glacier. Altitude really bolsters my creativity.

How do I traverse this daunting thing to reach the gendarmes and a possible camp? There is but one choice. The narrowest bit of a ledge begins on this side of the slope and ends 200 feet on the other side, where it intersects the rocky outcroppings. It appears wide enough most of its length. But it's very narrow at several locations, with not much pathway visible from my vantage point. When I step out upon it, things go well, at first. The constricted sections, however, don't allow me to walk across its entirety facing forward. Instead, at one spot, it requires turning to the mountain and sidestepping. Once I'm past this, the shelf widens but then shrinks from three feet wide down to two. Now I must face and almost hug the mountain. When I lean farther forward, my moves become tentative. I edge across sideways, carefully placing one boot and then the other. A fall here will tumble me downwards to the glacier and I'll shoot off the mountain in abject imitation of a skier in a jump competition. The path widens once more before shrinking to two feet at the point where it meets the tortured rocks. Two more steps and I've made it!

PHOTO: The site of the author's Camp II at 19,200', a Brigadoon-like place for him. (Photo 7.14 on the website.)

I strain through the gendarmes and sharply angled boulders, and the most wonderful place, a Brigadoon-like place, soon comes in view. It's a bowl-shaped enclosure strewn with various sized rocks with an expansive center area composed of soft, granulated sand. It's a perfect spot for a campsite -- a rich surprise at this height. The elevated sides of the basin offer protection from the wind, while the sandy area offers a perfect place for Blue. What's more, there are several snow patches nearby. It stretches in length 150 feet due west to east and in breadth two-thirds the same distance. And the altitude is ideal at 19,200 feet. This is a giant fortress battlement, an exquisite cirque of stones rarely, perhaps never, seen by another human being. How may I expect anyone to comprehend the unusual exhilaration I feel from its barren isolation? It happens occasionally that I place a magnificent camp at a magnificent location on a magnificent mountain, and this is one of those times. After I drop my first load of gear, the return to Camp I via the narrow path across the shelf causes me tense moments. Still, I'm able to manage it without incident.

In the evening, there is nothing of real importance, no more than an indistinct disquiet, a feeling of vagueness uncommon to my nature. Then a strange foreboding seems to spring from the world around me, sweating from the sand, the feeling I'm not to return home but to remain here forever, frozen in time, my body lost to the world. My family won't even get my Marine dog tags. As soon as the premonition arrives, it leaves. Why does such a thought arise now, and on this mountain? Perhaps this is not the right place for me, a place where I will have to pay for the things I've done as well as for the things I haven't done, a crazy kind of place turned upside down where they kill you as a criminal or they kill you as a saint.

Except for the wind's occasional noises, the impenetrable silence grips me like a vise. There is such an arresting power in silence. I suspect myself of deafness. Later, the dark comes and I'm blind as well, all in an instant. Solitude fills this soundless vacuum, the solitude of silence. It's a haven, a protective cocoon against all I seek protection from, like the inhumanity and self-flagellation a crazed world society visits daily upon itself. My wish is to remain in this paradise forever, if not in body, then in spirit, for it fits me perfectly. Out here, I am never less inactive than when I have nothing to do and never less lonely than when I am by myself.

Upon leaving Camp I, I tuck my trash under a small rock for pickup on my way back down the mountain. It snowed briefly during the night. A steady breeze rustled Baby Blue and disturbed my rest. But now the sun shines in a clear morning sky. The steep slope to Camp II poses real difficulty once more, as the rest of my gear weighs twice that of the first lift yesterday. It is not a matter of climbing now, but of hauling myself higher. I force my body forward by pulling my legs after. The weight of my pack? I try no longer to notice it. My sole concern is for the torture to cease. The incline's unforgiving steepness exacts its unforgiving price. I pause and pant and fight for that essential commodity -- air! What a hellish business. I struggle to right myself once more and fight for every yard upwards. At one moment, I feel surrender enter my thoughts. But something has a grip upon my innermost being, and that something will not allow me to give up. I must move up. I must move higher.

In an hour, I can't even maintain my rest step pace, that pace that blocks out all pain, all sensation, and I find myself appallingly, disappointingly, tired. I drop to the slope and gasp for more air in huge gulps. I urge myself forward once more, driven by something within the core of my being that forces me onward. So on I go, indescribably weary now. But I obey the orders of my mountain-charged psyche, which has only one focus -- to get higher. My body rebels, but I move up in a haze of altitude-induced hypnosis.

After ages of agony, I attain the slope's high point and traverse right; the dangerous path above the Banana Glacier is soon underfoot. All that is required for disaster is a sudden wind to catch my pack and send me pitching to the glacier below. I feel the insufferable load on my back as I carefully sidestep across the narrow parts of the ledge. My luck holds and I reach Camp II at 2 p.m., the close of another punishing day. I offer up my suffering to shorten my time in Purgatory.

I don't feel well. My pulse is still too high and I have a persistent headache. Enough water and time usually prove effective, but not this time. After I have Baby Blue in place at 3 p.m., my headache is the worst in memory. My pulse remains high and my urine dark, foreshadowing a physically uncomfortable night.

An aspirin and warm broth ease things somewhat, and I try to take my mind off the present by thinking back to Giancarlo's fate. Why did he leave his truck at such a late hour? He knew he faced a long walk back and should have waited until the next day. There's a rule determining life's drawing of lots. It's not justice that rules our fates but the dealings of chance, choice, and Divine Providence holding a fair and even balance. Who may say which or how many of them rule our lives? Perhaps they all work in tandem in a manner I don't understand completely. Maybe my friend tapped the bare wire connecting them all and the volt surge proved too great. He had little chance against any one of them and he didn't stand a chance against all three. *Requiescat in pace*, old friend.

At 4 p.m., the physical movement of crawling from my home chases the headaches for the moment and I take the time to inspect this wonderful piece of property. It's snowing on the mountains in the north and the salars to the east. Here, the grateful land is peaceful and serene. When I return to Blue, the headaches are upon me with a vengeance. I suspect cerebral edema, a killer illness at altitude. I review the symptoms meticulously. My vision is clear. My thought is rational. I'm able to walk heel to toe without losing balance. My conclusion is that I have regular altitude sickness and not edema. Tonight will be a rough night, but I must endure it. If the headaches persist into the next day, I might have to return to Camp I to recover.

My head thumps and pounds as I lie nestled in my bag. Then, the passage of time produces the right effect as the pain flees at midnight. Still, I will rest tomorrow. There are several thousand more feet to the summit, and the efforts to come will test my physical and psychological fitness to the limit. The extra day will benefit both. Out here, I have to hold the position and perimeter of my emotions, at all costs. Otherwise, every bad psychological phantom will breach my psyche and play orgiastic hell with my entire being. And that can cause a mental catastrophe. At 1 a.m., threatening thunder shatters the thin air with a shuddering as snowflakes gently patter against Blue's walls. A heavy load of snow could jeopardize the climb. But the storm harangues itself out, dying upon a faint, barely perceptible thunder peal harder to detect than a sigh.

With the new day, I amble over the rising ground to the northern border of my home. The sky is clear, and it portends a good day. At the topmost part of the rim, I peer intently at the majestically brooding hulks to the north -- Jotabeche,[45] in form resembling a reclining maiden; Tres Cruces, the double crested; and Ojos del Salado, the volcanic sentinel. It hasn't snowed out there, so the passage is clear to Paso Valle Ancho. My hope is that the terrain from Ancho to Base Camp will remain snow free until Patricio returns.

The western edge of the bowl draws my attention. I begin the tramp towards it, for looking south from there I will be able to see the route for the single haul to Camp III tomorrow. Thirty minutes later, the immensity of the mountain's western walls spreads before me to the south. This is a colossal mountain whose ramparts stretch to the horizon. I plan my route as I scan the terrain. First, I will cross a sheer slope, canted at thirty-five degrees, that ends hundreds of feet below on a glacier that flows from higher up to the base of the peak. On this slope, four outcroppings of rock, each resembling a shark's fin, protrude ten to fifteen feet outwards. Among the four fins lie three chutes or gullies, each choked with loose rocks and debris. Then, beyond the fins, I must traverse ground that metamorphoses into a vast rock garden. It's tilted and rises to meet the upper top of the aforementioned glacier. From there, I'll need crampons part of the way to wherever I place Camp III.

When I finish designing the route, I glance west to the hill where I fought the all-night windstorm in 1994. It seems so far below me. In minutes, I'm seized by an uneasiness that this mountain is unlucky. Is my mountaineering intuition warning me of danger? Should I retreat down the mountain? Or should I ignore my apprehension? The air turns frigid as clouds settle in, and I reach Blue just as snow drums against

---

[45]   19,286 feet.

147

her protecting, welcoming walls. An abrupt rumble reverberates off the high surrounding rocks, falls away, and then hurries back with greater immediacy. It seems another harbinger of something sinister, which has been brewing and simmering since my arrival. However, it stops snowing after two hours and my confident mood returns.

A light dusting of snow cloaks the ground at daybreak of my seventh day on the mountain. Clouds hide the main summit, 3,000 feet above, but here it's clear overhead and to the north. At 8 a.m., all my gear is on my shoulders for the single haul to Camp III. When I reach the western end of the bowl, I mount the lip and step onto the steep incline of the fins. The angle is so sharp that I must face the slope, lean over, and sidestep my way across. The route requires delicate balancing and delicate attentiveness. I take the first fin by climbing its flank to the top and clambering over it. The chute on the other side is loose scree, and I negotiate it with precise motions, using my ice axe for stability. At the second protrusion, I glance hastily down to the glacier below while I cling precariously to the jagged rocks. It's exhilarating, as I clutch the mountain and stare into the void. It reminds me of the vastness below my feet when I was halfway up El Capitan in Yosemite many years before. I climb laterally across this fin rather than above it and reach the next gully, identical to the first in its composition, and handle it with care and deliberation. The third fin is as large as the second one and part of it provides a resting place; it's a wind-carved formation shaped like a lounge chair. Soft, fine sand covers the seat, and smooth rocks on either side provide armrests. It gives real pleasure, the physical, touchable proximity to what, before that instant, I knew only through the intermediaries of images and words. When I cross the next chute, the last fin is like the first, and once I'm over it the boulder field is securely underfoot. As I continue on, the rocks, the incline, and the altitude punish every hard-won step.

During a stop to rest, I recall that this is Easter Sunday. It's near dinnertime at home and I can see my wife and girls preparing the ham, potatoes, green bean casserole, sweet potato pie, biscuits, and apple pie. What a feast it will be! And my grandson is sleeping soundly nearby. Here, I pant for breath. I imagine their rich, warm smiles. "Be sure to save some for me!"

After an hour, I reach the glacier and strap up my crampons. Their hard steel teeth soon crush and grind the yielding snow and ice. When I stop for pictures, I notice great clouds running up from behind. They hang there as they plot their descent, then crash down in ineffable fury and spread out on all sides into an enveloping sheet of white froth and white bluster. They say seasoned high altitude mountaineers have a sixth sense that signals an approaching catastrophe, and I sensed this one coming. I now feel danger in every pore of my being. Thick snow falls through the darkling sky and wraps the land in its frozen, stolid embrace. A snowy fog darkens the atmosphere, like the mist that sealed the fate of Flaminius and the Roman legions on Lake Trasimene at the hands of Hannibal. The snow falls so thickly it obscures all but the nearby ground. I'm dangerously exposed. To stop and set the tent is perilous and foolhardy; the rock slope is too steep and jumbled. A return to Camp II might provide retreat and respite, but the falling snow hides the route as the flakes hurry down to envelop all underneath in a deadly, ivory colored shroud. Besides, to retreat would suggest surrender, and I don't want to surrender. It's all a palpitating moment of charged emotion.

"Bob, watch it, son, you may be in over your head." It's my Guardian Angel, Robert, doing what he does best, watching out for my wellbeing. "I know. It's all in sight very clearly. I want it, but not at any price. Stay close and all will be well."

I continue ever higher, earnestly anticipating a break in the clouds. Then, with the flash of one hurried glance, I grasp the meaning of what must be my impending annihilation -- a whiteout. It's a whiteout! The word itself is enough to strike sheer, unadulterated terror into the heart and soul of any high altitude climber. Of all the words in all the dictionaries in all the libraries in all the world, this is one of the most dreaded, the most feared, the most frightening for me, and I suppress the sudden urge to pass water. Alone. Blind. At 20,000 feet. With no hope of rescue. The white mist is more blinding than night's darkness. Memories of 1988 and the whiteout on the summit of Bolivia's Illimani, at 21,003 feet, play through my mind in disturbing slide-show-like vignettes. We exited that near-nightmare 200 feet below the top on the descent, three of us roped to our guide. Our saving maneuver turned on continuous motion and we survived, barely.

Another premonition seizes my soul in its distressing grip. It may be my time soon; it may be my time now. Will my odyssey end on this frozen Elysian Field? Please, Lord, I pray, take me at Your mercy, just not yet. I continue into the snowy landscape as it envelops me, as desert sands smothered remnants of long-ago civilizations. There is no hope of a breakout, and death threats come from every quarter and from all about. Should my fate find an ending here or anywhere on this mountain, the knowing of my going would be lost, for rescuers summoned by Patricio would never discover my lifeless form amongst the shifting snows, not this high, not this remote on this giant of a peak. My epitaph will read: Lost, disappeared, somewhere on the slopes of the mighty Pissis. If sight of the sun be vouchsafed once more to me, it will be like recuperation from illness.

The glacier is dangerous; if I slip and don't self-arrest the fall with my ice axe, I'll wind up at the bottom several thousand feet below, so I abandon it for the rock garden. My movements are slow and halting. I feel like one more wraith in mankind's inevitable, Thanatopsis-like procession to the mysterious chamber of destiny's fulfillment. The rocks are hazardous in their own way, for the mists conceal their shapes and that makes boot placement precarious. A faulty step here might result in a broken knee or leg, a cataclysmic ending to everything. I continue to stumble over unseen rocks but continue to gain altitude. The snow falls so heavy and dense not even God Himself might know my true whereabouts. A moment's weakening of the will might spell doom. A man bears his own destiny, and sometimes there arrives a moment when he confronts his helplessness in a stark way. Such a time is now. I can neither return nor stop, but must keep going higher, for there I will find the light. I have to hold to continuous motion, for it will provide the thinnest possibility that I am on the path to life. I trust that if I pass through the gloom perhaps there resides a broad, sunlit highland to welcome my journey home.

I have no choice but to keep moving, keep climbing. But the steep angles, the altitude, the insufferable load on my back, all take a toll upon my physical and spiritual strength. I do not say I know when I do not know. And I know the whiteout must end soon or I risk residing on Pissis forever. All my life I have found the courage to live. Now I may have to find the courage to die. If there's an answer to my dilemma, it must be none, for what mere mortal may stay the hand of God? The thickened whiteness enveloping me becomes in my mind the boundary between the real and the unreal, between life and death. I contemplate that everything is endurable. At other times of peril, I thought all was lost and was not bothered in the least. I witnessed everything from a distance as though it was an event of little concern. But this time things seem of greater significance. I am experienced enough of a mountaineer to realize that even on known ground it is easy to make mistakes in weather such as this. I sense approaching desperation even though I trust completely in my high altitude intuition and instincts.

Should tragedy strike, I have Vicodin. I carry it with me in case I'm injured and need relief from pain. Several pills will cast me into a deep sleep and I will die in the night from the cold. My body will lie slumped, like a poppy weighed down by a sudden shower, a hastened, unheard farewell to my wife and daughters upon my frozen lips. For me to die in this manner is a painless and elegant way to leave this life. My body will recline forever on the snowy shrouds of Monte Pissis. And what of my family? Surely they will wonder when and how I died. Sadly, theirs will be a lifelong search for the manner and meaning of my going.

I continue from one point to another, each time thinking I have found the right path. If the pestilential mist lifts, if the pestilential snow relents, I might find the true way. The snow becomes deeper and it makes my steps forward even more fatiguing. This may be the last for me, and I reconcile myself to the end. Why continue at this? I should simply let myself drift away and permit the mountain to fold me forever within its embrace. I will allow one hour more in this situation and then, wherever I am, I shall lean down upon the earth, take my pills, and allow myself to go peacefully. The kindness of nature will grant me a comfortable state of unconsciousness and free me from my predicament. I will be done with it and sleep contentedly through the ages. I'm in no pain. I feel the end is near; it is the end I wish -- an end amidst the mountains of my dreams. I am grateful to Pissis for being so beneficent to me today, and its existence awes me as though I'm in church. I have always desired to die well. This is a fitting place for the end.

"Bob, do not doubt things. I am at your side."

Robert provides the right words at the right moment, and a measure of hopefulness restores my confidence. I cannot afford this. I cannot think of death or allow thoughts of desolation when I am on my own. That leads to ultimate calamity. The will to live becomes overpowering and my mountain personality revives. I know I can do whatever is possible. I do not intend to die here. With a superhuman effort, I forge ahead. The slow pace could dismay the most determined of climbers. But I will not give up.

I wish for sunshine after the darkness. If granted, I shall rejoice. And then. And then! In the end, the mountain yields to my tenacity. As if by merciful Divine decree, there is the palest glimmering in the opaque shadows, the palest brightening of the clouds that envelop me as the falling snow lessens in intensity. In an instance of deliverance, the clouds melt away, the gauzy vapors retreat, and all is in sunshine on the other side of the curtain. As pure luck has it, in the near distance the rock slope ends, with the barest hint of gravel and sand now visible at its border. I heave a thankful sigh of relief. I feel I have forsaken a load so weighted I had nearly broken beneath it.

"Dear Lord," I whisper. "Thank you. Thank you for your mercy."

PHOTO: The whiteout has lifted. There must be a place for Camp III just beyond the glacier. (Photo 7.16 on the site.)

I set out with a fresh sense of determination. I exit the boulder field and climb over a sand and talus slope that leads to a small platform, a site for Camp III, at 20,200 feet. There are rocks for anchors and sand for a soft floor. My home is up and secured to the slope in thirty minutes.

PHOTO: Camp III, on the western slopes. (Photo 7.17 on the site.)

Danger lies only twenty feet away, however. The small area of my home drops off dramatically on the south and west sides. Is this a bad place? Is this the wrong place? Is this my final place? The advantage is that this site sits at the bottom of a couloir leading higher and due east, a staircase to the mountain's summit area. I look out over my boots from my fragile and precarious position at the depths 4,000 feet below; the view hardly affects me, so apathetic I've become. I waver between appreciative thoughts of great hope and desultory thoughts of great despair. Why this should be so I am not certain. Perhaps the altitude and the recent struggle through the whiteout have affected my psychological equilibrium. In the end, I decide to stay at my present site.

A stolen glance back over the way I've come reveals the blazing sun igniting the western walls. But it leaves off after an hour and the clouds just exited return to capture me. Snowflakes play softly against Blue's walls. If this continues, snow will choke the gully that leads to the summit area and will force me to retreat to Base Camp. Flakes fall with distressing violence, then lessen, as I wait, patiently, stoically. Later, a stiff wind blows for hours, scouring snow from the peak. A snowfield in the wind is of many things in existence the most agitated, for its surface constantly moves and flutters and forms ever-changing tableaux. This is a propitious wind, for it is clearing a path to the summit.

A check of my vital signs is encouraging -- heart rate near normal, urine clear, no headaches. My adjustment is going well. But my appetite remains in Copiapo because of the altitude. I manage some cheese and salami, but all further desire for food is gone. Eating at altitude can be a thoroughly uninteresting piece of business. And because I do not eat much on a climb and because of the exertion, I lose five to seven pounds each trip, even thirteen on the climb of Aconcagua.

During the long night, as the wind wails and whines demonically, the climb to the summit plays through my mind. There's no telling the condition of the upper slopes. If the main peak is cloud-covered, a subsidiary summit must suffice, if one is nearby. My thoughts turn to my adventures today and how the whiteout was a close thing. This time, I made it. But the next time? A correct choice one day may be the wrong choice the next.

Why do I do this? Why have I striven these years, these months, these weeks, these days, these hours, these minutes, to reach this speck of gravel and sand? The answer never reveals itself. I'm just here, at another high place. I have yet to understand my need to do this, to reach the Great Andes' highest summits alone and by myself. The effort brings neither riches nor fame, only the furthest reaches of obscurity.

But I have enjoyed great adventure in my travels, and that must suffice. I know of no other words for it.

At 7 a.m., after another sleepless night, Baby Blue is behind me. With several hundred feet of mountain blocking the sun's faint rays from the east, a pale ruddiness suffuses everything. The high winds of the night have blown most of the gully free of snow, but clouds have devoured the main summit. If they remain, they will prevent a summit attempt.

My load is light -- just a water bottle, camera, and candy bars. But the gully is steep enough to force a three-step rest step. My climbing mood is exultant and I labor in a euphoric state. All is in tune, mentally, physically, physiologically, and psychologically. Would that each day on a mountain were like this. When I top the couloir in two hours, the major summit, to the left, remains cloaked in clouds, although here I stand in sunshine. As luck has it, a subsidiary summit is to the east-southeast. It's high and looks worthy of a solo ascent. Should my goal be the main summit with all the risks that accompany climbing a peak in clouds? Or, should it be the lower peak, with less risk? I decide in just brief minutes. It will be the subsidiary peak.

To my front, due east, is an immense bowl rimmed by rocks and boulders and choked with deep snow. The subsidiary summit, to the right of this basin, is approachable by a rock rib that angles to the south. As I move off amidst a landscape of large and small boulders and rocks, the rising incline causes me to gasp for air every few steps despite my light load. My altimeter's limit is 21,000 feet and it registers that now, so my present altitude is above that height.

Then an episode of delightful strangeness occurs. First I feel it -- something is about to happen. Then I hear it -- an enchanting horn or flute sound that is so foreign in this remote part of the high Andes that I scarce believe my ears. Then I see it -- a large boulder twenty yards away with holes hollowed out through it; the wind plays through the openings and the sound mimics a trombonist or flutist playing his instrument. This astonishing contrivance is the result of wind and sand erosion, the movement of His hand over thousands of years. In one tube are two small basins sculpted by the winds. Within these little bowls, grains of sand move as the wind moves them, scalloping out the rock as they have for millennia. As the wind blows through the holes and over the little basins, it creates a sound differential that causes the musical notes. Here I've found a celestial symphony orchestra tuned for His pleasure and hearing -- and mine, on this singular occasion.

I leave my "symphony rock" and travel through a shallow ravine towards the subsidiary summit on the opposite side. Once I exit the gully, the slope steepens dramatically, and it forces me to two steps with one of rest. A wonderful happiness suffuses my being, one I cannot describe. Here exists a different universe, deserted, lifeless -- a wonderful universe that does not anticipate the presence of man. I'm defying a boundary, crossing a limit; yet I have no fear as I continue higher. I stop every few steps and try to recover my breath and calm my racing heart. I am terribly tired, more than I have known. At my age, how can I endure this? I reach to the depths of my being for stability, strength, sustenance. I trudge ever upwards and risk much, but not all, for the summit. The top means less to me than my survival.

PHOTO: A glance over at the main Pissis summit as I near the top of West I. (Photo 7.23 on the website.)

I stop. Am I there yet? A slight deviation to the right, followed by a traverse to the left and . . . . yes! I'm there. Above, there is nothing but sky. The small stones and sand waver beneath the novel weight of my boots. A brisk wind from the east flows to the west over the summit. The top is a blank crest of rocks, stones, and isolated ice patches. Is this all there is? Of course. It's just paltry pieces of rocks and stones fashioned in a kind of crown of meaningless importance. And here I am, at one more summit. Here I am, at a place that has never felt the burden of the human presence.[46] How humbling is that?

PHOTO: Pissis West II (22,074') from West I. (Photo 7.25 on the site.)

---

[46] The author has learned recently that Stefan Osiecki and Jan Szczepanski of the Second Polish Andes Expedition of 1936-1937 are credited with the first ascent of this sub-summit. Today it is known as Pissis West I. The author is confident that his ascent is the first solo ascent of the peak. Its elevation is 22,135 feet.

PHOTO: View south from the summit of West I (22,135'). Bonete Chico and Veladero are in the distance. (Photo 7.27 on the site.)

An astonishing mountain scene plays out before me, and I struggle even now to describe it. There are not one or two peaks here but five, perhaps six. The highest point of Pissis sits at the northernmost part of this massive arrangement of subsidiary peaks. Three thrust skyward in the east, similar in elevation to mine. Where I stand is on the western side of the Pissis massif. Immediately to the south of my peak sits another of similar height and one south of that of lesser elevation.[47] A lower one has a crater for its summit with a sparkling blue pond at its center. Over the entire panorama lacy, luminescent sheets of snow-laden mist swirl like Spanish mantillas; one minute they conceal a peak or vista, the next moment they disappear and return everything to full view. Lazy breezes blow chuffing cloudlets between summits and back again, a celestial tennis match to delight the mountain gods. It holds me in thrall, and quiets the thoughts of leaving. In the south shimmer distant ice castles veiled in mountain vapors, charming, compelling, exciting. Veladero (19,916 feet) is in clear view, as are Bonete Chico (22,169 feet)[48] and Bonete Grande (19,472 feet).[49] They thrust up from the high desert floor like upraised stones in a precious amulet. It is a land so beauteous that meager words are too meager to tell of it. My imagined Paradise in the next world exists as a spacious upland presided over by mountains such as these. This view from this place shall remain my vision through my remaining years.

Although my wish always is for anonymity on my journeys, I indulge myself a moment for recognition by placing a collection of nearby stones in a small cairn.[50] It is no more than three inches high. I am very exact

---

[47] The Shuttle Radar Topography Mission (SRTM) of 2000 measured the main summit at 22,293 feet and two eastern summits at 22,270 feet and 22,263 feet. In total, the SRTM identified six peaks, the principal summit and five subsidiaries.

[48] The fourth highest peak in the Andes.

[49] The elevation of the Bonetes are not borne out by their "Grande" and "Chico" appellations, the result of confusion by early Argentine cartographers.

[50] The author encourages some future climbers of this summit to notice, but not disturb, the little pile of stones and to notify him of its continued existence.

in the number of stones, for they represent the number of those in our family -- my wife, my daughters, my son-in-law, and my new grandson. This is a moment of deep joy, a moment of deep wonder, a moment of deep appreciation. It is a moment to treasure forever. Abruptly, a cold, gentle lifting, as a plane lifts on an updraft, signals the time to leave.

I approach my "symphony rock" on the way down and ache to take the beautiful instrument home so its music might charm me the rest of my life. We part reluctantly, its tunes still cheerily playing upon the wind, like an angelus summoning me to deeper knowledge. Then, a faint uneasiness arises from the land, indiscernibly, silently, like the emergence of fog in the night. It stirs in me a sudden dread of my own mortality. I felt nervousness like this before I entered the whiteout trap. I push the thought away and turn my attention to the dangerous task of going down. Still, I remain on edge. Are there other dangers ahead?

I enter Camp III at 2 p.m. I would descend to Camp II if it resided immediately below me. But it sits one quarter of the way around the peak over dangerous ground. Since the hour is late, withdrawal must wait for the coming day.

When I'm safely within the comforting confines of home, I reflect upon what may be the first ascent of the subsidiary summit, and certainly the first solo ascent, as I light my stove; its hissing sounds and lively, undulating flames brighten my mood. This instrument is a treasure, the MSR Internationale. It burns almost anything -- white gas, auto gas, kerosene, or jet fuel -- and it's the best high-altitude stove on the market. I've had one with me on every climb so far. To prime it, you release liquid gas into a shallow pan by opening the gas bottle's control valve for just a second. The light hissing noise this causes indicates that the liquid is flowing, and one confirms this by visually checking the pan. The wick, the bottom of which rests on the pan, is then ready to light. The resulting flame heats the generator tube, the pipe that feeds the fire ring. This tube, when hot, vaporizes the liquid gas flowing through it, and this causes gas vapor to stream to the fire ring. When the wick flame begins to recede and weaken, ten to fifteen seconds later, you open the control valve and the gas vapor becomes fire as it exits the openings in the ring. I obsess over my stoves and assure myself prior to each climb that these pure engineering delights are in perfect running order.

The long, monotonous, dark hours drag by. I am locked away in my world as I settle into my own version of eternity, that endured by each of us, each individually. My poor little camp is lost completely and known only to me. The cold descends and strikes right through my being. My sleeping bag and generous layers of clothing provide the minimum of comfort. I doze in a semi-conscious state, barely aware of time's passage. There are instants when I see my situation in a true light, but for the rest of the time I feel imprisoned within a mysterious trance and I wonder if Fate will exact a price for reaching the summit. Hateful rumbles echo throughout the upper slopes.

I awake in near darkness and feel a vague agitation; it's the second time in hours that I feel something is not right. I take the measure of the dimness outside, now faintly illuminated by the distant dawning of the sun, and seek to read its depths, like some medieval necromantic soothsayer of the darkened heavens. A momentary breeze causes the walls to flap and dance to its soughing cadence. It's time for morning coffee. My headlamp is positioned so that its light tilts upwards and not upon the stove's pan, a near deadly mistake. I open the gas bottle's control valve a brief second. The wind rustling the walls damps the sound of the liquid gas squirting into the pan. A flick of my lighter produces sparks but not a flame. I position it directly over the pan, whose contents I can't see, and flick it once more. It still will not light, although the sparks should light off the gas anyway. I suspect a line blockage and open the control valve again. Wall movements and wind muffle the noise of gas flowing into the pan and, as before, I fail to visually check what is happening. Since I still assume the pan is empty, I open the valve a full four seconds. My lighter once more produces only sparks and fails to light the gas.

I bend the lamp down for a visual inspection and, to my shock and horror, see that gas has overflowed the pan and streams down the floor into the rightmost corner of the tent, where it collects in a death pool now five inches in diameter! I shudder involuntarily as I stare into oblivion, into eternity. Everything here is highly flammable -- my home, my sleeping bag, my windsuit. The effect of a fire caused by a gas explosion is more than I can comprehend. A swelling grows too large for my chest and chokes me in the cavity of my throat. Is this actually happening? Or is it a distorted, distended dream scene recording my own death? This must have been the cause of the premonitions. They were warnings of my end in a fiery inferno. Burned beyond recognition. Self-immolation on a high Andean peak. The emotional shock transfixes me, and several seconds pass before I understand the magnitude of my error. I have put my life at the highest level of risk. It must be the altitude. I'm not thinking clearly. Fate has been tempted to the limit this day. Only just. Only just that close. Had there been a flame, barely my name would survive, the rest of me written on the wind and lost to history.

I cannot think about this right now. I need all my concentration to clean up the gas mess and escape the mountain. The climb down a big peak can be more dangerous than the climb up. The danger of down. The problem isn't simply the use of leg and thigh muscles unaccustomed to the unnatural strain and awkward movements. There is also the difficulty of weight. Gear hauled up the mountain must be hauled back down the mountain. Then, too, mind and emotion are vital factors. If I have reached the top, the tendency is to dwell on the success, not on the hazard of every descending step. If the summit attempt was unsuccessful, there is disappointment at failing to realize a desired goal dreamed of for many months. Dwelling on any of this is so much luxury and must be put aside and forgotten during a descent. The only thought, the only focus, must be the next step, the next placement of the ice axe or poles. One moment of inattention can mean serious injury or death.

Dawn colors the heavens above. I take scant notice, so deep is my focus upon "down." I avoid the glacier. It's too steep and the weight on my back is too heavy. The snow from the other day has melted off and the rock garden is clearly visible. I glance back at Camp III. A snowy veil has captured that part of the mountain and my recent home location is no longer in sight. I approach the fins and chutes and pause for breath; here the sun has crested the mountain and there is weak sunshine. I move over and past these obstructions carefully. When I am safely through them, I pause for ten minutes to regain my breath.

I reach the site of Camp II at 2 p.m., grab the garbage bag, and in thirty minutes reach the delicate ledge above the Banana Glacier. Occasional breezes blow as I make my way across, slowly, methodically, my heart in my throat. Finally I'm across, and a great weight lifts from my shoulders. I'm almost down. But the descent so far has proven grueling, physically and psychologically. I lapse into a state of weariness from which I lose all desire to escape. I feel as though I might simply sit down and rest for the balance of eternity. I feel no danger at my strength slipping away; I only wish my ordeal to end. Still, I must press on. I must not think or feel. I must continue the descent.

After the garbage pickup at Camp I, Base Camp is in view at 5 p.m., my rainbow-colored shelter the most welcome of sights. I'm physically and emotionally spent and haven't an appetite, simply the most compelling desire to lie down and sleep forever.

The next day, I reflect upon the events of the past days. My sole conclusion is that His Hand protected me three times. First, my exit from the dreaded whiteout was not the result of chance or choice. Quite simply, Divine Providence was at my side. Second, He was there to prevent the lighter from igniting the stove gas. But there is more. It happens that the lighter only functions below about 17,000 feet. Above that height, the thinness of the air renders it inoperable and instead I use special matches coated with unique flammables that are guaranteed to light every time. On this occasion, I continued with the lighter, never remembering the matches, even though I had used them back at Camp II. Most will say, without hesitation, that the altitude fogged my brain and caused me to persist with the lighter. Perhaps. But I am convinced that Providence settled at my side, right there at Camp III, not only to prevent the lighter from igniting but also to withhold my hand's reach for the sure light of a match. Up there, one is so far from earth yet so close to God. Thoughts of His merciful intervention will be mine until the last breath. They say God offers His protective hand to little children, inebriates, and the mentally disabled. But there is one more for the Divine list: careless mountaineers.

The following day I begin my vigil awaiting Patricio, and I endure it in a more peaceful frame of mind than in 1994 during my wait for Giancarlo. The mantle of a golden morning falls upon my part of the Great Andes, and I hail warmly the friendliness of things. There is no cause for anxiety about Pat's return. The twenty-five miles to Valle

Ancho are snow free and I pick up the sun flashes off his truck windows at 11 a.m. Fortune proves kind and not cruel. At 12:30 p.m., he roars up the slope and jumps from the truck.

"Bob, how are you?"

"Something very special happened up there," I say, motioning towards the mountain. "I'll tell you about it on the ride back."

Once over Valle Ancho, we connect with the road below Mina Marte that leads to Laguna Negro Francisco and decide to visit the place where Giancarlo met his fate. There, under the large red cross marking the spot, we pray silently that his memory may always remain bright. He was a virtuous man who took one too many risks. "Welcome home, young man. You were ours once and they took you away. You are no more. Suns may set and suns may rise, but you must sleep on during one never-ending night."

Upon my return to the world, I view the climb from a distance of space and time and realize that the stove incident was one instance in the mountains when I almost caused my own death. My priorities as to what to worry about on a climb rarely include me. The focus is always on the mountain, the weather, all the things that can do harm to me, seldom what I might do to myself.

Amidst the travails of this climb, I remember with affection my "symphony rock." She will reside through eternity performing her songs without a deserved and appreciative audience, for now she must play her solitary notes only for herself. But I hear her tunes even now despite the distance of time and space from the far away Pissis heights.

It remains for me to marvel that I still breathe. And I reflect that we either live and die by accident or we live and die by plan. Some say we shall never know and that we are like small bugs that children kill on a summer afternoon. But some say as I do to the contrary, that even the sparrow does not fly without a gentle push from the Hand of God.

My Baptism of Fire at altitude occurred on Aconcagua, the highest peak in the Andes. My Confirmation, on the first trip to Pissis, for I came to a higher level of belief. On this trip, I entered the mountain priesthood, as one who has passed through the curtain of the unknown and emerged hardened on the other side.

GOOGLE TOUR: The Tour for this Chapter resides on the site.

PANORAMIO: Select the tag "Llullaillaco" to view the photos.

MOVIES: The November, 1998 movie contains footage of a Llullaillaco climb.

> *I'm the only one to have ever seen these exact*
> *stones and probably the only one who ever will.*
> *The real proof of their existence is my viewing them,*
> *for this grants them life. If man is the measure*
> *of all things, then they do not exist to the rest of mankind.*
> ----
> *My body slumps next to them, weary beyond the*
> *knowing, exulting as an explorer entranced*
> *by an unexpected discovery exults. I wonder,*
> *how did those guys do it, anyway? How could*
> *they do it, without stoves, warm clothes, sturdy tents,*
> *without plastic boots, warm socks, warm gloves,*
> *without freeze-dried meals, dark glasses, warm*
> *sleeping bags, and without . . . . cigarettes?*
>
> *--From the author's personal climbing journal*

CHAPTER 8

Llullaillaco, Chile: How Did Those Guys Do It, Anyway?

The passage has begun and I, withdrawing from "that" world, continue like an asteroid in orbit into "my" world, the mysterious realm of solo high altitude mountaineering. It's November, 1999, mid-Spring here in the Southern Hemisphere. This is my fifth trip to Llullaillaco, the "Flaming Mountain." This time my determination to reach the sacred summit and see the Inca buildings is all consuming, a dream that invests nighttime hours and waking ones too with mesmerizing visions of their rocky existences expectantly awaiting my arrival. Patricio Rios sits next to me behind the wheel, doing what he does best, driving me to and from a peak. This man I trust with my life, because honest and true men communicate in subtle ways, and I know Pat will never, of his own doing, leave me in the lurch. This assurance, never uttered between us, still exists as a surety, like the guarantee the sun will rise and the sun will set. As the tout says, "You can take it to the bank."

What is the "mysterious realm" of solo high altitude climbing? To one who has never sought peace and sanctuary from the "team" and "group" mentality which labor and health psychologists insist are so important to our worth as individuals, all this must seem beyond understanding. Yet, I contend that every breathing, hoping, and thinking human being on this planet must admit at least one time in his life wishing for the solemnity of aloneness, wanting to conduct affairs completely on his own without the intrusions of others, just a single moment to say, "Here, here is an instant when I, I, accomplished something without the help of others." And this need for individuality may take place anywhere and at any instant in our lives. I saw once an old man, using a cane for balance, work his way up a sidewalk's moderate incline in my neighborhood. He stopped several times to gather strength and then set off again. And when he reached the top of the hill, my exultation in his accomplishment was heartfelt. He did it on his own and without "team" support. I will arrive at that man's situation in a few years, and my resolve is to regard a similar sidewalk climb a triumph equal to my ascents in the Andes, solo. A large trouble today is that we have lost respect for individuality, and we are the less for it.

The Pan-American Highway from Copiapo to Antofagasta in the north hums beneath our treads until we turn off at the Mina Guanaco sign. Soon, we pass the mine on our left and it's bustling with activity. From here, it's a sixty-mile drive to the abandoned borax mine, our day's destination. We've been on this road so often we resemble somnambulant commuters proceeding to and from their workaday worlds. We soon encounter a number of *oficinas*, abandoned nitrate collection stations that knew their better days before WW I, when the entire world clambered to obtain their output, an ingredient in black powder. They lie scattered throughout this part of northern Chile to the east of Antofagasta, once busy places of commerce that now sit in silent decay and repose. At one point, we bisect the route followed by Inca Yupanqui's[51] three conquering armies, each 10,000 strong, on their journey from Cuzco, Peru, through northern Bolivia, to Chile,[52] sometime in the 1480's.

PHOTO: Volcan Lastarria. The winds on the peak have disturbed the steam rising from its vents. (Photo 8.3 on the site.)

---

[51] The tenth Inca king, who reigned 1471-1493.
[52] See "Royal Commentaries of the Incas" by Inca Garcilasso de la Vega, Vol. II.

When we reach Laguna Aguas Calientes at 12,000 feet, the flamingoes sporting about and the puffing of steam from Volcan Lastarria to the south welcome us. It's warm, eighty-five degrees, so warm it's as though a second sun is at the zenith, next to the burning globe already there, both shining brightly through the rarified air. We take residence at our usual lodgings at the borax mine and revel in its quiet and imperturbable nature, protected as it is from winds by the walls of nearby rocky battlements. The mine's name? I haven't been able to devise an answer over the years. Those who toiled here did so amidst the most agreeable surroundings, deep within the calm and quiet of the stoic Atacama land.

At sunset, the flames of alpenglow bathe the mountain in glowing splendor. The light is so intense Patricio and I wear our sunglasses.

"Bob. I like this every time I see it." A low, extended whistle escapes his lips in emphasis.

A wonderful stillness pervades everything. Later, the stars and the tranquility of their light convey an assurance of comforting solitude. In the evening, Patricio's dry humor amuses me as he tells of his response to a letter from a South African "Prince" seeking help to restore his fortune by soliciting the dollars and assistance of others and promising high returns to the donors. Pat actually traveled to South Africa to see this man and returned with an anecdote of woe, for the "Prince's" letter was all a hoax. He tells his story with occasional laughs that enhance the telling, and I laugh too. We share a hopeless romanticism about human nature that makes us susceptible to occasional disappointments, and so we understand each other very well.

My personal health is rather fragile. I contracted a nasty cold two days before leaving home and it has progressed straight to my lungs. I cough frequently and there's heaviness in my chest; it's a dreary, rotten kind of thing to have on a climb. For now, my choice is to continue higher and hope for the best.

I think late into the night. How did the Inca build their monument for the ages on this immense mountain's summit? To this day, the Llullaillaco buildings are the highest yet discovered in the Andes, and the story of how the Inca accomplished such a feat remains an archaeological mystery. I burn with a fevered intensity to see them "in situ."[53]

I think, too, about what some observers might call the oddities of my mountaineering personality. Part of me thirsts for the facts. Where are the conclusions, the data, the deductions, the figures, the knowledge of approach and summit routes, the weather pattern details? I'm uncomfortable without these. Some climbers become agitated over a lack of information. "You can't even get weather reports out there? Forget it." You can obsess about it, if you let it take you over. I might have followed the common course, stayed true to my nature, and insisted upon having all the data before going out. If so, I would have remained at home in a rocking chair writing a book of fiction. Instead, I went to Incahuasi, Llullaillaco, Ojos del Salado, Pissis, Tres Cruces and other peaks with the thinnest scraps of information, so dismal in content some would have reckoned the risk too great to even set foot on one of those giants. On my first climbs of those mountains, I hadn't even a picture, let alone anything about climbing history. How strung out was that? But I repressed the need to know everything about everything. It wasn't that I didn't care; indeed, my continued existence was vitally important. Yet I convinced myself that understanding the whole lot was a contrivance, a crutch, a prop for my insecurities. To remain true to my solo ethic, I had to accept incomplete knowledge.

And this is the liberating thing about my climbing career. I let go of the obsession, offered myself to the vagaries of chance, choice, and Divine Providence, and allowed things to evolve. Not that I abandoned all concern for my personal well-being. The part of a climb within my control I did control, relentlessly, ruthlessly, and without hesitation. My deeper understanding, however, was that there are things beyond one's

---

[53] How they may have done it is discussed in the second letter of the author's manuscript, "The Chronicle of Pedro de Merida: Travels to Chile in the Years of Our Lord 1535-1537; Being an Account of That Journey to the Farthest Most Region of the Inca Empire; As Related to His Most Catholic Majesty, King Don Philip II, Our Most Sovereign Ruler" In the letter, de Merida interviews one of the builders of the huts, who explains how they accomplished their amazing feat. (This discussion also appears in Appendix C of this book.)

ability to influence. And this caused an adventure, a voyage of the soul, of the spirit, one of those times in life when definition of existence and meaning here on earth are most vibrant. I learned that if I needed all those things to climb, I shouldn't be out there in the first place. And as for adventure, if its spirit infused any human being, that being was me.

At dawn, we rise with the sun, and leave for Base Camp an hour later. The disk's rays bathe all in their wondrous light, warming, illuminating the path upwards. The ground is still the tortured terrain we remember so well, and progress is slow, deliberate, with an occasional jolt. All is still, with hardly a breeze. In an hour, we reach the campsite I've used on previous trips. And the most wonderfully stunning thing occurs. A welcoming party of several butterflies flits about in the still air, an event we have never witnessed, certainly not at 14,600 feet. They remind me of my little cricket companion at 16,000 feet on Pissis in 1994. And the temperature? It's difficult to imagine but my thermometer confirms it: eighty-one degrees. We hug and Patricio gives me a reassuring pat on the back. After we trade pieces of paper with his return date, he is off for the eight-hour run back to town.

I study Llullaillaco intently. There's little snow on this side of the mountain, but there is a spot between two narrow fingerlings of white where I will place Camp I. There is another slender notion close to the Camp II location, which means my route will have enough snow along the way to satisfy my needs.

PHOTO: My location for Camp I is between the two fingers of snow on the left. Camp II is at the top of the ice cliffs above Camp I. (Photo 8.6 on the site.)

Now the "altitude hack," the exasperating annoyance spawned by altitude's dryness, joins my cold's cough. It's all a miserable affair, enough to take the heart out of an enterprise and dash it to ground. Chewing gum helps to keep my mouth moist, but fails to offer complete relief. My resolution is to remain optimistic and positive; otherwise, the chances of success will recede each passing day. Once I secure my tent of many colors, her company cheers me immensely. Our tiny camp is as isolated as though it resided in a distant galaxy. Everything here is all my own and beyond the knowledge of anyone in the entire universe. This is my preference. Here I have my own sun. Here I have my own moon. Here I have my own earth. It's good to be home once again.

The sun retreats behind low hills to the west and, later, the high desert moon casts its glowing brightness over the darkened earth, now made akin to the light of day as trillions of sand grains become sources of light as they cast their tiny sparks over the shadows of darkness. The warmth of the day is a remote memory by 10 p.m., the temperature having fallen fifty-one degrees in those few hours. My heart rate is 70; acclimation goes well. I still have headaches, more the result of the cold wracking my lungs and chest rather than the altitude. Here in the warmth and close confines of my bag, I exhort myself to greater expenditures of stoicism and stolidity in the face of increasing personal discomfort. I nod off with a renewed purpose midst the quiet beauty of the night.

I spend the following two days at Base Camp to ensure my adjustment to the elevation and hope the rest will cure my cold. I make occasional forays outside and the light in a clear sky is blinding. Only mirrored dark glasses protect my eyes from harm. It remains cloudless, warm, and windless during these days, nothing like the weather on previous trips. On one venture out, a glance up the mountain makes perfectly clear how the mistake happened on the first visit here, for the subsidiary summit blocks the view of the main summit, which sits behind it. And the other failures here through the years. Bad joss. Bad karma. My vow is to make things right this time out.

PHOTO: My Camp I, named "Camp Apricot" on a previous climb. (Photo 8.7 on the site.)

The rest days at Base fail to improve my chest cold. The first and second carries to Camp I (Camp "Apricot," 16,500 feet) transpire without incident, other than the irritating cough and pain in my chest and throat. The warmth and pleasant weather persist, with the daytime temperature at seventy-two degrees. It's all quite baffling and perplexing, the benign conditions. My prayer is that they will continue.

The first lift to Camp II (18,300 feet) is grueling over tough ground, but it proves more exhausting with my need to pause often to cough and gather strength. It's cooler at this camp, fifty-eight degrees, but still warm for the elevation. When I return to Camp I in the afternoon, a heavy weariness is upon me. Today things turned difficult; my chest cold caused constant aggravation and loss of concentration as my mind wandered from the task before me to deal with the pain. Will this never end? It is its own bit of hell here on earth and threatens to weaken my resolve. Tomorrow's second haul will be the toughest day so far, and I search within me for the spark of motivation to see it through. It's been there countless times before. Will it be there for me once more?

In another moment of high altitude reverie, I stare in desultory fashion at the rocks and stones strewn around Blue. I'm the only one to have ever seen these exact stones and probably the only one who ever will. The real proof of their existence is my viewing them, for this grants them life. If man is the measure of all things, then they do not exist to the rest of mankind. They're here, and here thousands of years gone by and will remain thousands more, disturbed solely by the imperceptible movements of nature's hand.

I prize the solitude of this land, yet loneliness comes to any man, and my thoughts turn often to my wife, girls, and grandson. I miss them keenly. I've been out here six days and would love dearly to have a plate of my wife's spaghetti and meatballs. And my grandson, Alex. He is all of three years old now.

The punishing second carry to Camp II proves fatiguing but uneventful. And a change in the weather seems possible. As I look upon the scene below from camp, clouds creep up the mountain's flank. The first wisps probe my tiny site with stealthy fingers of haze that threaten a double envelopment of milky grey. By late afternoon, the mists close about Blue and me like an incoming tide. The bleak afternoon is bleakest and the dense clouds densest at this moment. A sudden upset stomach causes the need for evacuation. Amidst stiff, cold winds, I exit the tent to find a suitable spot. These moments are always an experience, better left imagined than described.

The winds died out early last night. This morning, hesitant breezes stir my home at first light but never return. It's been another bad night with little sleep. Today will be difficult, but it requires only a single move to Camp III and not a return, so I can leave later in the morning.

Though I coughed through the night, a faint resolve began to grow there in the dark, and that ray of confidence promises today will prove a satisfying one. It comes from nowhere, or seemingly so. Perhaps my desire to see the huts is pushing me forward. Or my personality, emphasizing the positive, is coloring the situation once more. Whatever the cause, this sliver of motivation is welcome.

I'm packed and ready at 10 a.m. and push upwards with a determined intention to reach the snow plateau. I have decided to follow the scree and sand couloir instead of cramponing up the narrow snowfield that almost broke me on a previous visit here. The clouds of yesterday have vanished; the sky is clear, with no wind, and the temperature a pleasant forty-nine degrees. The gully is similar to others I've encountered over the years, a heart-breaking trap that demands determination and patience. Its steepness requires traversing, so back and forth I go, occasionally slipping down the incline as the loose stones fail to hold my weight. The going becomes brutal right below the edge of the ice table. I pause a full five minutes, to admonish myself, to cough, to pant, to rekindle the flame of resolve and keep it burning. Three hours after my departure from Camp II, the plateau's rim at 19,300 feet is underfoot and I slump to its surface, wearied beyond the telling. The terrain is somewhat different from what I've seen on previous trips here, since some of the table's ice has melted, especially at the northern rim of the wonderfully sapphire blue pond still residing here.

The subsidiary summit stands before me and blocks sight of the main peak behind it. After I consume water and cookies, I'm off to the Camp III site using the 1995 route, when high winds blew me off the peak. As I tramp over sand and small rocks rather than ice, I sense nothing, I notice nothing of the strange specter that dogged my steps on that climb.

PHOTO: A look back at the ice plateau as I near Camp III. (Photo 8.9 on the site.)

The ground steepens as I tread the plateau. The subsidiary summit is to my left, to the east, and the rock-studded lava flow is to the south, directly to my front. At 20,700 feet, a place seems suitable for a Camp III. But this is a dangerous place, exposed to rockfall from the subsidiary summit. A safer spot resides another 150 feet higher, and this location is my new home. It's 3 p.m. Despite coughing, hacking, and a slight headache, I quickly have Baby Blue in place to serve as my mountain refuge. The weather remains ideal. Still, one can never rest assured on a big mountain. Chance may turn on the instant and change this place into a deadly trap.

PHOTO: Camp III. The main summit is out of sight to the left. (Photo 8.11 on the website.)

Wearied by the day's effort, wearied by the chest pain and the constant coughing, wearied by the crushing load on my back, I ponder a rest day tomorrow. It will be an emotionally and physically draining climb to the summit, one that will require strength and fortitude. There are two freeze-dried meals remaining, so I have enough food. There are two extra days in the timetable, so the schedule isn't in jeopardy. Still, I might be tempting Fate by staying here, because the weather cannot remain so benign. My mountaineering instinct cautions me to seize the instant, that to remain an extra day here is to increase the risk that the weather will turn against me and dash my cherished hopes to see the Inca buildings. That goal argues for forward progress without delay. Yet, my physical condition is such that I resolve that success depends on my physical and emotional well-being, and an extra day here will restore both. So my decision is to stay here tomorrow, despite the possibility that the weather may change. I must gather strength and courage for the last push higher.

Small pleasures, insignificant at sea level, can assume monumental significance up here. I now desire a bit of fruitcake and some hot chocolate. In twenty minutes, the warmth of the cocoa descends straight to the ends of my toes. Studies suggest a climber needs at least three quarts of liquid a day to stay hydrated, but I rarely drink that amount. I have a few sips of coffee in the morning, a half-quart of water during the day's climb, and a quart of broth in the evening.

What do I do on my rest day? Not much. I sleep. I drink soup. I read. I think about my family. I wish for good luck tomorrow. I ponder those Inca huts sitting above me. I wish to see them tomorrow.

In late afternoon, light winds agitate Blue. It isn't anything enduring, just momentary. The sun shines on the tent walls and I let my thoughts carry me where they will. I reflect that the land here seems strange, unearthly. Back in the world, everything is conquered, cut up, and carved by man to work his purpose. Here the world is enormous and unfettered, unknown and untouched by the marching Ages of Man. I reflect on these bleak, cold places, cold since the beginnings of time, and wonder at their hold upon me, fast in their eternal embrace these many years.

Rest and sleep are impossible during the night; the altitude and persistent coughing cause endless discomfort. Yet, the weather remains pleasant. And my pulse is near the norm, so things bode well for tomorrow. Am I strong enough to reach the summit as the ancients did who constructed the summit huts? Surely I am, what with 500 years of technical improvements in gear separating our efforts. Still . . . .

The night of personal irritation fails to damp my mood. Today is the day to see the Inca huts at last, and this tugs at my imagination. I leave Blue at 5 a.m., the stars of the Milky Way and my headlamp guiding my steps. The darkest hour is the hour before dawn. I know this from personal experience on mornings like this one when I strike out from camp at an early morning departure. And the cold!

My route avoids the loose boulders of the lava flow that leads to the summit couloir. Instead, my choice is to labor in the gully east of camp. The lava flow rocks demand full daylight and not the faint light of my feeble headlamp. The couloir route rises due south and connects with another that proceeds east to the summit. I failed in this little bit of hell once before, but I don't intend to fail this time. At its base at 7 a.m., my struggle begins over the small stones and loose gravel that distinguish all these gullies. The angle is brutal and the angle wears me out. My cough and the altitude continue to play havoc with my breathing as I use a two-to-one rest step with a crossing traverse. By 9 a.m., the sun crests the summit and its light bathes the gully with its molten rays. It finds me laboring through the endless scree, the cough tearing at my lungs and throat, mucous streaming from my nose, everything now accompanied by annoying earaches. Each movement becomes a small act of great effort. My normal mental powers are numb and thinking is an effort. I realize, through the haze of altitude that I comprehend only that I am pursuing the desire to get higher, with my body in danger of giving up entirely. I move ever upwards in a kind of self-induced hypnosis.

At 11 a.m., I reach a point where I'm almost even with the subsidiary summit to the northwest and wish to photograph it. I remember my astonishment at reaching that lower peak years before, when, looking across to where I now stand, the real summit was in full view.[54] I take the photo, the last one of the roll. When I insert the new roll of film, without removing my gloves, my trusty Ricoh tumbles from my grasp and onto the rocks at my feet! I'm able to retrieve it, but I'm crestfallen to see that the lens is shattered. (It just goes to show that when one thinks things could not get worse, yet another calamity presents itself.) So much for filming the magic at the summit for later enjoyment through the years. It's a disappointment that darkens my entire mood. What an abject, sorry undertaking this climb has become.

PHOTO: A glance over at the subsidiary summit the author mistakenly thought the main one several years before. Right after taking the photo, the camera slipped from his hands. (Photo 8.15 on the website.)

This solitary incident has an outsized influence on my psyche. Now things are seen that unsettle me, a rotten feeling of failure formerly and largely unknown to me, and I rail against this entire cursed business. The camera, the cough, the interminable pain in lungs and throat, the punishing altitude -- all the negative forces gather and seek to destroy my resolve to continue climbing. "This is not meant to go," I tell myself. "I can't make it." These words play repeatedly in my head and threaten to unhinge my intention, my purpose, my resolve. The never-ending slog higher, fraught with frequent stops to blow, cough, and spit, the continual pain in chest, lips, and throat, all cause me to declare surrender. I'm beaten. Too many things conspire against me and make this entire situation an unmitigated catastrophe. "I'm done. Through." The words play repeatedly in my head. This entire enterprise reeks of disappointing failure. Yet, I still forge upwards.

I don't know how long I spent amongst the spirits of despair. It may have been an hour; it may have been a minute. But I awake to the

---

[54] See Chapter 3, "Cerro Llullaillaco: A Case of Mistaken Identity."

173

present when to the left appears the base of the couloir to the summit. My inner conversation has absorbed my complete attention. My eyes fasten upon it in muted comprehension until my altitude-addled brain realizes the top is within my reach. Here at the apex of the first gully is the pivot point east to the summit! It's the transformative moment of the climb; all doubt evaporates as emotional strength floods back in a momentous surge that pushes me on with renewed enthusiasm. With such unforeseen occurrences is the mountaineer sometimes presented. Unforeseen or not, it's a pristine moment of awareness and I assail the new gully immediately, confident that success is mine. I encourage myself with a beat in my head that urges on the lunges, the strokes, the inexorable steps higher. It is apparent now that I must take my chance for the summit or all chance to take it may vanish.

Several times I rest after ten minutes of intense effort. I wish each time to stay longer, now seized as I am by bouts of lethargic lassitude. But I must continue to climb. The desire to see the huts drives me; a fevered energy fuels my steps -- one, then another, and another. I decide not to look up to the summit. Instead, I fix my eyes upon a point only several yards away, and that is my goal for the moment. I am no longer interested in the summit. My attention is upon the next boot fall, the next rock ledge, the next turn on the ridge, the next slope's inclination, and not until I reach that point do I look farther above, and then only another ten or twenty yards. At these times, the summit is secondary. I have ceased focusing upon it. I have ceased focusing upon anything but the getting higher. I climb and climb over scree, over talus, over sand. For hours, my singular mountaineering motivation drives and compels me not to stop until I reach that next objective.

The top of the gully is in sight at 1:45 p.m., and in thirty minutes Argentina comes in full view to the east, a magnificent panorama brimming in gleaming, golden phosphorescence. The highest point is actually forty feet above me, the tip of a nastily contorted rock massif. Its rocks are fractured by frost yet glued back together by ice -- a stone and ice structure steep enough in some places that horizontal breaks are like giant steps. It is beyond my strength to climb it. Besides, my simple, singular wish is to see the huts. I sense them before I see them, for, without introduction, there they are, before me, here under the high point of 22,109 feet. I sink upon the sand and snow and thrust my ice axe into the surface terrain. I exult that I do not have to climb anymore or keep asking the question, "Will I ever reach the top?" It seems unfathomable I should have reached the summit. Yet here I am. I have a sense of joy at seeing the buildings and view them with profound respect. After all, those who placed them here surpass all my strength and surpass all my understanding. Superhumans they were, superior to all that we feeble, ineffectual beings are today.

My body slumps next to the huts and I exult as an explorer entranced by an unexpected discovery exults. I wonder, "How did those guys do it, anyway?" How could they do it, without stoves, warm clothes, sturdy tents, without plastic boots, warm socks, warm gloves, without freeze-dried meals, dark glasses, warm sleeping bags, and without . . . . cigarettes?[55]

PHOTO: Despite the loss of his camera, the author still has a shot of the huts, thanks to his friend Chuck. Chuck Huss Collection. (Photo 8.16 on the website.)

As I stare at the stones in amazement, I marvel at the visual incongruity; a basic contradiction invests the entire scene. My eyes see buildings, but my mind refuses to comprehend human structures at 22,100 feet! They simply cannot exist, do not exist. My intellect rejects as false what my vision insists is true.

PHOTOS: The famed National Geographic high altitude archaeologist, Dr. Johan Reinhard, and his team, excavate the huts on the summit of Llullaillaco. (Photos 8.17 and 8.18 on the website.)

And how have I done it, how have I reached the top? I have been miserable for ten days. But somewhere inside, beyond my immediate knowing, I found the determination to keep going higher. And I cannot

---

[55] The author again suggests the reader consult Appendix C for a possible explanation.

help but wonder at my wish to climb alone. Others desire companions to climb at the great heights. I desire only to be by myself. What accounts for this? I don't know. Perhaps I cannot know. The self is often indecipherable and beyond all understanding. I climb alone because I wish to climb alone, and that is the sum of it.

A hasty look tells me the sky is no longer as fine as when I started my journey. But I don't want to go down just now. I want a few minutes more of indulgence. I am all alone here. There are 100 square miles around me absent any sensible, rational being. This place is as solitary as a mountain upon the moon. Maria Ester's words about the spirits of Inca children come to mind. Are there mummies somewhere on this mountain? Who knows?

At two forty-five, it's time to leave; the route back is long and a biting wind suddenly beats up the eastern slopes. When I turn to go, a glance back fills me with a longing to return so I might see again this living testament to man's determination and will. As I approach the gully on the downward trip, I can't help wondering, "Did I really see buildings here?"[56] This has been a hard-won day, a wonderful day, a day of wonderful memories. I feel a change in my being, no doubt because I have attained a goal I have sought many times over many years.

I plunge downward easily and methodically on ground over which I had staggered on the way up. The bottom of the summit gully is soon underfoot and I'm into the next one, completely absorbed by the dangers of down. It's clear to the west. I hesitate several minutes as the sun sinks on the horizon. I hope to see the Green Flash, but once again it fails to materialize. The sun has vanished from the heavens when Baby Blue comes into view; her protective walls assure my safety at 7 p.m. A day

---

[56] As the world now knows, thanks to the determined work of Dr. Johan Reinhard over many years, more than huts exist on the summit. His team's discoveries of mummies, statues, jewelry, and much more is detailed in his book "The Ice Maiden," (National Geographic Society, 2005). His latest work, "Inca Rituals and Sacred Mountains," (Cotsen Institute of Archaeology Press, 2011), is a stunning portrayal of high Andean archaeology sites, with particular attention paid to Llullaillaco. And how was the author to know all this resided underneath his boots! He called Maria Ester when the book was published and told her, "You were right!"

of magnificent experience draws to a close, a day to cherish in my long climbing career, a day to cherish forever. I feel a deep happiness, a deep joy at having seen one of the great accomplishments of Andean history.

The next morning, a bright-eyed dawn greets my world in a clear sky, a favorable omen for the trip back to Base Camp. There have been several things of real surprise on this climb, the weather certainly one of them. There has not been a day of inhospitable conditions, except for the one afternoon of clouds and wind, a remarkable thing to happen on this mountain at this time of year.

At the rim of the plateau, I pause to look down upon the Atacama Desert as it reclines in burnished splendor in the morning sun. As I gaze, events of long ago spring to life. Figures come into view, vacant and distant at first, then in sharper focus in the high, vacuous mountain air, a scene conjured up by my fevered imagination. It's one of Inca Yupanqui's armies of 10,000 men tramping south to their appointed encounter with the Chilean people. These soldiers are the forefathers of my adopted, Andean-born daughters, who have Inca blood coursing through their tender veins. The army marches in two long columns. Oases at varied distances, located and marked in painstaking detail by those charged with finding the way, determine their route, for man cannot pass this way without a ready source of water. At the Inca's order, runners return to Cuzco with news of the army's progress every seven miles.[57]

On they come at the urgings of the *hortater*, who beats the cadence on a drum with two hollowed-out wooden branches, accompanied by the shrill notes of highland flutes resonating in the high mountain air and followed by several thousand llamas and their herders. In the middle of the columns, the general rides in a festooned chair supported at the four ends by poles clutched by determined, sturdy infantry. This is the way of the Inca, the projection of his power throughout the land to the south of Cuzco, the sacred heart of the Inca Empire. They march determinedly to the beat of the sticks, in a display of inevitability and irresistibility that confounds nations with its intent and secures those nations to the Inca's purpose. They advance until lost to view behind

---

[57] From "Royal Commentaries of the Incas" by Garcilasso de la Vega, Vol. 2.

intervening ridges and hills, still proceeding towards their ultimate goal to the south, where they will establish hegemony over the stoic Chilean natives. My pulsating vision shimmers to nothing, vapors on the air, an expiring mirage. I return to the present. It is time to flee this place.

Back at Base Camp (eighty-two degrees warm), waiting for Pat's arrival, my thoughts drift back to the climb. It's a mystery as to what happened in the lower couloir. When I was halfway up, failure was in my mind and on my lips. Yet, while I was telling myself the journey was over, I continued climbing, which is puzzling. Perhaps my will, so fixed on seeing the huts, kept me moving higher. Then again, maybe my personality, which usually sees the positive, played a role. In the end, who's to know? I do know, though, that there is a part of me I don't understand completely. This excites me, because the search to know one's self is a high pursuit for any person. I believe this to be one of the great endeavors of all human beings, to seek continually for self-understanding.

Later, in my journal, I write my impressions of the lonely, but rewarding climb up the mountain. At times, I look out through Blue's door towards the impressive contours and shapes of the mountain. How did I reach those lofty places? How did I endure the hardships? I recall all the hours spent at the heights and I come to know that the spirit of adventure and the spirit of discovery have infused my soul on this climb, as they have on all my climbs. My thoughts turn to the struggle for the summit, for it now seems unreal, just as the vision of the Inca buildings seems unreal. This entire adventure shall remain a dream, a dream that is difficult to believe, but a dream I shall treasure the remainder of my life.

Later in the day, I focus my binoculars on Aguas Calientes far below and the brief portion of dirt track leading to the mine from the west. Right on time, at 3 p.m, a cloud of dust smudges the road, a tiny puff at this distance. Of course, it can only be Patricio. He's here at 4:30 p.m. and honks in response to my waves. In the evening at the mine, he springs a surprise -- a fat pork roast sandwich from my favorite deli in Copiapo, *Bavaria*. What a feast!

In the morning, we're off early. I think often about the Inca buildings as we motor back to town. High altitude archaeologists estimate their construction at near 500 years ago, some time after Inca Yupanqui's death in 1493. And how, exactly, did they do it, accomplish such a feat? It seems impossible, incomprehensible.

But I have a theory. In brief, I believe the Indians built the huts away from the mountain, in today's Antofagasta, on the Pacific shore. They chipped local stones to fashion the walls and then transported them to the peak using llamas. Then they hauled all the stones to the summit, where the same stonemasons who had constructed the buildings erected the very huts they had built back in Antofagasta. I believe they did it this way because it is too cold and too high on the peak for men to chip at rocks for days on end. Anyway, that's my hypothesis, for whatever it's worth.[58]

My thoughts often wander to the indomitable spirit of the Indians who placed those small buildings on the summit of the great mountain. Marvels are many, but of all those is man the most marvelous. Through his inventiveness, he became lord of all he surveyed amongst the noble Andes mountains, because he became their masters and lord of all the animals living under their lofty roofs. He learned to speak, think, and live within cities perched upon the most precarious of precipices and planted the slanting land with all manner of fruits and vegetables for his people amidst the difficulties of altitude and cold. He understood the art of medicine, even the delicate procedure of brain trepanning. Possessed of resource and talent, I now wonder little at his indefatigability and ingenuity in building and placing the huts on the lofty head of the mighty Llullaillaco. All time decreed that it was his destiny to do so.

---

[58] Please see Appendix C for the author's expansion upon this theme. Also, the account of how the Indians built the huts appears in the author's soon-to-be-published book, "The Chronicle of Pedro de Merida"

GOOGLE TOUR: The Tour for this Chapter is on the website.

PANORAMIO: In the Panoramio section, choose the "Tres Cruces" tag.

MOVIES: The April, 1999, and the Chapter 9 and 10 movies are appropriate for this Chapter.

"I saw the most amazing thing and have a photo to prove it."

"Yeah, what's that?"

"A guanador. My first sighting." I cannot disguise my enthusiasm and happiness at my incredible fortune.

"A what?"

"A guanador. They're a cross between a guanaco and a condor. They're very shy, so to get a picture is quite a feat. They're akin to the jackalopes out in Arizona. You know, seldom seen, and then only on postcards."

Chuck looks at Dan for several seconds. It takes time until things sink in, since their headaches are a distraction; still, they eventually manage wan smiles.

"Bob, if you have a picture of this creature in that camera of yours, you'd better protect it from me the rest of the trip. It's priceless!"

In an existential way, I feel the mountain's pleasure at my return. My presence here lends a price to the sand, a value known only to the mountain and to me.

--From the author's personal climbing journal

CHAPTER 9

Tres Cruces, Chile: Climbing
with Friends

"Grandpa."

"Yes, Alex."

"When can I go on a climb with you?"

"Well, we might want to talk about that when you get a bit older."

I wish my grandson were with me as I disembark the Los Angeles to Santiago de Chile night flight on February 22, 2009, with the heartfelt desire and resolve to relive the wonder years of my forties and fifties. Why did I decide to end my absence from my beloved Andes Mountains and return for my twenty-ninth climb? One of the answers shakes my hand near the Foreign Exchange office on the airport concourse. It's Chuck, an ER doctor for twenty-one years. Until this climb, we have known each other only through the mails. He persuaded me months before to accompany him and Dan, his climbing partner, to Tres Cruces on their first trip to the peak. We both celebrate milestone birthdays this year -- he, his 60th; me, in July, my 65th. "Let's celebrate together," he said. And so, on that thinnest of suggestions, I succumbed to temptation and invitation. How will my body perform at altitude at my age? I am about to find out.

What caused me to stop climbing in 2001? A combination of things came together, until their cumulative effect became too considerable to ignore. For one, the risk factor increased with each successive climb, and that weighed heavily upon me. It seemed just a matter of time before a catastrophe would present itself, one demanded by fate for my dangerous behavior over the years. How many times can one reject the statistical verity that continued risky behavior results in the risk's fulfillment? Also, pain in my right knee and hip required an increasing level of commitment and effort, although knee surgery in 2002 and a hip replacement in 2004 remedied these problems somewhat. Reluctantly, I decided 2001 was to be my last year in the mountains. Chuck's invitation, however, resurrected memories of my climbing days and I could not resist the chance to experience those times again.

At the new Copiapo airport, I'm reunited after eight years with Patricio Rios, now thirty-eight years old. Until now, we have corresponded by e-mail since I last saw him. He was twenty-five when he drove me to Pissis on our first trip together. He has the same affable manner and subtle sense of humor I remember so well. It's a real joy to see him once more.

Another special moment is seeing Maria Ester, Giancarlo's widow. She still runs the La Casona hotel she owns, and she looks the same as the last time I saw her. It must be the northern Chile climate. This night is special, because she has prepared dinner at her home and with her are Caterina, her daughter, who lives and works in Santiago, and Giancarlito (now a practicing lawyer licensed to argue cases before the Chilean Supreme Court) and his girlfriend, Natalia. Over the years, I have stayed in touch with Maria and the children by e-mail. To see them once again face to face and hear their voices makes this a memorable occasion, and I listen intently as they share some of their experiences over the years. It's all a perfect beginning to one more Andean adventure.

Next day, we pick up one rental truck and use it to shop for food, white gas, several five-gallon plastic containers (we fill them with water at the hotel for our needs at base camp), and the other few items not brought from home. It's exciting to notice the changes in Copiapo's food markets over the years. On my first trip here in November, 1991, to climb Ojos del Salado, grocery stores were basic, with no frills. Now there are several huge mega markets that offer bakeries, full-service butchers, and fast food outlets.

That evening I learn more about my two companions. Chuck has a stellar climbing resume. I write down the high points as he relates them in a matter-of-fact fashion, as though it is of little significance. He's a man of enormous humility.

"I have been at this a long time and with passion. I love the excitement of planning an expedition, training for it, and pulling it off with a group of close friends. Most of my climbing partners are like brothers and go back twenty-five years. I have climbed in the Himalaya five times (four Everest expeditions, one Shishapangma), climbed on all seven continents, summited five of the seven highest summits in the world, seven 22,000 foot peaks in the Western Hemisphere,[59] the highest peaks in nineteen countries, and all (seventy) of the lower forty-eight states' 14,000 foot peaks. I love the outdoors, and aerobic sports and mountaineering have sated those passions. My favorite climbs are the second ascent of Centennial Ridge on Mt. Logan, the traverse of Mt. Cook in New Zealand, and the Brodkin route on Peak Communism in Central Asia. My peak book has almost 500 different ascents."

I ask if he's had any narrow escapes.

"I have been humbled by the forces of nature, the relative insignificance of man in the scope of the mountains. It was my luck in having been at Camp I on Peak Lenin on July 13, 1990, when forty-three people died in an avalanche that leveled Camp II (where we would have been had it not been for a sick climbing teammate). I was also fortunate on Mercedario, Argentina, in November, 2007, when we missed a flash flood by only hours."

Dan's climbing history is extensive also. He has more than thirty-eight expeditions to peaks all around the globe. These companions are mountaineering royalty, and it is an honor to climb with them. They remind me of another mountaineering legend, my friend Sverre

---

[59]   He and Dan climbed the eighth, Tres Cruces Sur, in January, 2011.

Aarseth.[60] Together, the three of them are a part of the Chosen Few brethren.

The following morning we rent the second truck, load all our food, gear, and water jugs aboard both vehicles, fill the ten-gallon containers with extra gasoline, and set off for Tres Cruces, my twelfth visit to the peak. If there had been the slightest hint of the problems my piece of wheeled junk would present over the coming days, I would have demanded a replacement immediately. But, such is life. I've brought hand-held walkie-talkies so we can stay in touch, and they prove useful on occasion. We drive the packed dirt road that eventually reaches Argentina and, within an hour, branch off on the Mina Marte road that leads to Laguna Santa Rosa.

My thoughts drift back through the years. I remember each exit from Copiapo, for every drive to a peak causes the same set of events to occur. As the miles roll by, the truck's cold metal frame becomes a warm chrysalis from which my transfigured being emerges when I reach a base camp. It is the birth of one who, merely hours later, will confront the vagaries of chance, choice, and Divine Providence upon one of the Andes' great mountains. And this time is like the rest, for I feel the transformation of my being from mere mortal to one clawing for the stars.

After two hours, we approach the pass overlooking Laguna Santa Rosa and see Tres Cruces fifteen miles to the east. What a mountain! We stop by the side of the road next to a small white car and a larger

---

[60] The author's good friend Sverre and he attempted Llullaillaco in 1998. He loves adventure and has climbed around the world, South America, Russia, Antarctica, Alaska, Turkey, Africa, a total of eighty-three peaks, nineteen solo. His most harrowing experience was in 1978 when a storm trapped him at night on Mt. Sabalan, in Persia. As a result, he suffered the dreaded "bite" and lost all ten toes. He was and is a man of great courage and a mountaineering legend. In addition, he was 64 years old at the time of our climb together (the author was 54). His enduring Andean achievement is the first solo of the Pissis main summit by a climber over 60 years of age (he was 62). During his working years, he was a post-doctorate Research Associate at Cambridge University in England. We stay in touch regularly.

white SUV, their owners surveying the brilliant scene before us. The vehicles shimmy slightly from the buffeting winds.

I gaze upon the mountain with eager anticipation, and a measure of dread, since it is unpredictable due to its volatile weather patterns. The sky is clear blue; the Laguna, 2,000 feet below, is a greenish-blue shimmering gem. Tres Cruces stands in regal splendor, a giant among giants as it jabs its spires towards the midday heavens. A blanket of snow drapes the Central and Sur summits. The couloir that leads to the col, dusted white at the margins, is snow free at the center, so the peak looks in good shape at present for a climb. Out of sight is the route to the summit of Sur, the goal for Chuck and Dan, and that won't come into view until they reach the col. My proposed route for Central looks clear the entire way. Though the assessment is favorable from here, little did we know what the mountain had in store for us and was preparing, even now, in welcome.[61]

As we approach the Refugio at the lake, the memories stream back from years past. It still sits upon a wooden platform, with a cooking area and three small rooms and measures some fifteen feet wide by thirty-five feet in length. It faces east, towards the Laguna and the distant Tres Cruces. The rough dirt track that connects with the Mina Marte road lies between the Refugio and the lake, which sits 120 feet from the building. My truck faces the lake and rests on a gently inclined slope.

PHOTO: A flamingo in flight over the Laguna. Chuck Huss Collection. (Photo 9.12 on the site.)

Chuck and Dan become immediate hostages to the beauty of this place and both amble off to photograph obliging flamingoes, with their tiny young, and the ambulating, retreating guanaco. I indulge myself

---

[61] When this was written (December, 2010), the accumulated data for the Oceanic Nino Index (ONI), the accepted standard, indicates 2009 was a strong El Niño year, as opposed to a moderate or weak one, which most likely accounts for the problems to come on this trip. Since the first year of ONI compilation in 1950, this is only the seventh "strong" year.

in a silent reverie, recalling moments spent here over twenty years, a mere speck in the life of these huge massifs and their surrounding compatriots, but significant to me, whose existence is measured in minutes and hours rather than in centuries and millennia.

PHOTO: The author and his truck are about to take off on an impromptu ride. (Photo 9.3 on the site.)

I decide to retrieve some items for the approaching night and step onto the rear bumper of the truck to search for the things I need. Immediately, the contraption begins to lurch forward. I jump off and grab the bumper with both hands, a 155-pound weakling attempting to halt a 4,000-pound truck inexorably rolling downhill. I scrape my knees and legs as the thing glides towards the lake. Fortunately, the hulk comes to rest on the earthen berm at the side of the road, thirty feet from the water. I don't see any undercarriage damage and it's drivable, so I return it to its original position in front of the hut, this time with the transmission in gear and rocks firmly placed before each front wheel. I now know I can't trust the parking brake again. It goes to show you, you can't take anything for granted out here. I have avoided real problems, at least for the present. Though the Laguna is only a foot deep, the muck on its bottom might have required a difficult rescue using Chuck and Dan's truck.

Now things become even more interesting, for in fifteen minutes an additional adventure presents itself as a small white sedan glides towards me from the Marte road. It's one of the vehicles we saw on the pass. Inside are a young married couple who introduce themselves as Tristan and Lucy. They are French and on an education loan program. They're vacationing here to marvel at the beauty of this part of the Andes. They speak some English, Lucy the more proficiently, and we converse in broken Spanish, halting English, and expressive hand gestures.

When I suggest they turn off their motor to save gas while we talk, Lucy says they're afraid to because the battery's dead. Tristan says they intend to return to Copiapo in several hours to purchase a new one.

Soon, they drive off to explore and promise to stop and talk some more before they head back to town. When they disappear behind a low-lying ridge to the north, Chuck and Dan trundle up. They complain of altitude headaches and choose to sit and relax on the hut balcony.

Twenty minutes later, two figures appear to the north, indistinct at this distance. Who could they be? Do people roam around out here without a vehicle? Not likely. Finally, I recognize Tristan and Lucy and drive out to meet them.

"Car not start," says Lucy, as she mimics turning the ignition key and accompanies this with the sound of a failed starter.

It's not clear what happened; Tristan must have killed the engine, probably by mismanaging the clutch.

Chuck and Dan drive out to help. At first, we use our jumper cables, but for some reason they don't work. Is the electrolyte level too low in their battery? No. Next, we try to tow it. When we hook my truck's tow cable to his front bumper, I tell Tristan to turn on the ignition, place the gearshift in second gear, and keep the clutch depressed. When we reach fifteen mph, I'll slow, to take the tension off the cable, and wave. He's then to "pop" the clutch. Lucy repeats all this in French, hopefully in the right order. We try this once and the engine fails to turn over. We try towing it three times more, each with the same result. How can a manual transmission fail a tow start?

What should they do? "You have a tent and food, but I don't think you want to stay out here. We're leaving for the mountain tomorrow, so you need to do something now if I'm to help. It's already 3 p.m."

They are fully attentive and stoically calm, as though this is another day at the office for them. At least they aren't showing a great deal of stress.

"I'll drive you to the Customs Station and you can call town for a mechanic and tow. They'll be at the Station tomorrow."

Lucy watches me attentively, until she suddenly looks past and points excitedly over my right shoulder towards the Copiapo road.

"It family at pass! They go back to town." She's animated, energized, and bouncing on her toes. The white SUV is a mile distant and proceeds up the incline towards the pass.

"Please, Bob, can we catch? They take us to Copiapo."

"Of course. Let's go!"

We roar off, reach the road in short order, and the chase is on. The SUV has a commanding lead, so I gun the truck to catch up, since we need to overhaul him before he reaches the other side of the pass. The descent on that side will be infinitely more dangerous because of its steepness. I watch my speed, because the dirt road we travel is rutted, pitted, and strewn with stones of various sizes and shapes. When the SUV enters the switchbacks, we've gained some ground. On the last sharp bend, I toggle my headlights repeatedly to attract their attention. But they're now over the pass and out of sight. When we reach the top and start down, the combination of horn and lights finally works. The SUV slows and then stops as we pull up alongside. Lucy talks to the driver in Spanish for several minutes.

"He say he take us Copiapo. He wait here for us." She's excited and so is Tristan. We'll return to their car back at the Refugio to retrieve the things they'll need in town.

We say goodbye and speed back to the Laguna. Lucy and Tristan marvel aloud about this man and his willingness to help and their good fortune in general. Tristan says they met him and his family on the pass. Theirs were the two vehicles there when we arrived. So intense was my examination of Tres Cruces at the time, I hadn't noticed. Lucy tells me his name is John and he has with him his wife, two young sons, a daughter, and a six-month-old baby. What a prince of a man to do something like this for my new friends.

"A what? A six-month-old baby?" I'm amazed.

"Yes," says Lucy. "I know is hard to believe."

Wait until the guys learn this baby is acclimating out here better than we are!

Back at the Refugio, they start to pack the things they'll need for the night. By 4:45 p.m. they're ready and off we go. We reach John and his family at 5:30 p.m., the sun having set behind nearby ridges. They prove a delightful family, the children bright-eyed, cheerful, and well groomed. John is a true gentleman. His English is limited, as is my Spanish, yet his manner indicates a man of dignity and professionalism.

I linger a few minutes and receive hugs from Lucy and Tristan. Lucy begins to cry and says she can't believe there are so many nice people in the world. What a wonderful young couple they are, and I wish them the best of luck.

On my return to the Laguna, Tres Cruces conceals itself behind dark grey curtains, an ominous sign that the weather there may soon change. At the Refugio, Chuck and Dan are feeling the altitude. But they have been through this on so many climbs they are used to it. They sit, Chuck on the hut's bench, Dan on the floor, stoically sipping tea and conversing quietly.

They listen to my story and stare, vacantly uncommunicative. I'm all too familiar with feeling uncomfortable at altitude. I'm fortunate, however, this time. I feel fine. Yet I know it may hit me also, so I continue drinking water to ward off possible headaches. All this is an uncomfortable business at times, requiring equanimity and stoicism.

Despite their situation, I must tell them of my discovery.

"I saw the most amazing thing and have a photo to prove it."

"Yeah, what's that?"

"A guanador. My first sighting." I cannot disguise my enthusiasm and happiness at my incredible fortune.

"A what?"

"A guanador. They're a cross between a guanaco and a condor. They're very shy, so to get a picture of one is quite a feat. They're akin to the jackalopes out in Arizona. You know, seldom seen, and then only on postcards."

Chuck looks at Dan for several seconds. It takes time until things sink in, since their headaches are a distraction; still, they eventually manage wan smiles.

"Bob, if you have a picture of this creature in that camera of yours, you'd better protect it from me the rest of the trip. It's priceless!"

At least we all have a good laugh. It takes the edge off their discomfort.

"I'm sure you'll be better in the morning. I still would like us to drive to a base camp tomorrow."

They converse a bit and then Chuck says they will decide in the morning whether to spend an added night here. They are slow and deliberate in their decisions, a testament to their experience among the high peaks of the world.

"Okay. If you do stay, at least follow me to the peak so you know the route. From here, it's 2,400 feet to the base of the mountain. There you can see the way to a base site. After you see it, you can return here."

They discuss things for a time and still decide to make a decision in the morning.

Later, on the hut's narrow balcony, the Andean twilight welcomes the quiet of this place beneath the advancing dark in the east, black, black as infinity, the stars glowing midst a velvet veil in a blackened sky, the dark land darker than all the night. The determined journey of a solitary satellite comes to view, a pinpoint of illumination spinning through the jammed star traffic of *Centaurus* and *The Southern Cross*, a pinprick of light on its unerring path through the night. It moves like a planet on its inevitable track through the fathomless heavens and courses on with assurance, its calculated route known for all eternity. My disposition brightens at its destiny's fulfillment.

Next day, Chuck and Dan are uncomfortable and still not sure whether to proceed. I prepare to leave for base camp and hope they will at least follow me to the foot of the mountain. Then, what appears to the south but John's SUV! It's 9:30 a.m. on a brisk, clear morning and he's here this early? He drives up and out stream John, Lucy, Tristan, and John's two sons. Lucy tells me excitedly of their adventures since yesterday evening. They returned to Copiapo, where John and his wife insisted they stay with them for the night. They also bought a battery and left Copiapo early this morning.

PHOTO: Lucy is at the truck driver side door, Tristan is in the middle, John is in the green shirt, and John's son is to the right. Dan Smith Collection. (Photo 9.4 on the website.)

John and Tristan replace the battery but the ignition still fails, despite several attempts. It's probably the starter, which means a call to town for a tow back to Copiapo. While they wrestle with the problem, I complete my packing. A check with Chuck and Dan finds them suddenly ready to go, their acclimation problems having vanished. One's physical condition out here may change quickly, for good or ill, and I'm relieved at their buoyant moods.

"Roberto, you have . . . ." Lucy begins to cry and large tears roll down her cheeks as she hugs me goodbye.

"Thank you, we not forget your help," says Tristan as he grips my hand tightly.

PHOTO: A mother guanaco and her baby at Rio Lamas Falls. Chuck Huss Collection. (Photo 9.17 on the website.)

We wave as we drive off from Santa Rosa and proceed north by northeast across the Maricunga Salar. In less than an hour, we intersect the Argentina highway and turn right towards the mountain, which sits ten miles away to the south. A pause at the waterfalls of the Rio Lamas, a stream born from an underground aquifer with melted snow from Tres Cruces, provides some memorable moments. A mother guanaco and her baby stand near the pooled waters above the falls amongst green shrubs and grassy tufts. It's an idyllic natural scene and ones like it play through eternity in this high, secluded Paradise.

We leave the purling waters and are now firmly on the Great Plateau motoring east, with Tres Cruces immediately to the south. From here, the elevation of 14,300 feet is virtually constant to Laguna Verde, an hour away to the east.

I haven't been here in eight years and watch intently for the faint intersection with the dirt track that proceeds southwest to the foot of our base camp slope. A rectangular sign looms up on the right. "Tres Cruces," it announces in large letters. An arrow points to the mountain.

That's nice, I think. The police have seen fit to draw attention to one of the great Andean peaks for passing motorists.

I keep driving. Yet I still can't spot the road I want. It doesn't actually intersect the highway but starts some 150 feet from it.

"Bob." It's Chuck calling from their truck. "I think I saw a road back at that sign."

"No. It's up here a short ways. You'll see."

Three minutes later.

"Bob." It's Chuck again. "My map shows the intersecting road should be around kilometer marker thirty-five. And the thirty-five marker was just past that Tres Cruces sign ten minutes ago."

Whoops! How many times have I been to this peak? Twelve?

I stop and turn around. When they pull up even, I shout out, "Hey, it's the first mistake I've made all year!"

They both laugh and we set off once more. I've probably damaged my mountain credibility with them. Between the two, they have more climbs to their credit than there are days in two years.

When we reach the sign, I now see the track that will take us to the foot of the mountain. We follow it until I spot the most suitable ground to begin the drive up to a base site. Once we lock our hubs for four-wheel drive, we drive off-road and begin the jaunt upwards.

The trucks grind up the incline as we navigate through rock gardens and loose sand expanses. At 15,600 feet, the area I've used on previous trips for camps comes into sight. We've done a good job of off-roading -- no flat tires, no busted axles.

"Bob, this is too high to spend the night. We'll go back down a thousand feet and make camp." Chuck is worried a night at this height will be too hard on them, especially after yesterday's problems. It's a wise decision.

Their departure fulfills my desire to remain by myself, for this will allow me to climb, somewhat, as I used to climb. In half an hour, Baby Blue is up and, reunited after so many years of separation, we're ready for another journey. My camp area is still identifiable by the rocks I used many years before as supports. In an existential way, I feel the mountain's pleasure at my return. My presence here so many times gives a price to the sand, a value known only to the mountain and to me.

The moment I have anticipated nervously for months is now at hand. My climbing boots on and a full pack on my back, I intend to hike uphill, directly at times, traversing at others, to test my replacement hip's sturdiness and the effectiveness of my knee surgery. Both joints function fine at home, but the uneven surfaces out here give me pause. I'm pleasantly surprised at my performance. I feel as strong as I did during my climbing days, and this realization determines my decision: I will attempt Central. This effort won't be as demanding as in past years, because the plan is not to start from our Base Camps. Instead, we'll drive the trucks as high as we can and put in an Advanced Base Camp (ABC), leave the trucks, and go on foot from there.

At noon, clouds begin forming above as I drive down to talk with my neighbors. They're in good spirits and feeling well. Chuck is outside fiddling with his crampons and Dan lies in his sleeping bag inside their tent.

We talk about our routes up the mountain and our plans to climb separately. Then, I ask after their rapid change of physical condition this morning, when they seemed to feel well very quickly.

"Dan took a Diamox[62] this morning. It worked for him. I haven't had anything. How about you?"

"I just had an aspirin and feel fine."

"Really?" He turns to the tent door. "Dan, how many guys around the world have we come across who don't take stuff[63] at altitude?"

"There are a few." Dan hesitates a moment. "Remember that climb in the Caucasus? That strange guy with the German climbing team? He told me he was the only one who wasn't on something."

"Oh, the guy with the variegated hair dyes in his beard. He must have been on something else, don't you think?" He says this with a slow

---

[62] Diamox is a perfectly safe drug to take at altitude. It is a medication that encourages urination, and that forces the kidneys to excrete bicarbonate, the base form of carbon dioxide; this re-acidifies the blood, balancing the effects of the hyperventilation that occurs at altitude in an attempt to get oxygen. It also helps to lessen headaches and sleep disturbance. It is not classified as a "hard" drug.

[63] The "hard" drugs of choice are dexamethasone for High Altitude Cerebral Edema [HACE] and nifedipine for High Altitude Pulmonary Edema [HAPE].

chuckle, as though he doesn't want to let it go. The memory clearly pleases him.

"Yeah, probably."

For those who climb the big peaks using drugs, a summit won by artificial means, I suppose, gives the conqueror a title of exceptional intelligence and exceptional contrivance. Indeed, it would seem some climbers call this cheating by drugs cleverness and drug rejection dishonesty. They are proud of the first quality and mortified by the second.

"If you both feel up to it, why don't we see how high we can go in the trucks? I have a place in mind for an Advanced Base."

Even though we have already gained several thousand feet in elevation in a few short hours, the three of us feel fit enough to try to go higher.

The idea of an ABC site bothered me when I began to plan for the climb months ago. It offends my deep-seated notion of mountaineering honor not to double carry all my gear to Camp I from Base Camp. After all the years of doing so, I found it difficult to justify driving above Base as a concession to my age. But I accepted it as such.

We set off driving up the grade I recollect so well; the memories flood back as we go, a remembered boulder here, a remembered vista there, everything with meaning, everything with value beyond measure. At 16,500 feet, we approach the area I have in mind, a place near a small snowfield with several spots ideal for tents. After ten minutes of discussion, we agree that this will be the location for the higher camp. As we planned, we'll stay here for several hours to acclimate and then return to Base for the night. However, in this mountain world of faithfulness and harmony, our being here upsets that tranquility, for there's a sudden convulsion over the quiet land as dark clouds form above us. Could it be our being here has upset nature's ordering of things?

While Chuck and Dan hike about, I stare fixedly out across the Maricunga Salar far below. My past rushes back and I reflect with astonishment upon the overpowering, irrational, irrepressible desert, a thing to abhor, yet one to adore. There is no better companion than this land, silent in conversation yet welcoming in emotional bonding. I'm lonelier among others back in the world than in my world of the silent mountain fastnesses that offer the surety of seclusion.

And what of Chuck's comment? Are we the last of a breed of mountaineers, those who reject artificial means to help us attain the heights? I have had few contacts with other climbers through the years. My friends, however, have traveled the world extensively and they know more about this than most. Drugs probably do play a role. In the end, how others wish to climb is not my business. My business is to climb in as "pure" a way as possible, and that is all that is my business.

A knock at the window interrupts my reverie. It's Dan.

"It's snowing. We're going down."

He's right. My thoughts have absorbed me and I hadn't even noticed. Back at Base, I nestle within Blue's protecting walls. Some say you can't go home again, meaning, no doubt, that one cannot recapture the happiness enjoyed in prior years. But I am able to disprove that statement, for I am here and "back home again." I am back among the high peaks, confident that I retain the climbing strength and ability of the golden years of my past.

A stiff wind stirs up from somewhere and froths the falling snow to writhing sheets and veils. Dense eddies of snow race across the slopes, the winds raging with such vehemence that I'm concerned about my tent's stability. In short order, the winds become a full-blown gale reminiscent of those I've encountered on other journeys. Blue's gyrations indicate a weakening support anchor, possibly the northeast one. It requires resetting before it pulls. The temperature outside is twenty-five degrees Fahrenheit. If the wind speed is 80 mph, the wind chill is -10 degrees. In my full windsuit, I crawl from Blue into the shrieking maelstrom and waning light. My gloved fingers secure the door zippers after me. What a shock between my warm sleeping bag and the cold, raging tempest.

I'm unable to stand, so on hands and knees I use my "col crawl" to visit each pile of anchor stones as the spindrift beats against my suit with a steady drumming sound. As I glance about, tiny bits of ice and sand careening like loose bullets across the land sting the unprotected part of my face. A tug at each parachute cord reveals the northeast corner needs adjustment. The wind's force against Blue has pulled the support rocks towards the tent. That leaves slack in the line and causes the tent to buck. Eventually, the cord loop around the stone will work itself free and cause the tent to collapse. I reposition the stones and add two more large rocks to strengthen the support. The howling is deafening as the wind's freezing embrace coats my suit with icy rime. No man could survive in the open in this violent whirlpool of freezing Hell, frozen like Dante's Ninth Circle of the Inferno.

Back inside Blue, I'm weary from the effort; the altitude and wind have exacted their toll. As I rest, I ponder that my situation is different from previous years at times of danger like this. During those encounters with storms, there was no way for me to flee; the only thing I could do was submit myself to the tempest until it blew itself out. This time, though, I have a truck that can serve as my refuge of last resort and my means of escape, should my situation come to that.

I'm reasonably pleased with my physical situation. It was an elevation gain of 4,300 feet from Santa Rosa to Advanced Base today. We drove to it in four hours and stayed a couple of hours longer. Now, back here at Base Camp, my pulse is only slightly elevated. I've read that the aged body withstands high altitude better than the younger. To this point, my age has not hindered my movements, and this is quite surprising and welcome.

The winds continue to shriek as I settle in for a long night of noise. I can't light the stove because of Blue's movements, and I'm afraid that one huge blow will scatter things inside the tent. So, a Snickers and fruit cake must suffice. But my iPod provides wonderful entertainment. I never dreamed during my early climbing career that I might one day watch movies in my tent! Later, the continued jostling of Blue disturbs the night and the orderly arrangement of my gear -- clothes, food, pee bottle, loose equipment. The buffeting and screaming of the pounding gale recede at 3 a.m. and there are several hours of quiet.

PHOTO: Dan in front of their tent. (Photo 9.20 on the site.)

The warm rays of the sun winking above the Cruces' battlements reveal a white dusting of snow that covers the land and stretches below Chuck and Dan's tent. With the sun's warmth, most of it will melt off in two to three hours. Our plan is to acclimate further by driving up to the ABC site, spend several hours there, and then return. The following day, they will move into the higher camp while I'll spend an additional day here at Base. The next day, they'll make a single lift to a Camp I and I'll move to Advanced Base. There I will judge my ability to proceed higher.

Our plans are in jeopardy within hours. At 11 a.m., they motor up to me, yet my truck won't cooperate. It cranks, turns over, and then dies. Similar efforts produce similar results.

"Come on, baby. You have to show some life. I'll put in a good word for you with the rental people if you do." I can't believe I'm talking to an inanimate object, other than Baby Blue, at over 15,000 feet in the Andes!

I wait ten minutes before trying the ignition again. That and subsequent attempts fail. The battery is now completely, totally, unequivocally dead, a thoroughly wretched turn of events. Starting the heap by letting it roll down the slope proves successful, and things are fine. But when I drive back to my camp and stop next to the tent, my inept clutch coordination kills the engine. Of course, it won't start. This situation won't work. After discussing alternatives with the others, I make my decision.

"I'm going to start it on the slope again. Follow me down to the highway. I'll lock and leave it there and you can drive me to the Customs Station. Then you return here and continue climbing."

Chuck asks what I'll do after that.

"I'll call the rental office in Copiapo. They'll send a guy out tomorrow with a new battery. I'll spend the night at Customs and return tomorrow by noon. Go ahead to ABC without me. I'll drive back here and catch up with you."

Once I stuff my pack with food, gas, sleeping bag, stove, and other items, I let the truck roll downhill, pop the clutch, and we're off down the mountain. It's a beautiful Andean morning; still, something bothers my mountaineer's sixth sense. It seems as though the mountain is telling me something, yet I can't discern what. Is the success of our climb in jeopardy?

PHOTO: The San Francisco Customs Station on the Maricunga Salar. (Photo 9.22 on the site.)

The fellows at the San Francisco Customs Station are first class and friendly. The officer in charge is a Chilean Army Colonel. On his staff are two carabinero drug officers, four Chilean Customs inspectors, and several support personnel. Colonel Felipe Soto speaks good English and places a call to the rental company. They'll have someone out first thing tomorrow. He then offers me a spare room with a bed, my quarters for the night, and this makes me feel like an honored guest. In the afternoon, he offers a caution.

"You must be careful on the mountain, Señor Roberto. El Niño. Weather angry and strange." He says this with a conspiratorial air, as if it's an unspoken secret shared only with a few. My friends and I are aware that the weather is unsettled on the peak. Is more in store for us?

At sunset, I stroll through the small complex as the wind whistles around the Station structures. Intervening ridges and low hills block sight of Tres Cruces to the south. Behind them, dark and ominous clouds rear high into the heavens, foretelling some nasty business on the peak. My companions must be amidst a screaming storm that might continue into the night. What luck. I'll sleep snug in a warm, cozy chamber tonight.

At 9 a.m. next morning, Arturo arrives from Copiapo with a new battery. After I thank the Colonel for his hospitality, we're off, as the sun casts a wondrous light, the desert sands assuming orange and purplish hues seen only at sunrise and sunset -- magical times, times known here continuously for millennia. The clouds of yesterday have disappeared, so perhaps it wasn't too bad a night on the mountain. When we reach my truck at the base of the peak, Arturo exchanges the old battery with a new one and then leaves for the trip back to Copiapo. I turn the wheels to the incline and in half an hour rejoin Chuck and Dan at their camp.

"We wanted to wait until more snow melts up there before taking off for the high camp. New battery?"

"Yeah, things are fine now. I'll get some stuff from my tent and be ready when you are."

At 12:15 p.m., they have packed all their gear and we set out. The sky darkens immediately, and a heavy burden of grey overhangs the peak and obscures the mountain just as we reach the higher camp. They have their tent in place and are brewing soup when another snow-storm begins its daily dump. We could set our clocks by the regularity of these afternoon storms.

"Okay, I'm going down, but I'll return tomorrow. Good luck going to Camp I." I have to leave; otherwise I could be trapped here by falling snow.

Their plan is to make a single haul to a Camp I above the col, around 20,000 feet (an elevation gain of 3,500 feet), stay the night, and go for the summit the following day. It's a strategy that works for them but is inappropriate for me now or on past climbs. That's too much of an elevation gain. I prefer 2,000-2,500 feet between camps, with two carries to each one except my last camp. That was my style through the years, and I'd be foolish to adopt a different one now.

By the time I'm safely back with Blue, the snow cascades from the heavens. It's so thick the truck twenty feet away is almost lost to sight. My thoughts wander to the whiteout on Pissis years ago; the memory strikes me with a primitive kind of fear. But unlike previous climbs when I had no means of escape, I have a truck that will provide that, should things really become ugly. My thoughts turn to Chuck and Dan. My friends must really be catching it tonight.

At 6 p.m., the snowfall slackens, followed by rising winds that in thirty minutes become a shrieking typhoon that hurtles the new-fallen snow back into the vault of heaven from whence it came, in a reversal of nature's order of things. Angry and strange. That's what the Colonel said. El Niño this year. Angry and strange. Did he know the half of it? He certainly didn't know the sum of it, for he resides in his protected and warm castle keep, safe from nature's threatening behavior.

Baby Blue shudders and trembles on her upslope side amidst the hammer-and-anvil like blows of the winds. I press my body to that wall to protect against a tent collapse. As the storm continues, I realize that we are caught in a weather pattern impossible to understand, whether we are at its beginning or at its end. There's nothing for it but to wait it out for the present, knowing that at some point we may have to abandon the climb. Blowing snow flutters against Blue's northern side, then shifts to the eastern side. Blasts of wind batter us incessantly, while the never-ending snow continues to bury the tent. I have the unpleasant feeling of possible death by asphyxiation. I push outward on the walls several times with all the power I can muster to force away the cold heaps seeking to cover us. These labors cause me to pant from the altitude and the effort. I sink into a wearisome state, possessed by a growing dissatisfaction with this complete undertaking.

Amidst all of this, my thoughts drift home, to my wife, my daughters, my grandson, and my new granddaughter, and I wish them near me. I miss the meaning they give to my life.

At 2 a.m., the winds slacken, followed by a stillness that allows me several hours of rest, though not sleep. At 8 a.m., menacing dark clouds that envelop this side of the mountain block the sun, with occasional falling flakes the only movement. Snow covers my slope, with deep banks near large stones and ridges. I'm living in a world of translucent crystal, where a whitened burden like a weighted cloth silences all sound.

I will not attempt to go to Advanced Base today. Conditions higher on the peak will be worse than they are here, and my concern now is whether Chuck and Dan can retreat from their camp. By late morning, the sun breaks through the clouds and reveals the scene above. From ABC to the peaks and the couloir is plastered in snow. If my friends find themselves trapped where they are, they might not be able to escape for a day or more. We have enough time left in the schedule to accommodate a delay. Still . . . .

PHOTO: Chuck and Dan are somewhere in that mess. (Photo 9.24 on the site.)

In late afternoon, the strength of the sun's rays has melted most of the snow around my camp and on the incline to the higher camp. As I warm water for broth, a steady droning sound disturbs my vacant thoughts, a sound like the humming of bees leaving their hive. It's my friends' truck, 150 yards distant, Dan carefully picking a path through the rocks and boulders.

"We couldn't get to the top," Dan says. "We climbed to the col in blizzard conditions and retreated. The snow was so deep that going for the summit was out of the question. It was a struggle just to get back to camp. And we got it all on video!"

The drive down had proved grueling. "It took us two hours to get here. You know what it normally takes, forty-five minutes." It turns out they were twice stuck in the snow and the underlying sand, and had to dig themselves out with a shovel.

It's now 5 p.m. and flakes begin tumbling down upon us. It's not too heavy a load, but a biting, snapping wind gives it teeth. Inside their truck, we discuss tactics.

"We talked about this coming down. The snow up there isn't going to melt soon. We're thinking of calling this off," says Chuck.

"Yeah, I agree. We're in an El Niño weather pattern showing no sign of a letup."

Still, they want to spend more time out here.

"We could hang at Santa Rosa and enjoy the scenery the days we have left."

After more discussion, we decide to leave the mountain next day and perhaps drive south to the Negro Francisco Refugio and spend the night.[64] We've all been there before on previous trips to this area. Later in the evening, the storm lessens in intensity. As I wait for my

---

[64] In 1996, Giancarlo died a mile from this Refugio.

freeze-dried spaghetti to cook, my thoughts return to the many times I've been to the Andes. It makes me sad to end a trip that is certainly my last to the big mountains.

Morning dawns in a clear sky, and the truck is loaded and set to go by 10 a.m. A wave from the guys below says they're ready also. Right on cue, the truck, even with the new battery, refuses to cooperate, and it receives every oath and epithet the English language has at its disposal.

"OK, dude. You've had it. Forget the good word to your bosses!"

Of course, I've parked facing downhill, so I start the worthless thing on the incline and join the others in minutes. We stare back at the mountain before leaving. Gale-force winds scourge and flog the heights of both Central and Sur. They scour those cold, upper reaches and hurl snow into a cobalt blue sky. We decide to take a faster route off the peak and follow the road at the foot of the mountain directly west. It eventually links with the Mina Marte road, just three miles north of the mine. Once upon it, we work our way over an uneven plateau and pause often to watch the mountain drama behind us. On the massif's lower slopes, near our Advanced Base site and above it, blustering gusts blow clouds of snowdrift into the air, obscuring the lower reaches of the peak. The two summits, though, remain in view. They appear to hover in mid-air, floating unhinged without a visible foundation; the azure heavens serve as a backdrop for ice crystals streaming outwards for miles from the two summits in distinct snow-banner formations.

As Chuck clicks away with his Nikon at double speed, Dan remarks upon the wonderful scene holding us in thrall.

"I'm glad things worked out like they did. I wouldn't want to be up there right now." He says this as though he's been in similar circumstances on other mountains. I'm sure he has.

I agree. "Yeah, it might be a life-and-death struggle, believe me."

We drop over the western lip of the plateau on a steep slope that bottoms out at a rutted dirt track. Twice my truck falls heavily into nasty holes, even though my speed is no more than 8 mph. When we intercept the Marte-Copiapo road, we proceed south, towards the Refugio at Laguna Negro Francisco. I call my friends.

"We made it. I hit a couple of holes hard, though. And I mean hard."

"We did too. But our truck's in good shape."

Yet, something isn't right. There's no traffic on this road. Even though Mina Marte was abandoned years ago, a caretaker crew remained behind, so one might expect to see vehicles occasionally. There are none.

We pass on our left a rare sight, a *bofedal,* or wetland. These exist at several spots in this part of the Andes and each takes a different form. They are characterized by vegetation similar to a cushion, which could be compared to a sponge, because they are collectors of water. The water for this one comes from Tres Cruces glacier melt off. Andean ducks and other birds play on its surface.

PHOTO: An example of a *bofedal,* this one near the Refugio Negro Francisco. (Photo 2.3 in the Chapter 2 photo folder.)

"Bob, you have a problem," radios Chuck. "Your right front wheel is bent sideways."

What? There's been no hint of a problem through the steering. I'm out and by the wheel when they pull up.

"Can you believe it? The axle's busted." The wheel angles out at forty-five degrees, the tire's innermost tread the only part touching the road.

"I was in 4WD. What if the transfer case and differential are damaged?" I sense another impending adventure.

What to do? I have little choice. The truck should be drivable, as long as I keep the speed under 20 mph.

"Mina Marte isn't far. Let's find it and call Copiapo to have the rental company come out and haul this thing back to town."

Off we go, albeit at a tentative pace. There's no telling what the exact damage is. I checked that the left front tire and axle are intact, and there aren't any grinding noises from the right front. A check of the wheel well verified there's no oil leakage, although the 4WD spider gears dangle near the axle. As long as we remain on flat surfaces, I can manage.

I radio the others. "See the road on the right that rises and disappears around the hill? The Mine buildings are back there." I hope my friends are enjoying this.

As we crest the top of the road, I expect the Mine's structures to appear there on the dirt plateau. And they do. Or do they? At first, I don't understand that an absence of buildings means an absence of the Mine.

"What did they do? Underground it?" I radio back to the others.

The eyes and mind play funny tricks at even moderate altitude. I expect to see structures so intensely that I know they're here, they must be here; when they fail to materialize, it causes unbelieving denial. Eventually, I realize there are no buildings.

"They must have hauled everything to another mine. What do we do now?"

I have the answer to Dan's question.

"This thing will hold together. Let's try to reach the Customs Station. You guys follow me, just in case."

"How far is it from here?" asks Chuck.

"I'd say close to forty miles. We should be there around 3 o'clock; then you can split and do what you want."

"Should we try the Refugio at Negro Francisco first?"

"I would feel better if we head for the Customs Station. I don't want to inconvenience the rental company too much. Besides, the Station has both landline and satellite phones. Negro Francisco may have neither. If we get down there and can't call out, then it's some sixty miles from there to the Station. I don't think we would have enough gas to make it."

"Okay, the Station it is," says Chuck.

"Yeah, I agree," says Dan.

I still can't believe the Mine is no longer here.

My truck drives fine on the Marte-Copiapo road as our two-vehicle caravan limps along. Five miles east of Laguna Santa Rosa, we leave the road, strike out north over the evenness of the Maricunga Salar, and intersect the Chile-Argentina highway in an hour. Two miles from the Station, my friends radio good luck and turn around to continue their journey. We'll meet in town in several days.

As I near the Station, Colonel Soto comes out to greet me. When he sees the bent wheel, he gestures to two of his staff to join us and they all admire my truck's front-end asymmetry.

"Señor Roberto, where you come from?"

"From Mina Marte."

A Station customs agent lets out a low whistle, obviously in awe.

"Mina Marte? To here? That's sixty-five kilometers, Señor."[65]

He whistles again, this time in amazement.

"Well, Señor, welcome once more. I call Copiapo for you. You our guest tonight for dinner. Si? You must tell us of your journey on the mountain. And you have the room once again."

As I while away the late afternoon in the Customs checking area, three fellows enter and begin setting up a portable table and chairs. They also have several boxes of food and a propane stove.

The oldest nods in my direction, touches the rim of his wide-brimmed Panama, and greets me in Spanish. When I apologize for my lack of fluency, he responds with better English than my Spanish. It turns out Dr. de Silva is an archeologist and is accompanied by a younger assistant and their driver/cook. He studied several years in the States and has a grant from the Chilean government to examine ancient Indian structures and settlements in this part of Chile. With his knowledge and background, he's qualified to offer an assessment of my de Merida letters. I briefly tell him about the letters' description of the travels by the Spanish and the Indians over the Great Plateau.

"I'm impressed with their content and I can assure you, according to our historians and my research, Almagro journeyed over the Great Plateau, as de Merida calls it, from Laguna Verde, past Laguna Santa Rosa, and then to Copiapo. We have found several small settlements from the pass to the west of Santa Rosa, down to the Valley of Copiapo. That tells me that this was a trade route with San Miguel de Tucuman in Argentina many centuries before the Spanish Conquest. So the Indians in Argentina knew the route across the Plateau and to Copiapo and would have made it known to Almagro."

---

[65] Forty-five miles.

"I've read of the historians. Aren't the famous ones, Encina, Silva, and Villalobos?"

"Yes. I can tell you have done your research."

He presents maps of the region, and we examine them together. We converse for an hour in re-creation of those times long ago.

"Señor Roberto, please have dinner with us tonight. My cook is better than the uninspired butcher they employ here."

With regret, I tell him I must decline, since I've accepted the Colonel's invitation.

Dr. de Silva does not give up.

"Well, certainly breakfast?" He says this in a gently pleading tone.

"Of course. I look forward to it, Señor."

Next morning, the day of my return to Copiapo, I learn more about Dr. de Silva. He has one daughter and one son living in California. Two other daughters live in Santiago with him and his wife. He earned his doctorate at Columbia University and wrote his dissertation about Indian cultures of the Atacama Desert. Over the years, the Chilean government has awarded him several contracts to study the Indian societies of the Chilean Andes.

He asks about my climbs. As I talk briefly about some of them, I notice he is studying me intently. He seems to be contemplating the curious nature of the solo climber by watching me.

"You have come many times to the mountains alone, Señor Roberto. You must have a deep love for our Andes."

"Yes," I reply. "And a great desire for great adventure."

"Ah, I see. I understand." He says this with a reflective tone.

"You have a need few men share."

"Yes," I respond. "And that is how I prefer things to be."

A flatbed truck from the rental company pulls into the Station at 10 a.m. I wish Dr. de Silva good luck with his excavations; I regret I cannot accompany him for a few days, for this place is heavy with history.

"Here, Señor. Here is my e-mail address. Write me sometime about your travels."

"Of course, Señor. It will be an honor to do so."

When I thank Colonel Soto for his hospitality for the second time in several days, he responds quickly.

"Señor, the room is yours whenever you wish it!"

This trip ends, but there is the promise of a future one. In my recent correspondence with Dr. de Silva, he asked if I might join him on an archeological project that will examine ancient Indian settlements north of Llullaillaco. His efforts will begin in October, 2012. He says he will supply food but cannot offer a salary. Salary? I would pay to join him. I plan to go, if I am physically fit.[66]

---

[66] Unfortunately, we were not able to work things out for this trip. (The author, 1/30/13.)

GOOGLE TOUR: The Tour for this Chapter is on the website.

PANORAMIO: In the Panoramio section, choose the "Tres Cruces" tag.

MOVIES: The April, 1999, and the Chapter 9 and 10 movies are appropriate for this Chapter.

The passersby know nothing of my coming
climb or of my previous forays upon their
sacred peaks and would have given them scant
recognition if they had known. To move among
these strangers with the wonderful knowledge of
my Andean intent fills me with a vague pride. I
seem a lonesome sentinel guarding a favored treasure,
though the treasure seems valuable only to me.

Welcome to old age, macho man!

They say that when one dreams it can last but seconds.
But in those seconds one can live a lifetime. We can live
and we can dream, and who is to say which is the greater
reality, the one we know or the one we imagine?

--From the author's personal climbing journal

CHAPTER 10

Tres Cruces, Chile: The Last Climb

"Grandpa."

I gazed into the beautiful eyes of my eleven-year-old granddaughter. "Yes, Jasmine."

"Do you see God on the top of a mountain?"

I paused a moment before answering. "No. But I feel His presence up there just as you and I feel His presence down here."

My granddaughter's earnest question upon my return from the March, 2009, attempt on Tres Cruces Central kept spinning through my mind for weeks. It caused my thoughts to return to the high Andes and the disappointment of that trip. My wish for the final climb of my career was to have more climbing about it, and that March trip had little of it. It was a climb to remember and bring a smile, yet not a climb to cherish and hold dear the remainder of my days. I wanted an adventure like past ones, one that gave me self-insight and knowledge, one that touched upon the ultimate danger without realizing its fulfillment. Several days after my 65th birthday, my dreams turned into a craving, the craving a yearning, the yearning an uncontrollable desire that was realized only when I booked flights for climb number thirty in a twenty-one-year career.

Flying south to Santiago de Chile, in November, 2009, I ponder the uniqueness of my climbing career. I have been fortunate to climb alone at an advanced age and to comprehend and see things allowed to but a few. But what is it I seek? Why do I wish to assume such risk at my age? Here I am, still running against the common and expected behavior for one my age. What will occur this time out? Will I be able to see the climb through? Well, at least I shall try.

The in-flight monitor, with its depiction of our position over South America, places us above Ecuador, the country with hillsides and meadows that display every known variation of the color green. It holds a special place in my thoughts, since I began my high altitude career there, at the age of 44, guided by the best mountain guiding company in the U.S., the American Alpine Institute in Bellingham, Washington. The main mountain we climbed on that trip was Chimborazo, at 20,564 feet, the highest peak in Ecuador.[67] My career began with that climb and it's where I first learned the trade, a pastime that became a consuming passion the rest of my life. Little of note happened on the climb, except the exhilaration of gazing upon the world far below from high above, a summit I had expended much effort to reach. January, 1989. Was it so long ago?

PHOTO: Chimborazo. (Photo E.27 in the Ecuador photo section on the website.)

Soon, Bolivia is under our wings and more memories spring from the land below. June, 1990 -- a second guided climb with the same company. A wracking cough and persistent diarrhea plagued me on the approach to Illimani, at 21,195 feet, the second highest peak in Bolivia. The summit was a near-run thing; 150 feet from the top, we climbed in a foggy whiteout but still managed to reach the summit. Then, coming down, I removed my sunglasses for thirty minutes and felt nothing until that night, when my burning eyes startled me wide awake. I couldn't see, since the sun had seared my eyeballs in those brief minutes. We were a day ahead of schedule and stayed at our base camp an extra day before hiking out to meet our ride back to La Paz. That proved fortunate; it was too painful to open my eyes for 24 hours. Several years later our

---

[67] Because it lies on the bulge of the equator, Chimborazo's summit is the point on the Earth's surface farthest from its center.

guide, who led us so well when we were blinded by the thick falling snow, died tragically on Everest -- in a whiteout. He stumbled blindly about, went over the edge, and plunged 1,500 feet to the glacier below.

PHOTO: Illimani in the distance as we approach a small village. (Photo B.12 in the Bolivia photo section on the site.)

With Bolivia in our slipstream, in the cabin's dark there is perfect light, for all the peaks appear in dazzling intensity as they parade before my mind's eye. They seem to beckon me to return so that we may know each other once again. This is my chance to do just that.

The next afternoon, twenty minutes out of Santiago on the flight north to Copiapo, the third guided peak comes in view to the east, Aconcagua, at 22,834 feet, the highest mountain in the Great Andes. There, on summit-day in 1991, at 2 a.m., crampon problems caused me to fall behind the climbing team at the bottom of the Polish Glacier. I climbed behind them for an hour before catching up, telling myself during it all that my climb was over. Yet I continued until I caught them just as they were roping up. How can the body keep moving when the mind is convinced of failure?

PHOTO: The mighty Aconcagua, from Casa de Piedra. (Photo A.8 in the Aconcagua photo section on the website.)

I knew my true predicament on the summit when there was no feeling in my right thumb and index finger or the large toe and the one next to it of my right foot. When we arrived back at Camp II after eighteen hours to the summit and return, I prayed that sleep in the warmth of my bag might restore my freezing body. In the morning, I could not feel the damaged fingers and toes. My fingers were translucent and felt like sticks. I could hold nothing in their grasp. My toes were so swollen there was no question of putting my plastic boot on. I could manage only the pliant inner boot. It served me well and protected my injured toes from further damage as we left the mountain on the two-day hike back to our mountain hotel. My fingers and toes soon turned black, an incongruous sight -- strange in appearance, dark instead of pink, with a hardness as deep as the bone.

I left our lodgings before the rest of the team on a bus bound for Santiago. I needed to return home to receive treatment for the frostbite. All travelers were required to go through Argentine Customs at the border. One of the passengers, in perfect English, said, "May I assist you Señor? I see you are in some difficulty." What a gracious man. He asked about the climb. I told him of my ascent to the summit and about my frostbite.

My new friend said the Customs inspectors required a small tip for their "services."

"Con su permiso, I shall speak for you, Señor."

When we approached one of the inspectors, my friend said, "This man has climbed Aconcagua and paid a stiff price for it." He said it with some emotion in his voice.

The inspector looked my way warmly.

"You climb our mountain, Señor? Well done. Pase!" He waved me on without inspection or tip and gripped my left hand in congratulation.

Following seven months of recuperation, I lost part of my large right toe. Thumb and fingers, though saved, were so weak their pinch was like that of a young child's, and still are. The marks of the ordeal are still upon my body.

My thoughts return to the present. I'll miss Patricio on this trip. He and his wife had business in Santiago. He has owned an electronic repair business since his father retired several years ago. He is also a manager of the annual "Atacama Raid," an event that attracts desert dune driving enthusiasts from all over the world. It lasts for two weeks in February in the sand dunes to the west of Copiapo. There are driving competitions during the day and barbeque parties in the evening. He is also the personal trainer of Chile's driver in the Dakar road race in Africa.[68] His duties require biannual trips there for competitions and training. What a tough life!

---

[68] The Dakar race has since shifted to Chile, Bolivia, and Argentina. And Patricio is still a mechanic for the Chilean entries.

But I do have a ride to Copiapo. Giancarlito, Giancarlo's son, and his friend Natalia meet me at the Copiapo airport and we're off to lunch. Later, it is wonderful to see Maria Ester once more. Last year she added two more rooms to her hotel, La Casona, and she has saved one of them for me. She makes me feel like royalty!

The next day, before venturing out to purchase the items I need for the climb, I visit the main plaza, Plaza Prat, there to walk amongst the passersby. They know nothing of my coming climb or of my previous forays upon their sacred peaks and would have given them scant recognition if they had known. To move among these strangers with the close-kept knowledge of my Andean intent fills me with a vague pride. I seem a lonesome sentinel guarding a favored treasure, though the treasure seems valuable only to me. The Plaza inhabitants know nothing of me. What might they know of the perils soon to come my way, of the stars that one by one going out will signal my possible undoing? Neither they nor I were receiving the messages from the messengers of the night that great winds now are gathering to trouble my climb and threaten my fragile existence. Although they care not, all this suits my purpose, because I seek complete anonymity and exist in a world of solo mountaineering not theirs, nor one that might ever be theirs.

For this last climb, I have chosen Tres Cruces Central. I'll drive to Laguna Santa Rosa for the first night and move to a base camp next day in the usual location at around 15,000 feet for a stay of two nights. As on the March trip, I'll place an Advanced Base Camp (ABC) at 16,500 feet. From there, I'll make double carries to Camp I at the col at 18,600 feet, make a single carry to Camp II at 20,000 feet, use one day for the climb to the summit and the return to Camp II, take an added day to return to the 4x4 and drive back to Copiapo, and allow one day for contingencies, a total of six days from ABC. Driving the truck to Advanced Base, rather than walking to it, makes this time frame possible.

This journey is completely different from my previous ones, for I am driving to and from the mountain on my own. One advantage is that I can drive off the peak and back to civilization any time I choose. But if the truck fails me? I know that this is risky business. A busted axle, dead battery, flat tire, damaged cooling system -- any one of these will present serious difficulties. In that case, I have an escape plan. The Chile-Argentina road is only two miles from the foot of the peak and an easy walk, if I'm able to walk. From there I can flag a ride to the Customs Station.

Since I remember the many problems with the diesel on my last trip, I choose a gas model this time in the hope it might fare better at altitude. Between Copiapo and the pass overlooking Laguna Santa Rosa, the truck overheats on the steepening grade. I stop to let it cool near a meadow of green grasses and plants. A burbling rivulet of water flows its length. A shabby, silent hut sits to the side of the road; someone keeps this place. This oasis in the middle of the golden desert sands amazes the eye. The contradiction of wet and dry and the juxtaposition of green and gold give the place a magical aura. I have found several such places on this road over the years, and that strengthens my contention that the Almagro expedition, on its way from Cuzco to Chile in the search for gold, trod this same land on their march to Copiapo in 1536. The several oases provided water for the men and grass for the horses and llamas.[69]

PHOTO: One of the oases on the Mina Marte road. (Photo 10.1 on the site.)

These green sanctuaries, here, in the middle of nowhere, are tiny islands of existence, a few hundred feet across, where a few people live their lives, knowing little and caring less. These signs of a life I can barely envision and certainly never know. They look like the leftovers of a primitive paradise rescued long ago from the ruins of the world around them.

I'm on the road for no more than another forty-five minutes when the steep grade forces another stop because of overheating. In half an hour, I'm going again. Then I have to stop once more. Llamas could make the trip faster. The antifreeze reservoir is empty, so the gallon jug I

---

[69] The author's soon to be published manuscript, mentioned in previous chapters, tells of the Expedition's experiences as it passed this way in 1536.

purchased in town receives its first use. It never dawned on me to verify the antifreeze level, a sure sign I've succumbed to advancing years and the altitude. Welcome to old age, macho man!

Upon the pass above Laguna Santa Rosa, high winds pummel the truck as I sit and admire the scene before me. The beauty of Tres Cruces shimmers in the distance; there is little snow lower on the mountain. That's different from the scene in March and past years, when snow blanketed much of the peak. I can see snow patches near an ABC site, but the top of the col is not in full view, so it's impossible to know what conditions are like up there.

PHOTO: View from the pass above Laguna Santa Rosa. The Laguna lies below, with Tres Cruces in the distance. (Photo 10.2 on the website.)

When I descend from the pass, the Refugio Laguna Santa Rosa at 12,100 feet is in sight. I have lost count of the number of trips here through the years. The scene still makes me smile with pleasure. The wondrous blue Laguna waters sparkle in the light of the afternoon sun. It's a primal joy to be amongst the high peaks again. Primal because this pleasure springs from within, from a place unknown to me. A joy because I'm happiest when among them.

A high wind blows here, an insistent wind. It's as if an unseen force wishes to deter me from my intentions, and it occurs to me that this may be an omen of things to come. It's a dismaying thought. Climbing on the mountain in wind like this will be impossible. Is this trip fated to end in disappointment like the one several months before?

When I pull up to the Refugio, I check the cooling system; again the antifreeze reservoir is empty and the radiator dry. This is puzzling; there's been no hissing of boiling water, no warning from the gauges, no steam pluming from under the hood. The truck is the weak link on this trip. What kind of physics is operating underneath its hood? Perhaps physics has little to do with it. This entire operation is disturbing; my mountaineering intuition detects something isn't right. It takes the full force of my personality to keep me optimistic.

That evening and night, the wind howls around the sturdy Refugio structure, but slackens in the early morning hours. I awake at first light amidst the still darkened land. The moon's light clings to the Refugio like a frozen mist. There is drama here at sunrise, and I am eager to see it for, perhaps, my last time. Shade by shade, the dark flooding the land lessens, and poorly outlined shapes appear. Forms provide poor definition, lacking clarity and color, here a faint boulder or the pale outline of the Laguna, there the growing immensity of Tres Cruces. Golden rays of light strike the retreating moon that sinks as though withered by the warmth of the coming dawn. Dim tints flee the land as the golden shield comes into view, spouting flames of golden fire, just as when comets glow. Across the dry lakebed, the sun's shafts fall obliquely upon its calm, stoic immensity, there to splinter into sparkling dust, and then into a stunning spray of light that blinds the eye with its intensity. It is daybreak on the Maricunga Salar.

Granted the comfort of packing without the interfering winds, I soon drive off at a leisurely speed from Santa Rosa and enjoy a cigarette and coffee, all the while fastening the clutch of instruments with a grandfatherly gaze. The calm, the clouds, the mountains, the sun, the wisps of light, make the drive relaxed and unhurried. The desert, yielding to my passage, speeds the ride to the Chile-Argentina road, my sole companion a towering dust devil that rears up to the west. It stretches hundreds of feet into the sky. I wonder, is it strong enough to lift a guanaco?

PHOTO: Approaching Tres Cruces from the north. (Photo 10.7 on the website.)

At the waterfalls of the Rio Lamas, I'm on Pedro de Merida's "Great Plateau." High winds scour the place and hint at the possible disruption of my trip. I follow the road leading to the northern base of the peak and soon begin the grind upwards, dodging rocks to protect the tires and watching the terrain for loose sand that might trap my wheels. Here the wind is greater than down below on the Plateau, and it nudges the truck occasionally from side to side.

At 14,800 feet, I'm startled by an image off to my right 100 feet away. It's a guanaco! I've never seen one this high. It watches me intently and then lopes off down the mountain. I've probably saved her life. I don't think guanaco or llamas can remain long at this elevation.

When I reach Base Camp at 15,200 feet, the wind howls in welcome at my arrival. Its strength prevents me from raising Baby Blue. So I sit, and I think. Will this be a trying climb? The conditions must be favorable to climb a big mountain, and sometimes these conditions are unfavorable on a given day. When the weather turns inclement, nothing else matters. If the winds continue with their present force then, yes, this will be a trying climb. I must trust to luck entirely where the weather is concerned.

Within an hour the blusterings lessen somewhat, and I wrestle Blue into position and secure the four lengths of parachute cord at the corners to surrounding rocks. As I do so, I touch her sides with caresses I thought affection. She has been a faithful companion through all my climbs. When I transfer gear from the truck to the tent, the wind carries away the light foam mattress I place under my sleeping bag to provide insulation from the cold ground beneath the tent floor. It's annoying to lose it. I have had it with me on every climb.

PHOTO: Base Camp. The wind will soon reach near hurricane force. (Photo 10.8 on the site.)

My plan this first day is to use a strategy similar to the one in March -- drive to an ABC site at 16,500 feet and remain there several hours to acclimate. I leave Base in the screeching wind and start higher, but in fifteen minutes the truck overheats yet again. I filled it with water and antifreeze only yesterday. The piece of junk now joins the wind as the antagonists of my journey. I'm expending more energy worrying about them than seeing to my emotional and mental preparation for the climb. This entire situation is irritating.

The wind has picked up once more and is too strong for me to risk raising the hood; the gusts could wrench it loose and send it sailing like a metallic Frisbee. A deep lassitude settles upon me, a tiredness of body and soul, exhaustion brought on by the fight against two unrelenting adversaries. Because of the lateness of the hour, I set aside a further attempt to reach ABC and return to Base instead, where I can rest and recoup my strength. Later, I lie inside Blue fatigued by the perplexity of it all, weary with disappointment. This wind pattern on Tres Cruces is similar to those on other climbs here, and it might continue for days. I might not have enough time in my schedule to last it out. Within the hour, though, my personality restores my flagging spirits by choosing instead to see prospects of ultimate success.

As the afternoon advances, the land begins to pale and then evaporate completely. The desert sand retains a measure of sunlight, but there is already something of departure about it. A darkening in the north signals the light's exit to the east. Did I just hear thunder crack in the distance? Yes, I believe I did, and the heavy rumble interrupts my thoughts. The thunder rolls on as a searing stab of light lights up Blue as it seeks its earthly mark. My home is untouched by these outbursts of nature. When the bulk of the mountain is in darkness, one last point, the summit, remains in light a few seconds longer.

The winds ruffle Blue and disturb my musings. Tumultuous eddies of air continue to play upon my tent's frame, and she repels all in a heroic display of defiance as on trips in the past. Sometimes I think the tempest will blow us flat, and each gust requires leaning against the western wall that receives the worst pressure. The night is heavily laden with worry, and in the end I become worried too. Pissis. Just like Pissis in 1994. To this day, my escape from that near-catastrophe is a mystery. The difference on this trip is that I have a truck outside. If there's a problem, flight will be swift. Or will it?

Early next morning, the night's long journey is over and the long journey into day about to begin. But this new day is a world of cold, heavy clouds, and wind. As my plan is to drive up to Advanced Base to acclimate for several hours, I check the truck for problems. The battery is strong, yet the engine refuses to turn over. Ten minutes later, another attempt yields the same result. If it's not the battery, it must be the altitude. There isn't enough oxygen to provide a spark. Since the truck faces downhill, a short roll provides enough speed to start the engine.

But on my drive back to camp, I botch clutch management and stall before I have a chance to park it facing downward. Repeated attempts to start it prove fruitless.

I'm now deeper in the morass of ill luck. I've lost the advantage of the truck facing down slope, and this poses the prospect of an inconvenient trudge to the Customs Station. I try to maneuver the metal hulk into a favorable position. It's a tiring task. I have to turn the wheels and then shovel sand from underneath each tire so they will roll more easily. In thirty minutes, I still do not have it pointed downhill. I collapse inside Blue. The altitude and my lack of strength cause an overwhelming tiredness.

But I must keep at it. I have some warm broth and then return to the task of positioning the truck correctly. It's too dangerous to push it from outside the cab. If it starts to roll, with me still outside, the contraption will stop who knows where. On three separate occasions, it lurches forward and suddenly stops; each time it requires more digging. An hour of this, with the altitude, the wind, and the cold conspiring against all my efforts, is emotionally and physically exhausting. It may be time to retreat from the mountain.

I rest inside Blue and ponder departure. My badly damaged confidence needs a boost, and soon. My friend Paula had given me a small card when I left home. On it are the simple words "EXPECT A MIRACLE." I stare at it and my flagging spirits begin to revive. Another friend, Lina, provided further solace with a copy of Psalm 121, "A SONG OF ASCENTS." I lift my eyes from reading it with renewed resolve. Did my friends know their kindnesses might repair my damaged self-assurance? I suspect in an existential way they hoped their offerings might benefit me no matter what circumstances caused the need for them. This is the love human beings may extend to one another.

Climbers need little miracles or small favors each day in the mountains, some days more so than most. This is one of those days for me. I decide on another attempt at ignition; a turn of the key produces no spark. The wind wails about the truck with a note of glee; it rejoices at my wretched situation. It blows in fierce and unremitting gusts, as if it wants to blast me from this place forever. Then the moment comes for one last attempt before leaving the mountain. I turn the key, and the engine explodes to roaring life! I sit, exulting, and let it growl several minutes, reveling in this latest instance of fortuitous luck.

Finally, I can leave for the higher camp. The engine hums reassuringly. But the drive is still a delicate exercise. I must choose the best terrain, know when to apply full power and when less, and watch the surface for signs that loose sand lies underneath. It's a kabuki-like dance requiring concentration; a mistake will require the long march off the mountain. And if a sharp rock punctures a tire, changing one at this elevation in loose sand in a demonic wind …. well, I would not want to try it.

The truck's sudden spring to life and the absence of overheating manage to instill in me confidence that things will turn positive. My plan calls for six days from ABC to climb to the summit and return to the truck. But before deciding to make that first carry to Camp I, I need an indication that the weather pattern has changed. It must be in my favor if I am to proceed higher. I decide that 24 hours of little or no wind at the higher camp will be the indicator. It must stop. It has to stop. This is my last climb in the mountains and I wish to have a chance for the last time to be the best time.

Here at Advanced Base, the wind whips and screams around the truck as I read my book and watch my movies. There has been no hint of a storm, despite the high winds, except yesterday's far-off thunder and lightning and this morning's early clouds. My personal condition is optimum, and this buoys my spirits. The mountain's climbing conditions are optimum, too. I can see a snowfield just peeking over the top of the col, with small white areas on the flanks of Central, and that means enough snow to melt for my water needs. It certainly is not in the same condition as in years past, but this is an El Niño year and that always means strange weather.

When I prepare to leave the high camp in late afternoon, another ignition failure sends me back to my recurring bad dream. This problem has now become a routine event. I have to jump-start the truck on the incline again. It rolls easily downhill, I pop the clutch, the engine roars to life, and the adventure continues. Just as I reach Base Camp, I notice the gauges again signal overheating. This, too, has now become a commonplace event. More water and more antifreeze set things right.

At night, as the wind continues its ferocity, it's obvious that this is a pattern of unknown duration and it now threatens my climb, because to climb in wind is to climb in adversity. Moving forward with gusts in one's face, the effort demanded increases arithmetically, geometrically at high altitude. Strong gusts at a climber's back cause quicker steps, and he risks a faulty boot placement on dangerous ground. Wind that blows directly from either side makes the heavy pack act like a nautical sail, and that could cause a misstep or fall. Only a fool or a desperate climber will venture out onto the slopes with even moderate breezes blowing about.

At daylight, with gusts blowing hard, I break camp and start back towards the high camp, there to spend the night at the higher elevation. My fervent desire is for an immediate end to the relentless gale. The truck sways slightly as it struggles higher, and I'm anxious about it overheating again. The sun is directly above camp when I arrive. To honor my 24-hour "rule," I will remain here tomorrow in the hope that the winds will slacken. If they do not, I will have to abandon the climb.

PHOTO: It will be a cramped night in the truck. (Photo 10.9 on the site.)

I occupy myself with my iPod movies and music in the truck as the hours drift by. An occasional sideways movement reminds me of the tempest raging outside. A jerry-rigged stove support allows me to heat water for my freeze-dried dinner. The boiling point of water at this elevation is lower than at sea level. As one climbs higher, it drops farther. This means tepid water for my meals.

Later, as the sun abandons the land, it's impossible to sleep. The cramped confines of the back seat require contorting my body to find a comfortable position. The door entries of Chilean vehicles are lower and the insides less spacious than stateside vehicles. Still, it's warmer inside than out, and it saves Blue and me from a thrashing by the gale.

I become aware of it only after it happens. Without forewarning, the winds vanish at midnight and leave this part of the Andes for promising ground elsewhere. The continual wailing had become background noise, and its exit almost went unnoticed. Twenty-four hours. My fervent prayer is for a 24-hour respite from the wind that signals a possible break in the pattern. How wonderful it is to know that in hours I might resume the climb and the summit will be within my grasp in a few days.

My thoughts turn to my wife, daughters, and grandchildren. This is my seventh day since leaving home and I miss them terribly. What exactly is happening there beyond my knowing? Why is it that when I am here I wish to be there and when I am there I wish to be here? Such is my passion and my ambivalence for my mountains. Once the stars make their appearance, I reflect that, here in the Southern Hemisphere, these stars do not shine over my family. I feel even more distant from them than mere miles and hours.

The new day arrives in a clear sky, with the wind now a discordant memory. I spend the hours dozing, reading, writing, with occasional forays outside to test my legs in preparation for the climb to Camp I tomorrow. An assessment of my personal condition reveals I am acclimating well, just as on the March expedition. I marvel at the human body. Yet, I have a sense of impending danger. My intuition causes the thought that it's useless to continue the climb. But am I looking at my situation through the wrong end of the telescope? My usually optimistic personality thinks so. It wishes me to continue higher. So, I soldier on.

I'm confident the wind has left off, but I'm still wary. This plan of mine to use one day without wind as an indication the cycle is at an end is without scientific merit. A single day's respite is merely a contrivance, and it might prove dangerous as the days unfold. If I proceed higher and the winds return while I'm at the col or above, I might stay up there forever.

As night descends upon the land, I drift into a deep sleep. The following dream came to me, I believe, by the realization that this is to be my last climb, and our thoughts have an effect upon our sleep. In this case, my many climbs cause me endless memories, and Robert, my Guardian Angel, stands before me, the lifelong protector against threats to my well-being. At first, his appearance startles me, for this may be the moment of my final reckoning and atonement.

"Do not worry, Bob, I am here so we might reminisce about our times together. We have been to the Andes' highest places and known their most enduring hardships. I wish to recall the adventures by taking you to where they happened."

He gestures me to accompany him.

"But I am a mere mortal and cannot fly."

"Touch my hand, Bob, and you will be raised up in more than this."

Together we call to mind all our past climbs as they parade by like kaleidoscopic vignettes, a Dream of Scipio-like[70] re-creation of my life's most memorable moments in the high Andes. On the first part of our trip, we return to Aconcagua.

"Aconcagua was an unforgettable experience for you and for me. Here we stand at the foot of the Polish Glacier, where your team started towards the summit without you because of your crampon problems. You soon caught up with them but, when you withdrew from the summit, you felt the cold in your feet and hands."

"I remember it well. I didn't do anything to counteract the cold as it seeped into my fingers and toes. But you weren't with me."

"I am different from the soul. I do not reside in your body and do not share your bodily sensations. I learned of your frostbite, or, the "bite" as you call it, when you did, the morning after. But understand the good that came from it. Do you realize how vigilant you became on the following climbs, the extra precautions you took to combat the cold? And, what's more, when you lost your toe, you vowed never to seek the Himalayan peaks because of it. I can tell you, because of my knowledge of such matters, that you would have perished on Dhaulagiri (26,795 feet)[71] in 1998, should you have gone. Remember your friend Mike, who called to invite you on that climb? You would have perished there, along with him."

"Yes, Aconcagua was a pivotal climb. And it had exactly the effect upon me that you say. I didn't know of the dangers awaiting Mike and me on Dhaulagiri."

---

[70] The "Somnium Scipionis" in Cicero's "De re publica."

[71] Located in Nepal, Dhaulagiri is the sixth highest peak in the world.

The scene begins to rock slightly from side to side, and then stops. My dream continues.

"Do you remember the time I thought I had cerebral edema?"

"That was the Ojos del Salado climb when you worried about the swelling of your right temple. Here we are at the Tejos Refugio where it happened."

"I recall during several moments wanting to flee down as fast as I could go. But you helped me to see there was no danger. I learned that things are not always what they seem and matters must be examined calmly, even though one fears the worst. I almost came to grief, too, on Llullaillaco, you know, with snow blindness."

We move in moments to that great peak.

"This is the site of your Base Camp. You awoke in early morning and knew the situation immediately. When you were blinded on Illimani, you had the climbing team to assist you, so I wasn't worried. Here, you were alone, and when you needed a brief word of encouragement, I gave it to you. You were fine from then on."

"And what of the trip here when I felt the presence on the snow plateau? Remember? What was it, exactly?"

"I cannot account for the presence; it was not one of us. My conclusion is that the altitude influenced your imagination with a mild hallucination. My involvement came, not from a concern about any danger it posed to you, it was harmless, but because winds from above were rushing down to engulf you. Fortunately, you took my advice."

"Let us turn another page and move to a different peak."

"I know this place," I blurt out. "It's the col between Tres Cruces Central and Sur."

A moaning sound of disturbed winds interrupts our conversation. Then, without notice, it leaves off.

"It is. This was where your tent door failed to zip fully and became progressively worse the higher you went. I was there and provided a measure of comfort. Ultimately, however, I was unable to do more. You should have ended the climb here. As it happens, you learned a valuable lesson -- that sometimes one must admit defeat, especially when confronted with the failure of a piece of equipment that jeopardizes your safety."

"May we visit Pissis? I wish to see again the spot where that tremendous gust of wind flattened Blue and me."

Instantly, the five summits of the peak are directly below us.

Robert gestures to the place we remember so well.

"Here we are, and this place brings back the memory full and strong. Who might have foreseen such an explosion of wind? I felt you there with me. You gave me the strength to last it through."

"Can you recall the climb when I was most agitated? Two things happened that might have turned events ugly, and ugly very fast."

"Yes, I remember it well -- this same peak, Pissis, March, 1997," I answer.

"That is correct. And here is the slope leading to Camp III. Memory of the whiteout will remain with us forever. I gave you terse admonitions to keep your composure and confidence and, to your credit, you did. You knew that climbing higher would save you. Look over there and above. There's the small promontory upon which you placed Camp III."

"The site of the stove incident. You were there, too. Your real fear was I would abandon the lighter and strike a match. That would have been the end of things."

"My worry exactly. I do not know what might have happened. Still, I think you know that at this height and in this remote part of the Andes, well . . . ."

Other summits nudge the golden blue horizon. Those I have gained are more than rock and snow. Those high places were the fulfillment of myself. The magical world of the Andes acted as a stimulant to a man who confirmed himself, conquered himself, and understood himself through the struggles for the summits. In the acute strain of those efforts, on the fringe of life's passing, all evaporated and fell away beneath. Fear, space, suffering, time, no longer had meaning. This is when I understood all is very simple. There is a part of me that is indestructible, against which nothing may triumph. And this spark, once struck, may never be put out. It was this certainty that granted me the will to endure my ordeals.

Something beneath me moves, followed by a thundering like the thumping of a massive drum, and it fills the air with shocks and shudders, all heard as though in a world far away, in a world beyond the senses. As my companion wishes me further safe passage, his image fades from sight.

"Robert. Thank you, Robert. Thank you for all you have meant to me through the years. I know you shall remain with me forever." They say that when one dreams it can last but seconds. But in those seconds one can live a lifetime. We can live and we can dream, and who is to say which is the greater reality, the one we know or the one we imagine?

I am fully awake in an instant. It's 2 a.m. and the winds have returned with a vengeance. They moan and wail at all in their path. The sky to the west remains clear; the soft, evanescent light of the declining moon drops upon the remote mountains as they sleep and bathes them in a soft, incandescent glow. But behind me, to the southeast above the mountain, an inky blackness blots out all starlight. Another storm is rising, and an urge to flee seizes me. Should it begin to snow, this place might turn into a deadly trap. Should I try to escape in the dark? Driving at night over dangerous ground poses its own risks. So I await the dawn, ready to leave if it begins to snow.

At daybreak, with the wind raging, I decide to retreat from the mountain. The moment gives me pause. At my age and with my advancing physical weakness, I will pass this way again only in my memories.

I'm ready to leave at 8 a.m., but the truck again refuses to start. I shovel sand from in front of each tire, but each time I attempt to get the hulk to roll it steals but a few inches from the mountain, yet even this I count as progress. I keep at it for more than an hour; I will not give up. But the mountain will not permit my departure. Inside the truck, out of the freezing wind, I sit, exhausted by my efforts, knowing I can't remain at it much longer. There's a tightness in my throat as I ponder the long walk out and the consequences of leaving a vehicle this high. My gear will remain here, until I can arrange for a rescue truck and driver from Copiapo to bring me back to retrieve everything. How will they get a tow truck up here? More important: will the driver agree to drive this high?

I gather my strength and exit the truck into the howling winds again to shovel sand and rocks from in front of all the tires. This time my efforts must pay off. I again create downward slopes in front of each one, but this time make them even more pronounced. I spend an hour at this, until I feel things are right. I also empty everything from the truck except the gasoline container, which is too heavy for me, to lighten the load. The extra pounds have created too much "drag." I hope this works. My body cannot continue with these efforts much longer in the cold and the wind.

I sit behind the wheel and murmur a fervent prayer. I place the transmission in second gear, depress the clutch, and release the parking brake. She's going! She's rolling! She's sliding! At the right moment, I pop the clutch. The engine roars to life in a tremendous burst that is like a symphony to my ears. I'm jubilant. I drive back to the gear I had thrown from the truck, reload it, and drive carefully down the mountain, the winds harassing me at every moment.

I pass through my Base Camp site and feel confident I will make it. In thirty more minutes I'm off the mountain and away from the winds, the sound of silence my welcome companion once more. I slump back in my seat and seek a few moments to myself and to offer thanks. What a mountain. What a deliverance.

I pause to eat some salami and cheese and my gaze wanders over the landscape. A rock gendarme nestled in a mound of earth and sand catches my attention because of its distinctive shape and size. I have seen it on every trip here and there is no other like it. Formed like a church's pulpit, it stands thirty feet high. The highest five feet resemble a church's spire. Below that, it widens to a small plinth or podium. It reminds me each time I see it of Pedro de Merida's letter recounting the expedition's journey over the Great Plateau. At the foot of a large mountain, the men paused while Father Molina led them in a service for three dead comrades who died on the Plateau. "All the Spaniards gathered while men placed the three crosses within a rocky alcove resembling a church's pulpit." This gendarme has to be the rocky alcove. It all makes sense. And this event quite probably led to the mountain being named, "Tres Cruces."

With the climb cut short, I wish to drive the length of the Plateau. This will be the third round trip over the years between its western limit, here at Tres Cruces, and its eastern boundary at Laguna Verde.

Though I worry about the truck's problems, I have plenty of water and antifreeze.

As I drive, I stare. Everything here has a meaning; everything here has a history. If the many mountains were able to speak, they would tell of the brave and grand deeds of the Indians and Spaniards who passed this way five centuries ago.

At Laguna Verde, I visit the Carabinero Station, the first Chilean structure this side of San Francisco Pass, amidst terrific winds. I open the truck door, but must hold it with both hands or the wind will rip it from its hinges. The Officer-in-Charge invites me to lunch with his men. He wishes to hear of my stay on Tres Cruces. Unfortunately, I have to decline. It's getting late and I must leave for Laguna Santa Rosa, where I'll spend the night. But I appreciate his hospitality. The Chilean people have generous hearts.

PHOTO: A last look at Tres Cruces. (Photo 10.10 on the website.)

I stop at Tres Cruces on the way back to the Laguna and look across to the mountain, my last time to do so at this close a distance. Stillness and tranquility bring the solemn mood I know so well, taught to me by my solo climbs amongst the Andes, taught to me by the great mountains themselves. Something within takes notice, not of the thought of growing old but of the thought I have grown old. All around me the panoramas and scenes remain unchanged. Yet, I have changed; my strength has ebbed and my skin become wrinkled, sacrificed to the remorseless ravages of old age. I understand that the landscape never changes. Only those who travel the landscape change.

I sense the mountain staring back at me. "You and your Andean sisters have remained comforts and mainstays for me these many years," I stammer. "But there comes a time when life stops giving us things and begins to take them away. Such is the turning of our lives and is mine now -- my strength is fading and my days are close to done. Yours are enduring for all eternity." In this seeming reversal of being and meaning, the mountain seems young, while I seem old; it seems fresh, while I seem tired; it seems cheery, while I seem gloomy.

I turn to go, since the journey here is at an end; the other, my journey through time, runs off my hands like the ageless sands of the Maricunga Salar and carries me forward towards an unknown future. A deep unwillingness to leave the mountain seizes me from deep inside. "And please know and hold close these parting words for you," I choke out. "I knew joys with you and your sisters I could not have realized elsewhere. The years with you have been the best years of my life, and memories of them will gladden me as I travel to my destiny's next port of call. Remember me with pleasure in the endless millennia to come, for my steps trod your virgin inclines in perfect comprehension of your meaning for all mortals. Though we soon pass away, you are forever, and I should be the less were you to dismiss or forget me."

PHOTO: A stunning sunset the evening before my return to Copiapo. (Photo 10.19 on the site.)

The next morning at the Refugio, the truck starts without a hitch. I hesitate to go. As I stare upon the lake and distant mountains, I long to feel the Andes again beneath me, to feel their sublime strengths, to feel their ancestral spirits. Sadly, this must be my final foray to the mountains of my dreams. Nevertheless, they will remain with me forever.

My return to town occurs without incident. But when I enter the rental company's driveway and stop next to the office, the manager comes to greet me. Something seems wrong. She has her left hand over her mouth and points to the back of the truck with her right.

"Señor Roberto," she says, gesturing towards the left rear tire, "do you know you have flat tire?"

It must have gone flat only in the last few minutes, for I felt nothing on the drive back to town. Sometimes, just sometimes, fate can be merciful.

Back home, Lina, who gave me the "Song of Ascents" in the hope that it would provide me comfort (it did), sent me the warmest of notes as a welcome back. I quote it here.

"Dear Bob:

I didn't have the heart to tell you way back in Spring of last year when you told me you were going back up again that I had a strong sense that your climb wasn't going to work. I so prayed for your safety before you even left because I knew you were determined. I prayed so much for you while you were gone; there were even times when I had a very strong sense to pray, which I obeyed very promptly. You cannot imagine how relieved and thrilled I was to hear that you were back and safe. I was very worried. That was the other reason why I so wanted to be sure you had the Psalm with you because that is the prayer the Jewish people would pray while making the dangerous and tough journey to Jerusalem for the major festivals. I know you had lots of angels watching over you. You said something once that leads me to think that you have had an amazing encounter with the Lord Almighty. I believe He will give you your dream because, as you said, you have a respect and reverence for His creation and you will be rewarded in His time.

Take good care my dear friend and may the Lord and all His angels continue to watch over you and protect you from all harm."

I count myself fortunate to have a friend like her.

My climbs made me interesting to myself.
Solo mountaineering made me different from
others and satisfied my desire for uniqueness
from the ordinary living of the rest of my life.
My understanding was that I needed this individuality
more than I needed friends.

I do not love my mountains because they are beautiful;
it is my love for them that makes them beautiful.

So for me, death holds no terror. And this knowledge,
learned during my time amongst the great peaks, permitted
me to see that it is better to attain the truth of self by not
locating it while seeking it than by deciding not to seek it
and never finding it.

From the author's personal reflections

REFLECTIONS: THE JOURNEY ENDS

Alex, you asked me to write about my climbs in the mountains, and I have tried my best to do so with this book. You also recently asked me why I endured the hardships and dangers of high altitude, alone, especially in the later years of my life. After a good deal of reflection over the years, I'm afraid I must own up to an incomplete understanding as to a reply. Your question, though, has prompted many thoughts about my adventures among the Great Andes. Perhaps if I share them with you, they might reveal some answers for you and for me.

My initial response is that I wanted to obtain a wealth of memories to entertain me in my later years, the years I'm now living, and the following years that may turn dark and lonely. Old age can overwhelm us if we don't store up a fair amount of pleasant recollections to accompany us on our way. And I am prepared for that journey, for I have remembrances in abundance.

There are other reasons for my magnificent obsession with the mountains. So much in our day extols the work and effort of the group, the "team," and the participation with a band of others to obtain whatever the goals may be. To many, the team is everything in their lives. Yet, for me, life must allow for the striving of the singular human being, those of us who wish to act alone occasionally as we live out our lives. Should that become nonexistent, then much will be lost to all Mankind. And, in the end, the team does not confront the ultimate fate we face as human beings, the battle with the incomprehensible, the inevitable, the final reality of death that we must encounter individually and alone. And that ending combat may be less threatening to those who have faced life's challenges with a measure of singularity, whether on a big mountain or in one's everyday life. Such men and women are best composed to face man's ultimate fate and thus better able to accept the final verdict of life's close in an equitable frame of mind.

I count it a benefit that solo altitude climbing allowed me to express myself as myself. I didn't live in my climbing world in a meaningful way until my very being entered it, and then it wasn't a concept any longer, it was actual experience. Life as climbing, climbing as climbing, climbing as life -- a complete process, if you're able to finish it. It's a definite path to travel, but only if followed consciously and deliberately; a kind of dramatic re-creation played out on a colossal stage. And I was on that stage in middle and old age. This was a grand advantage, for my later years conferred a certain amount of wisdom. For example, reaching the summit was of secondary importance to me. As a result, I took fewer risks than might have been the case. Also, I believe my body was better able to handle the high elevations because of my advanced years. I have no medical research to back up that statement. But other than occasional headaches, I didn't suffer from anything more serious than that.

My climbs gave me some important personal insights. For example, my career taught me that one climb connected to another like the linking of one minute with the next until they all wove my climbing experiences together in a rich tapestry of life. On the high peaks, one senses the harmony and the permanence of this embroidery, and that sends men and continents on their way. Life and death do not appear as solitary events, but as part of a drapery woven upon the looms of eternity. And part of the beauty one finds answers a thousand questions. It also grants self-definition.

My climbs made me interesting to myself. Solo mountaineering made me different from others and satisfied my desire for uniqueness from the ordinary living of the rest of my life. My understanding was that I needed this individuality more than I needed friends.

One result of enduring hardship and danger is that my mountains dwell with me every day of my life. I long for them as I long for my children and grandchildren. And I wish them to miss me as much as I miss them. My precious peaks are there, right over the horizon, out of view and out of touch, and to know they so exist without me is saddening. I envy the clouds that cloak their shoulders, the earth that bears their weight, the snows that wrap their heights, the winds that scour their sacred battlements. They are beautiful, each in a unique way. They derive their beauty from my knowing them, and each approaches the ideal, the universally valid reality that resides somewhere, imperceptible to the five senses and known only through pure mental abstraction. I do not love my mountains because they are beautiful; it is my love for them that makes them beautiful. They exist in my thoughts as stationary, undimmed to my sight, their presences suspended in a static, unchanging state. A good deal of me resides with them -- my aspirations, my failures, my fears, my qualms, my successes -- and they remain with me as I lived among them. One truth for me is that all my climbs would have been worth a final fall.

I think often of Giancarlo and Patricio. I always looked forward to seeing them and their families on each trip. They became like an extended family to me. They were brave men, for they risked a good deal driving me to the peaks and, at the time, I did not appreciate the possible hazards for them. Once they left me on the mountain, they returned home and then came back, completely alone over dangerous ground. A flat tire posed inconvenience, but one capable of remedy. Yet, a broken axle, a ruptured crankcase -- the list is long of things that might have stranded them miles from assistance. In dark, pensive moods, and with the distance of years, I chastise myself for not asking them what precautions they took, especially in Giancarlo's case. If we had discussed what his actions should be in case of a breakdown, he might have remained with his truck through that first night and then walked out the following morning, or stayed put until he was rescued. But, such is the turning of our lives.

It is true that a faint understanding of my fascination with the high Andes came to me at the end, the very end. At times during my career, high altitude mountaineering meant only great exertions and great heavings for breath. But in the years after, I have come to see those times with greater insight, often unknown to me at the time, when my step was halting and my breath was rasping. For isolation amongst the mountains caused me to ponder what is important in life: birth, life, death, the fate of me, my place in God's Plan and His universe, the ending of it all, the meaning of it all, the purpose of it all. I do not wish to exit with Kurtz's cursed lament upon my lips, "The horror! The horror!" Rather, I want my final words to be, "The beauty! The beauty!" We begin preparing our graves from the instant of our conception, and certainly I have prepared mine. I do not fear the physical act of dying, unless much suffering is involved. I do fear not having lived. But I have lived a life full and rich. So for me, death holds no terror. And this knowledge, learned during my time amongst the peaks, permitted me to see that it is better to attain the truth of self by not locating it while seeking it than by deciding not to seek it and never finding it.

My thoughts turn as well to my constant companions on my journeys. When I returned from my last climb, I lifted Baby Blue from my expedition bag for careful placement in storage. It caused me to realize that I would never know her on a mountain again. The thought gave a surprise and, for one long minute, my fingers closed about her blue being as I remembered all the times we shared of closeness and danger. To me she is a living testament to my survival in the mountains. She remained my friend throughout my career; she was always there for me and never expected anything in return. I shall hold her close in an occasional embrace in acknowledgment of our intrepid journeys amongst the high Andes mountains. She was my shield against adversity and unconsciously, unknowingly, I granted her personification.

I think also of Robert, my Guardian Angel. He has been with me all my life and will accompany my soul throughout all eternity, as St. Thomas teaches. In one chapter, I say that I never had an unseen companion upon my journeys and explained that Robert was something other than that. Now, however, with the reflective advantage of time, those instances when he was near me, talking to me, really were times when my psyche needed the calming effect of someone nearby to soothe me. And so, yes, he was an unseen friend anxious after my physical and spiritual welfare.

Such are my mountain memories -- snapshots in my head, some from long ago, others more recent, all fresh and vibrant as when I lived them. My memory wires are stretched so taut and tight, all that's needed is to dial the line with a peak picture or trip journal and data packets sing across the link, flooding my brain with remembrance filaments so dazzling and searing that, if touched, would incinerate me in a second. I revel in the memories, throughout the day and into the night, never pausing, never stopping, and never even slowing down, one climb linked to another by thoughts that bring increasing pleasure as the string lengthens and the years go by. And, in my twilight years, with the dark curtain of mortality inevitably and slowly descending upon my stay here, those white-hot, recollective fibers will be my welcome companions on the passage into the next, warming me along the way.

And what of me now, now that I have reached the advanced age of 69? Once, I was the embodiment of all I wished to be. I had that combination of determination, skill, and strength to climb the high Andean peaks late in life. But with age comes physical frailties, weaknesses I regard as another mountain to climb. I need grit, stoicism, and faith to confront the daily physical pains and tribulations. This is what my climbing career gave me -- the means to confront and live my later years with some measure of equanimity in the face of hardship.

I ask for a few things during my later years. One is that my contemplative and philosophic faculties resist the ravages of age and remain bright and strong, to compensate for the loss of physical strength. I also wish to continue viewing the big mountains, if just in my mind's eye. Last, I pray to retain the memories, all the precious and sacred memories, that I may relive again those astonishing days of years gone by. And, when I'm stooped and bent with age, within I will be smiling and happy as I remember the many occasions in life known but to a select band of climbers. Fortunate the high altitude mountaineer who lives to old age after so many mountain adventures, for he is many times blest. At the end of my days, I shall trust myself to a little pain, and then say to the world, "Godspeed."

What is the last, true mountain for the high altitude climber? It is that peak that poses life's summons to Eternity, warmly welcoming the mountaineer to that inexorable caravan moving to the mysterious realm we all must know, the silent, soothing sarcophagus of death, in a Paradise I know exists only amongst the highest mountains. And I shall be sustained throughout inestimable time in that sacrosanct realm by Baby Blue's drapery drawn about me, both of us reclining midst pleasant dreams within her calming, soothing embrace, amenable to the long, agreeable sleep of the ages within the everlasting fastnesses of our beloved Andes Mountains.

Well, Alex, my mountain journeys, and this book, are at an end. Thank you for asking me to write about my climbs. This may be an unexciting legacy to some but it is all that I am able to offer. I believe you now know something of why I kept returning to the mountains. Remember my adventures and me occasionally in your thoughts. That way I will be with you forever. Love always. Grandpa.

APPENDICES

Appendix A[72]

High Altitude Climbing Handbook

As an overall suggestion, I urge the beginning altitude climber to become a mountaineer rather than merely a climber. The mountaineer understands and is competent in all areas of the high altitude experience. Climbing ability is just one facet of this experience. The following outline develops the components necessary to be a well-rounded visitor in the mountains.

As a preamble to the following discussion, one might keep in mind a comment made by Frank Smythe, a famous member of several of the pre-war British expeditions to Everest. His observation was, "The great mountains are first climbed at home." Think about this and you will see the wisdom. The essential truth is that climbing knowledge cannot be learned or hope to be acquired at the time one first sets foot on the slopes of a big peak. This knowledge, such as proper gear selection and familiarity with the logistical requirements of an expedition, in most cases must be learned

---

[72] This Handbook was required reading for the author's clients.

at home, prior to even going out. In fact, some characteristics are innate. For example, certain climbing character traits like courage, decisiveness, patience, prudence, steadfastness, stoicism, and wisdom, which are important in this kind of activity, do not reside in a book. Instead, they appear over time through experience and development as we go about attending to the daily challenges and tasks of simply living our lives.

1. High altitude mountaineering is a system composed of the following components:

    A. Gear.
        - Having the proper gear is an obvious necessity. Seek advice from experienced climbers as to what does and does not work at altitude.

    B. Logistics.
        - A climb should be prepared for much in advance of the trip. Poor logistical planning has doomed many an expedition to failure.

    C. Physical readiness.
        - Concentrate on aerobic exercises to prepare for your climb.
        - Because altitude decreases the appetite, you will eat less the higher the elevation. Therefore, approach your climb a couple of pounds above your normal weight so that you have something to "give back" to the mountain.

    D. Psychological well being.

One should look for any fair "edge" over the mountain and psychological preparation is a way to do this. I no longer use meditation or visualization, but I did when I first began climbing.

        - Meditation techniques. Meditation isn't for everyone. But try it out to see if it might work for you.

- Visualization techniques.
- Subjective visualization. With this method, you become the performer in your visualization of climbing on the mountain.
- Objective visualization. With this, you view things as though you are watching a movie of yourself climbing.

Regardless of the method used, visualize by:

- using all your senses
- using photos, film, or video replay to strengthen the mental picture you have of your performance
- mentally rehearsing difficult situations that have given you problems on other climbs
- creating positive mental images of your past performances
- reviewing helpful mental and emotional responses to difficult situations you have encountered
- working to eliminate images of failure on other climbs and replacing them with positive experiences
- As an adjunct to meditation and visualization, there are other ways to set the proper "mood" for climbing at high altitude. One is the role color often plays. For example, here is a hierarchy of colors and their influence on the human psyche.
  - High positive energy: deep blue.
  - Low positive energy: light blue.
  - High negative energy: red.
  - Low negative energy: black.

One can use this data to purchase gear like a tent, sleeping bag, or windsuit in a color that will produce the effect that works for you. For example, the color red energizes me and makes me want to produce my maximum effort. So my windsuit is red. When I put it on, the color suffuses my being with motivation and I feel invincible as I leave my tent and set out for the higher elevations. But notice my feeling toward the color red doesn't conform to the color influence data above, and that cautions us to know ourselves well in this matter and not slavishly follow suggested guidelines. Also, the color of light blue calms and relaxes me. So the tent I take above base camp is blue, and its color sets a mood of tranquility that is restful and soothing after a day on the slopes.

     E. Physiological component.

    This refers to a climber's ability to acclimatize. You must understand that the mind plays the essential role in the body's ability to adjust to higher elevations. That is one of the reasons why climbing is often referred to as a "mental" game. You must plan carefully the elevations for your camps, knowing your body can take only so much altitude gain at a time. Also, you must exercise mental judgment as to the rapidity of ascension, when to use the rest step (see below), how often to rest, and how to choose the optimum route.

- The Cheyne/Stokes phenomenon. If this is experienced without being told of it beforehand (as happened to me), it can be unnerving. It occurs at night and is the body's reaction to the thinner air. You simply stop breathing, entirely. This can persist for as long as ninety seconds. Then the lungs suddenly begin to gasp for air. As I said, this is very disconcerting when you encounter it initially. But nothing is amiss. Your body is just trying to adjust. You can ameliorate the effects by taking a dosage of 125 mg or 250 mg of Diamox before going to sleep at night.
- The climber new to altitude may also experience crushing headaches. I don't suffer from migraines, but high altitude headaches can be extremely uncomfortable and must be similar. Again, this is a symptom of poor acclimatization, so one must take heed when headaches persist and don't diminish one to two hours after arriving at a new altitude. Aspirin helps, but occasionally an extra day at the new altitude is required.

- The use of Diamox. The FDA approved this medication in 1977. Doctors prescribe it for travelers to high altitude cities like Cuzco, La Paz, and Lhasa. One may take it prior to an ascent or when the symptoms of high altitude sickness first set in. It induces urination, and that helps the acclimatization process.

I leave it up to you to decide what you wish to do. You may take it when we leave Copiapo. Or, you can decide to take it if and when you feel poorly. I don't use it or any drugs on a climb. That is my own personal ethic. Whatever the case, have your doctor prescribe the regular pills of 250 mg, NOT the Sequel gels. The gels do not allow you to break off part of the pill for a smaller dosage.

You also need to take aspirin at high altitude. This helps thin the blood (as well as damp the headaches) and ward off clotting, which can lead to phlebitis and frost bite. However, one must be careful with the interaction of aspirin and Diamox. In heavy dosages, above 1000 mg for both and taken together, strokes have been known to occur. I don't take aspirin in a greater dosage than 250 mg. This has always served me well. I'll help you find your optimal dosage levels for both medications, if you choose to take them.

F.   Personality.

The ideal climber: stoical, logical, sense of humor, takes adversity in stride, deals effectively with uncertainty, possesses the ability to plan his own efforts as well as those of others, good team player. If you have taken personality assessments, like the Myers-Briggs, note how your personality characteristics play out on a big climb and document your findings and observations. It all goes towards knowing more about yourself.

2. Acclimatization.

The peaks covered by this guide are easily and quickly accessible from the Chilean coast cities of Copiapo and Antofagasta. In fact, from an acclimatization standpoint, they are too easily and quickly approachable. For example, base camps at 14,000 feet to 15,000 feet on any of these mountains are within 4-6 hours from the coast. The temptation to drive to base camp may be irresistible to some. But the dangers of altitude sickness that such a rapid rise will provoke is the reason we spend the first night at 12,000 feet.

Here is a quick review of the rules of acclimatizing properly and the successive levels of altitude sickness and their symptoms.

A. Rules of Acclimatization.
   - Acclimatize thoroughly at lower elevations before going higher. One night stops at 10,000 feet and 12,000 feet before going to a higher base camp will moderate the effects of altitude. Also, climbing a nearby peak 500-1,000 feet above one of these lower camps can help. But, exercise should be minimal since the body's physical abilities will be taxed to the fullest later on the climb.
   - Stay hydrated. Drinking liquids throughout the day will help minimize the altitude's effects.
   - Place camps no more than 2,500 vertical feet above the previous camp.
     We will climb expedition style, so we make double carries between each camp. This helps to reduce the effects of altitude.
   - Monitor the body's adaptation frequently. The heart's rate increases with higher elevations. Your normal pulse rate (number of beats at rest) should return within two to three hours of arrival at a new level. So, know your resting heart rate prior to leaving for the climb. Also, the urine's color should turn from a light brown to its normal color within the same period.
   - Proceed at a slow pace. There are no awards given on a big peak to the climber who beats his comrades to the next camp. Adopt a pace that is comfortable and seek to

maintain it. Only an emergency should force a climber out of the stride right for him.

- Maintain a steady rhythm. The heart and lungs have difficulty adjusting to the oxygen thin environment if there are erratic bursts of activity.
- Rest often. The body absorbs a tremendous beating at altitude, especially the cardio-vascular system. A deliberate pace with frequent stops for food, drink, picture taking, and conversation are the best bet here.
- Under no circumstances should any other medicines, such as dexamethasone for High Altitude Cerebral Edema or nefedipine for High Altitude Pulmonary Edema (see below for further discussion), be taken or administered unless prescribed or given by a physician thoroughly knowledgeable of the effects of high altitude.
- Each climber must determine through experience his body's unique timetable for acclimatization. Once it is understood, adhere to it rigidly, and depart from it only in the most compelling of circumstances.
- It should be noted that the body's reaction to altitude may be different on successive trips. This means the ability to acclimate on a climb does not guarantee acclimatization on a following one.

B. Levels of Altitude Sickness.
- Acute Mountain Sickness (AMS). This condition is felt most often near 12,000 feet but is also encountered at lower elevations. AMS usually begins with mild headaches that grow more intense. The pain is as bad reclining as it is standing. If one stays hydrated, the symptoms usually disappear in an hour or so.

Insomnia is another frequent symptom. Irregular or periodic breathing, called Cheyne-Stokes breathing, is common at altitude, most often at night. A short period of little or no breathing (apnea) is followed by a series of increasingly deep gasps, followed by a decrease, and again apnea.

Loss of appetite is also common at this stage. Favorite foods at sea level lose their appeal and taste and the act of eating often becomes a chore. This leads to lethargy and to gradual weight loss.

Diamox (see above) lessens the symptoms of AMS. You should discuss with your physician whether this drug is right for you.

- High Altitude Cerebral Edema (HACE). The symptoms are loss of muscle coordination (ataxia), mental confusion, hallucinations, headaches. HACE proceeds quickly to unconsciousness and death. One must descend at least 1,000 feet to recover.
- High Altitude Pulmonary Edema (HAPE). The symptoms are severe shortness of breath, with a deep cough accompanied by frothy or bloody sputum. Great fatigue, and now and again, a slight fever are all or individually present. This condition was and is, even today, mistaken for flu or pneumonia. HAPE progresses rapidly to coma and eventually death. A gurgling sound in the chest, along with other symptoms, is usually a good indicator that HAPE is present. One must descend at least 1,000 feet to survive.
- The use of "hard" drugs. The drugs of choice are dexamethasone for High Altitude Cerebral Edema [HACE] and nifedipine to treat High Altitude Pulmonary Edema [HAPE]. Discuss these serious medications with your doctor. I do not take these drugs, which is my choice.
- Blood Clotting. The symptoms of dangerous clotting are swelling in the legs or thighs and angry red blotches that appear on the skin and follow a vein right to the lungs. Should the clot reach the lungs, it will cause a pulmonary embolism and then death.

The best preventive for all levels of altitude sickness is a strict adherence to the basic rules of acclimatization. However, even following the rules may be insufficient. In the case of simple AMS, none of the symptoms are life threatening and they generally moderate within a few hours or so. The other conditions are life threatening and must be treated with respect and speed. Clotting is less time dependent but no less serious. Make every effort to get a person off the mountain entirely and to a hospital for treatment as soon as possible.

3. Expedition climbing.

Expedition climbing involves placing camps between 1,500 feet to 2,500 feet steadily up the mountain and making double carries to each of them. This is the method longest in use and the means used to climb all the world's highest mountains. From Base Camp, on our first haul, each of us will carry our food for the higher camps, a pint of white gas for our stoves, an extra layer of clothing, and other items. When we reach a Camp I location, we will drink, eat, leave our gear at the site, and return to Base Camp to sleep. The next day we will carry everything else we need for the camps, our tents, and sleeping bags. This load is always heavy, so prepare mentally beforehand. At Camp I, we place our tents and sleep the night. The next day we make the first carry to a Camp II site, drop our gear, and return to Camp I to sleep. The day following we make the second carry. And so on up the mountain. Climbing in this way allows our bodies to acclimate gradually to the higher elevations.

- Camp placement. We will discuss this once on the mountain.
- The timed interval rest stop method: one keeps climbing steadily until reaching an interval, such as five, ten, thirty minutes, before stopping to rest. This has its adherents among some climbers.
- The rest step method: one decides on a set number of steps as dictated by the terrain, load carried, and altitude. Those steps taken, the climber pauses briefly

until setting out once more. This has the beneficial side effect of occupying the brain in counting steps so that it has less time to process pain messages. It also staves off exhaustion and tiredness. This procedure also has its proponents.

- A third technique involves combining the two methods and using each according to the terrain and how one feels. This approach is the one that works for me.
- Planning what to take above Base Camp.
- The first question to ask of any item carried higher up the mountain from Base is, "Do I really need it?" If the answer is "yes," then continually ask yourself how you can find a lighter alternative or how you can modify the item so that it is lighter. A good deal of this you can do before you get to the peak. Stay current with gear that is lighter while still providing the same functionality as a heavier version. Do this by reading climbing magazines, talking with friends, etc. Also, stay current with new foods that will provide you with the same nutrition a heavier product does. This pursuit of lightness never ends. It's fun trying out new things. Several climbers go to extremes by cutting labels out of their clothes, cutting holes in their toothbrush handles, you name it, we all have tried it.

4. The far view of a peak. And the near view.

- From a distance of twelve to twenty miles, all high peaks appear intimidating. The mountain's slopes seem so steeply angled that an ascent appears all but impossible. And possible ascent routes are obscure and even hidden. One does not see all that is there. There is a likelihood of being "psyched out" by a big peak at this distance.
- At a distance of three to five miles, all mountains have many of their defenses and their weaknesses exposed. Those mountain walls so imposing miles away now

appear much gentler in angle than they seemed at a distance. And several routes will come to view that could scarcely be imagined miles back.

5. No "separate reality" on a summit.

For those who might think that reaching the top of a big peak will make them a better person or transform their lives, I have found this untrue for me. You must be your own judge on this. In my opinion, there is nothing on the top of a big mountain but rock, snow, tremendous views, and a sense of accomplishment.

6. Chance, Choice, Divine Providence.

Whatever you wish to call it, sometimes events are set in motion and no human intervention may change their course. We will discuss this further on the climb.

7. Escape strategy.

- Always know your escape routes, like where the nearest roads and mines or other sites are and the most efficient way to them.
- Once at an escape point, you may call Maria Ester (Hotel La Casona) at 217277 or Patricio Rios at 212714 (O) or 224018 (H).

8. Goals.

We will share together (only if you wish to, no one will be pressured to do so) what our short and long-term goals are once we are on the peak. For example, do you one day want to climb in the Himalaya? Whether you share with others, think to yourself why you are committing your time, money, effort, and quite possibly your earthly existence to such an undertaking. Can you rationalize this as a worthwhile activity?

9. Hygiene in the mountains.

    -   Personal hygiene. We will discuss this on the mountain.
    -   Garbage management. We will discuss this on the mountain.

10. Loss of judgment.

Perhaps the most serious consequence of the body's reaction to high altitude is the mind's loss of ability to process information the same way it does at sea level. There's a serious diminishment of one's capability to multi-process a multitude of data. As a result, you will find yourself treating information in single thread fashion. Given this is the case, it's essential that you remind yourself before making a serious decision that you fail to see the entire picture. Force yourself to go back over the data and try to tease out what you may have missed before rendering a final decision.

11. Learn your limits.

It's important to understand your strong and weak points when climbing at altitude. For example, are you lousy at logistical planning? That's important to know. In future, try to learn that skill or plan to climb with a person who does it well. Know, too, the circumstances that press you psychologically. Understand where your break point is and resolve to keep it at a distance. And you definitely must appreciate your physical boundaries. How many hours over what kind of terrain and in what conditions does it take to feel absolutely exhausted? Again, you must know that limit and vow only to approach it if it's a matter of life or death. This knowledge may come after many climbs. However, you may never know completely these boundaries. Still, you must continue to search for them in the pursuit of self-knowledge, the most important pursuit of all. Plato's admonition to "Know thyself" is an essential ingredient to success at high altitude.

12. Miscellaneous Rules.

- Always return by the way of ascent.
- Do not leave a ridge you are climbing to traverse a face.
- On the ascent, find firm ground such as small rocks and compacted sand. When descending, seek looser ground.
- Never try to move in a full-scale storm or a white out or in the wind unless not to do so is life threatening.
- Keep your party intact. Remain together.
- Never travel over a glacier unless roped up.
- Make sure others know of your whereabouts and your schedule.
- Always take a moment to assess the risk of whatever it is you are going to do.
- Always keep a reserve of energy. Climb at 80% of capacity by using a steady pace and a judicious use of the rest step. Do not be forced from your pace unless it's an emergency.
- Do not look up the mountain hoping to focus on your ultimate stopping point. Your slow progress upwards will just serve to weaken your resolve. Set your goals twenty to thirty feet ahead. Those incremental victories will get you eventually to a higher camp.
- Cook outside the tent unless conditions dictate otherwise and then only with proper ventilation. If you do cook indoors, always do so just inside the doorway with something underneath the stove to protect the tent floor. With the stove near the door, it can be flung outside if a fire flares.
- Prepare a list beforehand of gear for each of the two carries to the higher camps.
- Take enough food, fuel, and water, to Base Camp to last at least a week beyond your planned stay on the mountain.
- Make sure your tent is anchored for wind from any direction.

- Trust logic more than intuition on your first climbs. As your experience grows, you may trust more to intuition.
- A client should seek self-sufficiency. He should know how to get off a peak in case anything happens to the guide.
- One of the greatest dangers at altitude is the loss of judgment due to poor acclimatization. Hence, think things through before acting, if the situation permits.
- Always know how long it will take to return to your prior camps from wherever you are on the mountain.
- In extreme high wind conditions, it may become necessary to collapse your tent, with you inside. Taking into account your tent's characteristics, rehearse in your mind the sequential steps needed to make this happen.
- Do not hesitate to challenge your guide as to what he is doing and why. This will enhance your learning experience and his.

13. High altitude mountaineering -- a useless activity?

To many non-climbers, climbing at altitude is the ultimate in useless endeavors. Of course, measured by the standards of this or most other societies, that assessment is true. For the majority of people, those actions that result in making more money or in bettering one's position in life deserve their attention. To them, all human action must be cost-effective, else it has no meaning. But one may argue successfully with a seeming paradox that there is value in some few members of a society engaging in so-called "useless" undertakings, because these efforts provide meaning to society as a whole. In my case, altitude climbing is far from a useless activity. It provides me with the following:

- It's an escape from the everyday horrors that parade across the TV screen and reported in the daily newspapers -- the senseless killings of innocent human beings and the countless stories of man's inhumanity to his fellow man. All these remain suspended from knowledge while on a peak and it's a relief. One feels above and removed from all the tumult reigning far below.

- Life is usually quite simple on a big mountain. Things often are either black or they are white. One makes choices and the results can reveal themselves quickly as to whether or not the decision was a good one.
- Climbing on a big mountain is a perfect catalyst to learn more about oneself. And this is the highest form of learning.
- Climbing provides a sense of adventure that is difficult to replicate in daily life. The heights lure me on, beckoning with sights and occurrences men and women at sea level can never know or understand.

14. Uncertainty in the Universe and on a high peak.

One thing Quantum Mechanics has taught us is that uncertainty at the sub-atomic level is the norm in the Universe. For those of us who strive to control all we can in our lives (and I am such a person), it is humbling to know that there will always be elements in our existences that will forever remain outside our control. This we must accept. But despite the reality of uncertainty, this must not deter us from preparing and planning for a climb, and planning in a way that anticipates every possible occurrence. The caveat must be, however, that we cannot be so rigid in our thinking that we are unable to react to unexpected circumstances on the mountain due to weather, injury, or simply those things that go wrong. The ultimate test of the high altitude mountaineer is how well he reacts to unforeseen developments and their circumstances.

15. A story with several plots and sub-plots.

I liken a high altitude climbing expedition to a play with several mini stories occurring within the larger story of the climb. The climb itself is the over arching umbrella underneath which lesser tales involving the weather; one's ability to acclimate; the proper functioning of gear; the interaction with other climbers; one's physical, mental, and psychological state; play out during the climb. And all these lesser stories can and do affect the other sub plots and, ultimately, the major story line itself. Sometimes I think for weeks after a climb concerning the untangling of these various story themes and how they each came to affect the overall climb.

16. Risk assessment.

The control of risk stems from man's desire to control the events happening around him and it's an exercise I urge you to undertake as you foray into the world of high altitude. As you gain experience, you should take stock before every climb of all the factors that affect your success and failure and seek to quantify and codify your chances for success. But please keep in mind that events in the universe happen in a random manner, so even though we may attempt to control events, eventually uncertainty may win out, and we cannot change that.

17. High altitude tragedies.

This is not a study in morbidity. But the high altitude mountaineer should know the famous tragedies in climbing history so as to extract from these stories what went wrong, why, and what could have been done to prevent the fatal outcomes. In this way, we learn better how to survive "up there."

- The 1924 Everest expedition. This is the famous climb that resulted in the disappearance of George Mallory and Sandy Irvine. Everyone knows the story by now. Mallory's body was discovered on May 2, 1999 (see "Detectives on Everest," by Hemmleb and Simonson). The mystery still remains as to whether one or both ever reached the summit. The book: "Everest, The Challenge," by Francis Younghusband.
- The 1932 German expedition to Nanga Parbat. Willy Merkl, Willi Welzenbach, and two other Germans along with six porters died in the attempt. Exhaustion and the

difficulties posed by a raging storm trapped Merkl at 24,000 feet. In a touching gesture of friendship and devotion, Merkl's porter, Gay-Lay, refused to abandon his sahib, even though he was fit to do so, and stayed with him until both died. The book: "Nanga Parbat Adventure," by Fritz Bechtold.

- The 1939 American expedition to K2. This attempt, led by the world renowned Fritz Wiessner, almost succeeded in the first ascent of an 8,000 meter peak. Wiessner and a sherpa got within 800 feet of the top and were forced to turn back. Dudley Wolfe, a novice climber, who had stayed in the high camp not far below, joined them on the descent. Upon entering the lower camps, the party found them all stripped of supplies and deserted. Wiessner decided to descend farther to investigate, leaving Wolfe behind -- alone. Wiessner reached Base Camp to find that a young climber on the expedition, Jack Durrance, inexplicably had ordered the sherpas to clear out the supplies from all the camps they could reach on the peak. Later, unable to descend solo, Wolfe needed rescue. Two sherpas left Base Camp and climbed to Camp Six, a 7,000 feet elevation gain in one day. There they met two other sherpas and the four set out next morning to rescue Wolfe, several hundred feet above. That is the last anyone ever saw of the four brave sherpas or of Dudley Wolfe. The book: "K2, The 1939 Tragedy," by Andrew Kauffman and William Putnam.

- The 1953 American expedition to K2. Dr. Charles Houston led this expedition, his second attempt at the peak. In 1938 he led an expedition that saw the famous Teton climber, Paul Petzoldt, get near the top of this most difficult mountain. But tragedy struck the 1953 effort. Houston and his party found themselves at Camp VIII at just under 27,000 feet and ready to attempt the summit. But the next morning, one of the climbers, Art Gilkey, complained of a pain in his leg. Houston, an M.D., diagnosed it as due to phlebitis (a blood clot in a vein that, if it reaches the heart, can cause a heart attack) and ordered a retreat from the mountain. The ensuing descent by the team, bearing the weight of their companion, made for an ordeal in every sense of the word. A savage storm pinned them down for ten days. Only when the storm lifted were they able to continue. At one point, they stopped to rest and secured Gilkey and his carry litter to the slope of a shallow couloir. They went off a ways to discuss their plans for further progress down the mountain. When they returned for Gilkey, to resume the descent, he had vanished completely. The team mourned the loss of their friend and continued down to the safety of Base Camp. Climbing in two teams, one above the other, a member of the top most team lost his footing and slipped down the slope, pulling the rest of his team with him. This team fell onto the lower team and pulled all of them off their stances. Now all seven tumbled down the mountain to certain death. Then, in one of the great feats in all of mountaineering, Pete Schoening righted himself and thrust his axe deep into the snow. The lines of both teams wrapped about this single, thin shaft of steel, and this saved them all. We know this today as the "miracle belay of Pete Schoening." The team eventually made it down. Climbers discovered Gilkey's body several years ago and gave it a proper burial. And Pete Schoening, I believe all of 67 years of age, was a client, along with his nephew, on Scott Fischer's ill fated 1996 expedition to Everest (see "Into Thin Air"). He did not make it to the summit, but dropped out near the South Col. The book: "K2, The Savage Mountain" by Charles Houston and Robert Bates.

- The 1976 ascent of Nanda Devi. Several years after his famous first traverse of Everest, with Thomas Hornbein,

Willi Unsoeld climbed a peak near Nanda Devi. Viewing the mountain in the distance, he found himself mesmerized by its famous outline and vowed one day to climb it. He even named a daughter, Nanda Devi, as testimony to its beauty. When Nanda Devi reached 20 years old, she convinced her father to organize a climb of the peak. He established a team composed of some of the best American climbers, including John Roskelley and Lou Reichardt, to tackle the mountain. Nanda Devi, while not initially disposed to ascend to the summit, fell in love with the idea during the expedition. She pleaded with her father, who initially resisted the idea, to let her climb with the summit team even though she had no previous altitude experience. He eventually relented, to her and his regret, for she contracted altitude sickness at 20,000 feet. Soon after she developed the symptoms, a huge storm descended upon the mountain, preventing any movement down to Base Camp. After two days of entrapment, her symptoms worsened, and she died there in camp. This devastated Unsoeld. The storm still raged and all realized they must get down or they would all perish. The burden of carrying Devi's body might worsen their chances of survival. So Unsoeld made the painful decision to commit her body to the mountain. They placed her in her sleeping bag, and let her fall down a steep couloir to her final resting place. All made it off the mountain, but Willi carried this experience with him until his death several years later. He had led the members of a climbing club to the top of Mt. Rainier when, on the descent, he unclipped from his climbing harness. He fell into a crevasse and died when the other climbers could not pull him out. The book: "Nanda Devi, The Tragic Expedition," by John Roskelley.

- The 1982 British expedition to Everest. This was an attempt, by Peter Boardman and Joe Tasker, to climb the last unclimbed ridge on the peak, the North East Ridge, without supplemental oxygen. Chris Bonington was the expedition leader. Boardman and Tasker, experienced climbers, struggled for weeks to work their way up the Ridge. But they were thwarted by storms, sickness, and bad luck. Finally in a position to try for the summit, they were last seen above 8,000 meters, before clouds enveloped them, never to be seen alive again. Climbers found Boardman's body in 1997, but Tasker's is still lost. The book: "Everest, The Unclimbed Ridge," by Chris Bonington and Charles Clarke.

- The 1985 climb of Siula Grande in the Peruvian Andes. This is the climb made famous by Joe Simpson in his book, "Touching the Void." If you haven't read it, do so at your earliest.

- The 1986 events on K2. This horrific set of events and the numerous deaths that ensued Kurt Diemberger relates in "The Endless Knot" and Jim Curran in "Triumph and Tragedy." Both are must read books. In brief, what took place on the mountain became the greatest tragedy in the history of high altitude climbing. Thirteen men and women perished while making the attempt. An avalanche buried two Americans; a husband and wife team summited, and then disappeared; another climber, forced down by high winds, fell into a crevasse just above base camp; and the ultimate calamity was seven climbers were pinned down at 26,000 feet and only two able to finally escape. This story will break your heart.

- The 1996 ascent of Everest as chronicled in "Into Thin Air," Jon Krakauer. Again, most have read this one. Five climbers died in tragic circumstances. The sole problem I have with the narrative is that Krakauer trashes Anatoli Boukreev, with thin justification. Actually, Boukreev's rescue efforts on Everest were among the most heroic in all of high altitude climbing history.

Appendix B

Twelve Highest Peaks in the Andes and their First Ascents

PEAK	METERS	FEET
1. Aconcagua, Argentina	6960	22,834
2. Ojos del Salado, Chile	6893	22,609
3. Pissis, Argentina	6795	22,287
4. Bonete Chico, Argentina	6759	22,169
5. Tres Cruces, Sur, Chile	6748	22,133
6. Huascaran Sur, Peru	6746	22,126
7. Llullaillaco, Chile	6739	22,109
8. Mercedario, Argentina	6720	22,041
9. Cazadero, Argentina (aka: Walther Penck)	6658	21,838
10. Huascaran Norte, Peru	6655	21,828
11. Tres Cruces Central, Chile	6629	21,743
12. Incahuasi, Chile	6621	21,716

FIRST ASCENTS

1. Aconcagua: January, 1897, Mattias Zurbriggen (Swiss), lead guide on the Edmund Fitzgerald (British) Expedition.
2. Ojos del Salado: 1937, Polish Expedition.
3. Pissis: 1937, Polish Expedition.
4. Bonete Chico: 1970, Argentine Expedition.
5. Tres Cruces, Sur: 1937, Polish Expedition.
6. Huascaran Sur: 1932, German/Austrian Expedition.
7. Llullaillaco: 1952, Chilean climbing team.
8. Mercedario: 1934 Polish Expedition.
9. Cazadero: 1970, S. Kunstmann, et al, Chile.
10. Huascaran Norte: 1908, American Expedition.
11. Tres Cruces Central: 1937, Polish Expedition.
12. Incahuasi: 1913, Walther Penck, Germany.

Appendix C

The Conversation with Apani, The Indian

*I*n this appendix, I wish first to explain what the reader is about to
encounter. For here I present certain events during the Spanish Conquest
of the Incas that began in 1532. The history is contained in two letters
written to the King of Spain, King Philip II, by Pedro de Merida, a
conquistador of Peru and Chile, who was a member of Diego de Almagro's[73]
expedition to Chile in 1535-1537 looking for gold.[74]

De Merida's authorship, and the letters themselves, are historical
narrative. The missives are my way to recreate, as accurately as possible,
the tenor and general atmosphere of a long-lost era in a remote part of the
world. I have relied upon the historical record to present figures, actual
dates, and the events we know took place. To weave the story together, I
have supplied narrative based upon my personal research and knowledge of
the Spanish Conquest of Peru and Chile during thirty-five years of study.

---

[73] 1475-1538.

[74] The two letters in their entirety appear in the author's historical narrative, "The
Chronicle of Pedro de Merida: Travels to Chile, in the Years of our Lord 1535-
1537; Being an Account of That Journey to the Farthest Most Region of the Inca
Empire; As Related to His Most Catholic Majesty, King Don Philip II, Our Most
Sovereign Ruler" The letters offer an historical perspective to his climbing stories.
Spaniards and Incas preceded him on several of the big peaks, 500 years before.
Please visit the author's website for more about this book.

The date of the first letter is July 1, 1589. In it, de Merida tells of the journey from Cuzco to today's San Miguel de Tucuman in Argentina. From there, the expedition turned west and crossed the Andes over the Great Plateau, a high mountain table that stretches from the San Francisco Pass in Argentina to today's Laguna Santa Rosa in Chile. The first letter ends there at the Laguna.

The second letter, dated September 15, 1589, begins with the expedition's arrival in Copayapu.[75] De Merida then tells of the fruitless search for gold and the often perilous journey from that town south to the area north of present-day Santiago, Chile, and the return back to Copayapu. From there, they begin the long march back to Cuzco. In Antofagasta, de Merida and Ancohualla, one of the Inca princes assigned to the expedition, interview one of the men who helped build the huts on the summit of Llullaillaco. It's an astonishing recounting of one of the great feats of Andean history. I quote now from the second letter at the point that leads to the interview.

On July 15, 1536, we left Copayapu, heading due west towards the sea. From there, we turned our steps north, following the Inca road, with the ocean immediately on our left. It required thirty-eight days to reach the town, Angastu,[76] and we did so on August 21. This place reminded all of us of Cuquimpu, in the south, and we enjoyed our stay here immensely. The townspeople proved friendly enough. Anco (Ancohualla) dealt with them in a pleasant manner and they in turn viewed him as the Inca's representative among them. He asked after the whereabouts of men we wished to converse with and, within three days, one man made himself known.

What follows, Your Excellency, is a recounting of the extraordinary conversation we had with this man. He was one of the Indians who helped build and place the huts on the summit of Llullaillaco. I may tell his story because I have in my possession a copy of the detailed notes written out by the two scribes who recorded the interview. Formerly, this remained in the sole possession of Father Molina. Six years ago, at my request, Father had it copied and sent it to me for my personal collection.

---

[75] Today's Copiapo.
[76] Known today as Antofagasta.

THE CONVERSATION WITH THE MAN CALLED APANI, AS CONDUCTED BY PEDRO DE MERIDA AND ANCOHUALLA.[77]

- Pedro: I wish to start by asking your name.
- Apani: I will tell not my given name but the one they called me on the great mountain, Apani, which means "I carry."[78] They called me this because on the mountain, when others could not lift their loads, I offered to carry their burdens for them.
- Anco: How is it you found yourself a part of the undertaking to place religious structures on the top of Llullaillaco?
- Apani: In Peru, they made me join the military and placed me in the army here in central Chile as a replacement. When I reported to the general in Angastu, he assigned me to a special project; its nature he did not say. A month later, a large caravan of llamas and Indians approached our base. Our general dressed himself in his finest uniform to welcome them. These men came from Cuzco, dispatched to Angastu for important work. Inca Yupanqui, a great ruler of Peru for many years had died the year before.[79] The new arrivals came in regards to his death. The lead man of the entourage, an important official sent by the new Inca, Huayna Capac,[80] carried the title of the Inca's "master builder;" he planned and coordinated the construction of worship sites on high mountains to honor the Inca and our Lord the Sun. His caravan of men and llamas took two days to arrive at our camp.
- Anco: Your age at this time?
- Apani: I had eighteen summers. Today, I have sixty.
- Anco: Why did they send this man to Angastu?
- Apani: Inca Huayna Capac wanted a site built on a high mountain to honor Inca Yupanqui and to serve as a worship

---

[77] This was recorded on August 24, 1536.
[78] The word Apani is *Quechua*.
[79] In 1493. He reigned from 1471 to 1493.
[80] Reigned as Inca from 1493 to 1527.

place for our Lord the Sun. We addressed this master builder by his full name, Vitahuati, as we respected and admired him while we worked on this project and his demeanor and position demanded esteem.

- Anco: How did it happen that he chose Llullaillaco as the site?
- Apani: This man, Vita, as I may now call him at a distance of years, heard of the large mountain east of Angastu and decided it a most worthy place as a worship site.
- Pedro: Did the master builder control the entire effort from start to finish?
- Apani: Yes, as the chosen man to do this he had complete control, on orders of the High Inca. Moreover, as he told us, he had done this on four other mountains, so we trusted his knowledge and leadership. Our general appointed Vita our "general" until the work's completion and told us we must obey his orders as though they came from him. We had no battles to fight, the people of northern Chile proved congenial, and so our service to the master builder did not threaten the security or safety of the army. In truth, we thought it a welcome change from the boredom of daily military life. It offered us an adventure new to us. In addition, my mother once said she had a dream in which she visited the top of a high mountain so she could reside closer to the Sun. When she died, my father saved a lock of her hair that I have kept always. Now I thought, when on the top of this great peak, I would leave the lock of hair there so her spirit might realize her earthly dream.
- Anco: And what of your duties?
- Apani: At first, Vita told me to work with stonemasons to shape rocks for the two huts destined for the top of the mountain. He chose eight of us to perform the work, four assigned to each building. We all had worked with stone at home in Peru. Our goal was to construct the huts in Angastu and, when completed, to mark the stones to indicate their places in the structures, either the lower or the upper parts. It went in this manner: we daubed with a stroke of green paint the rocks comprising the

lower half of my building; the stones of the upper half with blue. We painted the lower part of the other hut's stones with a red mark, the higher half with white. I think you recognize the genius of this scheme, and I shall tell more of it at that point in our discussion. We disassembled the huts and transported the rocks to the mountain, where our men carried them to the top for reassembly there. Vita chose me to participate with the construction of the buildings, and this gave me pause as I had never been on a high peak before. By the way, Vita made sure of an accurate count of the number of stones composing each hut. The end walls we made of forty rocks of various sizes. With the four end walls of the two buildings, the total equaled 160 stones. The sidewalls comprised ninety rocks each, so the amount of the four sidewalls came to 360, giving a sum of 520 stones.

- Pedro: And the importance of the number?
- Apani: As I said, these men knew their business. With the rocks counted, they calculated how many individual loads would be needed to transport them to the top and hence how many carriers we required to complete the task. For example, Vita believed that if every man hauled three rocks approximately eighty-five men could carry 255 stones to the higher camp the first day and the remainder the second. So, the effort required two days to move the majority of stones from one camp to the next. Depending on the number of camps on the mountain, he could tell the total days required to complete the entire effort.
- Anco: Very ingenious.
- Apani: Vita wished to avoid men high on the mountain having to chip and cut the rocks. It is too cold there, it is hard to breathe, and it is persistently windy. The stones, marked as to their position in the structure, allowed the builders to put together the huts quickly after the rock-bearers hauled the stones to the top.
- Anco: This seems a sensible thing to do.
- Apani: Yes, we thought so too, especially when we got to the mountain and experienced the hardships there. And, a larger

design revealed itself. Vita told us the foundation stones would precede us up the mountain, followed by the second level's rocks, all marked, and piled in separate heaps on the summit, so when we arrived we could make short work of assembly. Also, it helped that we, the builders of the huts, would be the ones to reassemble them. As I mentioned, this man deserved the title of "master" and we grew to trust and admire him very much.

- Anco: You had other reasons to respect the master builder?

- Apani: Well, yes. Despite his position of royalty, he acted with and towards us without any airs or pretension. Here is an example. As a man close to the Inca, he deserved a litter as his conveyance, carried by bearers. Yet, when he arrived at our Angastu camp, he walked, as the others did in his entourage. This remained his habit throughout, to walk as a common Indian, though lameness in his right leg caused a noticeable limp. Nevertheless, he did not make his health an excuse for soft living, but his constant activity a cure for his health, as by long journeys, simple diet, sleeping in the open air (except when we resided near or on the mountain), and enduring hardships with the rest of us common soldiers, he fought off his physical troubles and kept his body strong against his infirmity.

- A further example. He always took his meals with the rest of us, out in the open, if the weather allowed, or with us in large tents during times of cold. On these occasions, he talked with whomever sat close, as though he was that man's friend or neighbor. He also cared about us in other ways. On the journey to the mountain, he walked behind a man herding several loaded llamas. All of a sudden, two of the animals, frightened by a large snake slithering across the ground in front of them, jerked wildly to the side and knocked the man to the ground where he hit his head against a sharp boulder. Vita ran to him, held him in his arms and tried to stop the bleeding with his tunic. The man died within the hour, Vita never leaving him. This was witnessed by others and me and I told many of my friends what had happened. Never had we heard of a man of such eminence

264

acting in this manner. By the subsequent day, all knew what had taken place and we held him in the highest regard as a result.

- Pedro: I am beginning to like him myself. To return to the buildings -- their size and dimensions?

- Apani: Ten feet long, four feet wide, three feet high and fitted with a roof of woven reeds pulled tight over small wooden beams.[81]

- Pedro: What other preparations did you make here in Angastu?

- Apani: Well, everyone remained busy. Many said later that they found the preparations here more demanding than climbing the mountain. Vita handled everything and directed the efforts with four aides he had brought with him from Peru. The responsibility of one of these lieutenants was transport, to make certain we had the proper number of llamas to carry all our equipment to the mountain. The responsibility of a different man included seeing to the availability of *charqui*, dried fruits, nuts, corn cakes, and hot chilies. An added job of his was to ensure that enough food found its way to the base of the mountain to feed those carrying the stones to the top. The third lieutenant saw to it that all other equipment, such as clothes and the special implements necessary to climb the big peak, stayed on hand while we worked. Fortunately, this man brought with him from Cuzco pants, jackets, gloves, and head scarves made from alpaca and vicuna wool. I remember it as the warmest clothing I had ever worn, and comfortable. A further duty included seeing we all had warm sandals on the mountain. The fourth man served to assist the other three, if they needed help. He knew the job requirements of each lieutenant and operated as Vita's "right hand man," as they say. He also instructed us in the construction of the buildings and planned the transportation of the rocks to the mountain.

- Anco: Did Vita bring others with him?

- Apani: Yes, and they proved important. He had with him four specialists who knew how to climb high mountains. Their

81 See Chapter Three of Johan Reinhard's "Inca Rituals and Sacred Mountains."

name, *cuntur runas*, or "condor men," they acquired because they go higher in the sky than the great bird of the mountains. The *cunturs*, as they told us to call them, found the best path up the mountain, located camps on the route, guided those hauling rocks to the top, and then led the builders so they might complete the work. Given that my duties included assembling the huts, these men remained important to me and to all of us.

- Pedro: And how did they find the necessary number to work on the project? I think you said the Inca army provided most of them.

- Apani: Yes, Inca Yupanqui sent three armies to Chile, each 10,000 strong, during his reign of twenty years. In 1494, one contingent billeted itself in the south near the border of the Araucanian Indians.[82] The second army resided in Limari. The third divided itself between Angastu and Copayapu. Vita had orders from Huayna Capac to use men as he saw fit, so we provided most of the labor. Also, many Angastu natives offered to join our force, like those who knew the road to the peak and the location of the water sources, things such as that. Others coordinated the gathering of local foods. Several chose to kill llamas and prepare vast amounts of *charqui*, one of our staples on the mountain. Other locals prepared dried fruits and cooked corn cakes from crops grown here and at other towns nearby.

- Pedro: What route did you follow to the mountain from Angastu?

- Apani: Actually, there is a road from here that connects with Saltiza, on the other side of the mountains. Traders used this road between our two towns over many years. It goes through a place called Monturaqui, which contains large stone structures built many years ago, their purpose unknown.[83] From Monturaqui, Llullaillaco is visible to the south, if one knows where to look. It is near eighteen miles distant.

---

[82] This area is some 240 miles south of present day Santiago.

[83] Today this site is known as Estacion Monturaqui. The ruins of these ancient buildings lie near the Estacion.

- Pedro: So, traders here in town knew the path?
- Apani: Yes. In fact Vita chose several to serve as our guides. They knew the locations of the water sources and the pastures of *ichu* grass.[84]
- Anco: So this place, Monturaqui, became a supply staging area?
- Apani: Yes. When Vita heard of it, he dispatched stonecutters and a lieutenant there to fit out buildings as storage depots. This worked well. Caravans from Angastu with food and provisions left every week, or when needed, to journey to Monturaqui, a trip there and back near to 300 miles. The round trip took thirty-three days, more or less.[85] When the caravans started on a regular basis from Angastu, they arrived at Monturaqui often. Vita began this early. And, along with the dispatch of the stonecutters to that place, he ordered a pack train out with our warm clothes and the first load of food. As I said, Vita had a genius for planning, organizing, and moving matters forward.
- Anco: And the nature of transport from this place to the peak?
- Apani: The *arrieros* and llamas used to move goods to the peak stayed separate from those making the journey between Angastu and Monturaqui. They remained dedicated strictly to the passage from the warehouses at Monturaqui to the storage depot on the peak and back.
- Pedro: Why?
- Apani: Vita, when at the peak, wanted to deal with *arrieros* he and his lieutenant in charge of the stores at Monturaqui knew and trusted. In his experience, this arrangement had worked well in the past, so he used a similar method here also.
- Pedro: And the equipment depot's location on the peak?
- Apani: We had two of them, actually. Our first we placed on the western side of Llullaillaco. When that route proved too strenuous, we built a new depot on the eastern side.

---

[84] *Ichu* grass is common in the high deserts of the Andes and is a favorite of the llama.

[85] Llamas have a daily range of seven to nine miles.

- Pedro: How long did it take to prepare everything before final movement from Angastu?
- Apani: It took several weeks of building, coordinating, and staging until all appeared ready. One day, Vita seemed satisfied with our progress and ordered us to strike off from Angastu at the end of August.
- Pedro: Is there significance to the date?
- Apani: Yes, very much so. Vita and the *cunturs* had talked with those who traded goods in Saltiza and an item of interest centered on storm activity on the mountain this time of year. It turns out the worst month is February, while the best months occur in spring and fall. Vita decided to devote the entire month of November to placing the huts on the mountain. Consequently, leaving when we did, it gave us time to reach the peak, deliver all the necessary equipment, and afterwards concentrate on placing the buildings on the top.
- Anco: Will you tell us of the journey and what happened on the western side of the mountain?
- Apani: Yes. The passage to Monturaqui seemed uninteresting to a number of men, yet exciting to many of us as it offered grand adventure. We began to sleep as we would on the mountain, four of us in each tent sewn of llama hides. Occasionally it proved uncomfortable sleeping that way; nevertheless, later on the peak we stayed warm. During the afternoons at our camps, the *cunturs* talked to the eighty-five selected to climb with them to place the several depots on the mountain.
- Anco: And what did the *cunturs* have to say?
- Apani: They talked of the coming venture to prepare us for what we would encounter. For example, the higher we went the more difficult our breathing would become. They also told us how to prevent our fingers and toes from freezing. We must avoid this from happening at all costs, they said, as the most likely result, frozen fingers and toes, might require cutting them off. The lead *cuntur* spoke from experience. He had lost two fingers and a toe to frostbite several years before. What to eat, how to light fires,

how to prevent water from freezing in our gourds, especially at night, all these matters they discussed and explained over and over until we understood and had memorized them. Also, they made plain that Vita exercised control at the bottom of the mountain, but when we found ourselves above and away from him the *cunturs* would be in command. If they told us to do something, we must obey immediately and without question. Failure to do so might endanger all of us.

- Pedro: And the aspect of Monturaqui?

- Apani: A bustling place, when we arrived at the end of September, during the spring. Builders had constructed two warehouses and fitted them out with reed roofs. The older structures there our men enlarged to accommodate our needs. Food, eating utensils, clothing, climbing packs, all lay around, and details of men busied themselves placing provisions in the storehouses, stacking other items outside, whatever the lieutenant there had ordered. A large area contained tents to house those working at the site and as a rest place to provide the *arrieros* from Angastu a place to stay until they returned to that town. It also housed the *arrieros* who traveled to and from the peak. It all resembled a small village, there in that remote part of the desert. It remained a cheery place, with everyone working hard and with purpose. Late on the day of our arrival, Vita made a speech and congratulated us on our efforts and reminded us we still had much to do. The spirit of Inca Yupanqui smiled down on us, he said, and our Lord the Sun would be pleased when our work ended.

- Anco: Please describe the western side of the mountain and why it proved unsuitable as a route to the top.

- Apani: I will tell you first of our journey there and what happened in the days afterward. From Monturaqui, the peak lies to the south and it took us two days to get there. Vita placed the first camp on the shore of a large, warm lake with many flamingoes on it.[86] Our unit numbered nearly 130, composed of Vita, the

---

[86] Today's Laguna Aguas Calientes, 12,000 feet.

cunturs, those of us to climb with them, men to haul the rocks and stores, and our *arrieros*. A few of us found it hard to believe that after a few days we might stand on the mountain's summit. At sunrise, we left to find a location for our Main Camp. We rose higher and higher and had to stop sporadically to catch our breath. Eventually, we attained a place Vita decided a suitable spot,[87] where the *ichu* grass became scarce. This site sat to the left of a strange flow of rocks that appeared to have its source higher on the mountain,[88] out of our sight. The walk to this camp is when I acquired my name, Apani, as I offered to carry the loads of several who found it strenuous at the new heights. We erected the tents, opened the food stores, started the fires, and within an hour the cooks had prepared fresh llama meat with vegetables, a meal most welcome following a hard day. We stayed at this place two days, until Vita decided to begin placing higher camps to support an eventual ascent to the top.[89] Just the *cunturs* took part in this. It required several days to get to a broad, level snow plateau, high on the mountain. Two small pools of deep blue water there remained unfrozen and would serve as a ready source of our drinking water.[90] Even with this available supply, the *cunturs* decided the route unsuitable, for this reason. On the plateau, an immense spike of rock rose before them. But it shielded the main peak that lay behind this spire. To reach the primary high point, the route lay to either right or left, bypassing the spire. To the left, a steep ramp posed ascent problems. At the crest of that slope, the ground fell off into a deep gully, beyond which a long, rising incline of various sized rocks and boulders led to the summit.[91] As the ramp and

---

[87] This broad slope at around 14,500 feet has several possible campsites. Please see Ch. 3, 4, and 8 in "Clawing for the Stars: A Solo Climber in the Highest Andes."

[88] This is the large lava flow that spills down onto the western slopes.

[89] Possible campsites they may have used lie at 16,700 feet and 18,300 feet.

[90] This plateau sits at 20,700 feet and is larger than the one on the eastern side at 19,200 feet (see below).

[91] This description is still true today.

ravine posed real problems to those who hauled loads to the top, an easier route needed discovery. Going to the right of the spire looked difficult too. That route rose slightly as it left the snow plateau, and quickly confronted a huge mass of rock debris from a long-ago eruption of the peak. Beyond this area, a steep gully rose towards the summit, choked by small rocks and stones. Going that way might exhaust us and cause us to fail. Due to these problems, the *cunturs* decided to return to Main Camp, report to Vita, and let him decide. Overall, it required seven days to complete this scouting climb.

- Pedro: And how did Vita feel about things?
- Apani: He trusted his *cunturs* because he and they had been a unit for many years and he knew their judgments to be sound.
- Anco: So what happened then?
- Apani: Well, Vita ordered us back down the mountain to our interim camp for the night. In the meantime, a new llama train joined us at the lake. Vita decided we ought to proceed to the northern side of the mountain and locate a different path to the top. If we found nothing suitable, we would examine conditions on the eastern slopes. As another mark of his planning skills, Vita ordered the hut rocks to remain at Monturaqui until the location of our major camp had been determined. This strategy paid off as it saved the *arrieros* needless effort and time.
- Pedro: It occurs to me to ask how you carried provisions from one camp to the other?
- Apani: Along with our fur clothing, Vita brought with him from Cuzco different kinds of bags that suited our purpose -- llama hides woven in two shapes. My favorite type we wore over both shoulders. It had two straps at either side and rested on the back below the neck. The other we wore over the shoulder. It had a long strap for resting round the neck, the bag falling to either right or left side at the man's hip.[92] On several days, principally lower down the mountain, a few used two of the over

---

[92] Examples of both types have been unearthed in Bolivia, Chile, Ecuador, and Peru.

the shoulder bags, in addition to the one on the back. Higher on the mountain, when breathing proved strenuous, many carried only a single shoulder bag.

- Anco: What of a route on the north side?
- Apani: We looked at it and the *cunturs* saw many possibilities, five as I recall, and Vita and they discussed them in front of us, so we might understand what they knew and what they thought. The possibilities looked, to my friends and me, as too steep for hauling heavy loads. In addition, the routes appeared to end at the snow plateau that the *cunturs* encountered on our western climb. In the end, the *cunturs* decided none of the routes suited our purpose.[93]
- Pedro: And what happened after that?
- Apani: We went to the northeastern side so Vita could evaluate conditions there. We walked past the huge northern part of the mountain, and much of the eastern side came to view. And there, as if put in place to match our needs, rose a ramp-like projection of the mountain that led from a height equal to where we stood to the top of the mountain, with several angled plateaus along the way. Most of us, though knowing little of these matters, nevertheless understood this to be the route higher. One of my friends, on seeing it, said in amazement, "That is the way! It must be. It looks perfect!"
- Anco: And did it prove as good a route when seen close up?
- Apani: Yes, it did. When we got closer, we recognized that the ramp appeared steep and uneven in several areas. Yet, it looked an improvement over the western and northern approaches as this path meant going higher rather than having to descend into gullies and mounting the other side, as on the western route. And, there appeared to be several places to locate camps.
- Pedro: And Vita and the *cunturs* approved of it?

---

[93] In November, 1998, the author attempted one of these steep routes and failed from sheer fatigue. Apani and his friends were correct!

- Apani: Yes. In fact, as we approached closer, Vita ordered a halt. As we rested, he and the *cunturs* talked amongst themselves in an excited manner. Presently, he left the group and motioned us to gather near him. This is the route, he said, and told us why he and the *cunturs* thought so. It looked like a good ramp, better than anything we had yet seen; it afforded several places to put our interim camps; and so on. He went on to say that we would spend the rest of the day attempting to find a spot to locate our equipment depot, which would be determined by how high the llamas reached. We had to attain this point before all else; we needed every animal to do as much of the carrying as possible to take the burden from us.
- Anco: And you found a place to put this camp?
- Apani: Yes. After two more days of climbing higher and diagonally over the slopes, we arrived at a location beyond which the llamas refused to go. Almost all the animals among them stopped as if by a predetermined command. Fortunately, this happened at an ideal spot, a broad, flat area, with a watercourse flowing nearby with melted water from the snows above.[94] Vita, with his experience, said the stream would freeze at night and flow in the daytime if the sun warmed the snow above us. He said the *arrieros* would return to Monturaqui the next day with instructions that the hut rocks and all the other stores must begin their movement by using all available llamas to do so. He also sent a request to his lieutenant to send twenty more men to serve as load-bearers on the mountain.
- Pedro: How did Vita organize this camp?
- Apani: He and the *cunturs* organized it as they had on other mountains. One place they designated as the latrine area, one more as tent quarters, another location as the spot to cook and eat, yet one other as the location for our clothes and food. Such was their design of the camps.

---

[94] This area is located at just over 15,000 feet. This site and the subsequent camps up the mountain are documented in Johan Reinhard's "The Ice Maiden."

- Anco: And the other days at this place?
- Apani: With luck, we erected the tents in the afternoon before a terrific windstorm, in a completely clear sky, raked the place. All our equipment and stores required tying down to prevent them from being blown away. Vita and his men had prepared for this. They supplied us with sturdy leather ropes made of dried llama hide. We attached one end to the corners of our tents and the other we tied to nearby rocks. We used this technique at all our camps.
- Pedro: So this place served as your Main Camp?
- Apani: No. It served as a staging depot to accommodate the llama trains arriving from Monturaqui. Our Main Camp they set higher, located on a wide plateau, with a stream of running water close by, the same that passed the staging depot.[95] Here we erected a large cooking area at Vita's direction. We builders gathered stones and constructed a sturdy enclosure that protected the cooks from the wind. In due course, we built two more rock huts here for their sleep and rest. We gave these men special treatment, always. Of course, we could exist on *charqui*, nuts, corn cakes, and dried fruits and vegetables. Here at our Main Camp, though, we desired warm food and our cooks pleased us every day of our stay. Vita ordered the cooking fires never extinguished so the cooks might prepare food at any hour of the day according to our needs. Main Camp remained a joy to us in this regard.
- Pedro: And on these days, how did you and the others spend your time?
- Apani: After the placement of Main Camp, the task began of hauling the rocks, food, llama dung, and other materials from the staging depot below up to this place. Now Vita conceived a project to occupy the builders, in addition to building the cooks' quarters. He directed us to construct rock huts to store all the goods to be delivered here over the ensuing weeks. As for the rest of the men, they stayed in constant motion and carried all

---

[95] This camp is at an elevation near 17,100 feet.

the stores from the lower camp to this camp. The llama trains from Monturaqui arrived every several days at the lower depot, and the provisions were made ready to proceed to Main Camp. One day the winds blew so hard through several afternoons that Vita stopped our work until the conditions became calmer. Still, we remained fortunate with the weather. Matters could have been much worse. And the days spent in stocking Main Camp helped all of us adjust to its high elevation.

- Pedro: The building of these structures seems to have been a demanding task.
- Apani: Well, we had our tools with us and plenty of stones of all sizes. Moreover, staying busy kept us warm. In several days, we built ten small storage structures.[96] In addition, it happens these shelters provided a storage space for the equipment arriving from the supply depot, and also a place to store religious items needed in the ceremonies to honor the Inca and the Sun.
- Pedro: Main Camp must have been crowded.
- Apani: Well, it was a large place and everything fit. Several died here from the cold or in accidents. Vita designated an area nearby for our cemetery, and he said comforting words at the burial ceremony of each man.[97]
- Pedro: How did they identify the higher camps?
- Apani: Vita directed the *cuntur runas* to ascend the mountain and locate the succeeding camps above that could accommodate a large number of men. If a water source resided nearby, all the better, although he doubted the existence of such a place above our Main Camp. He needed to know this so the proper number of water gourds would be available as we climbed higher.
- Anco: And they located such places, I assume.
- Apani: Yes, and they had luck in doing so. It were as though the mountain gods had prepared the peak to please us. They found

---

[96] Reinhard's teams found twelve such structures, as noted in "The Ice Maiden."
[97] Ruins of the small buildings at the main camp and the cemetery are Incaic, according to Reinhard. This confirms this is the route Vita and his men used.

a spot to place a camp on a wide table, this with an unfrozen pond of water on it,[98] a most fortunate discovery. The last camp they put right below the top of the mountain,[99] on a wide spot they found covered with snow. Of course, the *cunturs* felt tired when they came back eight days later. It had snowed lightly several nights at both camps, but they continued going higher. They told this to the builders and Vita on their return.

- Pedro: And all were ready to begin the climb?
- Apani: Well, we delayed awhile. One day it began to snow early in the morning and lasted until early evening. However, at the supply storehouse and to a lesser extent at Main Camp, it never stayed on the ground long. It is a dry snow, with little water content. And the air is so dry it causes the snow to disappear quickly.
- Anco: You wish to say more regarding this?
- Apani: No, not of the snow. I want to tell you that we received a great surprise here. Vita called us all together and said the High Priest, Anta-Aclla, would join us for three days and arrive on the morrow. He planned to say a prayer that our efforts might please our god the Sun. This caused a great deal of commotion and excitement as we knew this man and respected him. Befitting such a great honor, at Vita's instructions, we set up a tent to shelter him and his attendant. And we builders erected a small stone platform so he might conduct a brief ceremony. We stayed excited the rest of the day and in great anticipation of his appearance.
- Anco: And did he arrive as planned?
- Apani: Yes, and he seemed as if the climb from the depot (he had made it there two days before) had been just a pleasant walk on the ocean's shore! An amazing man. We crowded round him, preventing him from resting or taking refreshment after his exertions, and he minded not in the least. He touched the forehead of all those who crowded close and recited a brief prayer requesting the man's safety and well-being. When the

---

98 This is still a good camp site, at 19,125 feet.
99 This site lies at 21,950 feet.

High Priest had finished the blessings, Vita escorted him to his quarters, there to have food and drink and converse in private.

- Anco: This man seemed very special to all of you.
- Apani: Yes, absolutely. Late the following morning, with the sun shining, we gathered near the platform we had built for the occasion. At a signal from Vita, Anta-Aclla emerged from behind his tent, arrayed in his ceremonial garments. He presented a striking appearance in such a remote place. He conducted the ceremony, while flute players played solemn music, and said a prayer for our success. This moved and inspired us.
- Pedro: I am sure he has remembered the occasion also.
- Apani: Well, I know he has never forgotten it. A single instance stands out. A companion had addressed all of us the previous day, on Anta-Aclla's arrival, and suggested we call him Anta-Aclla Orqos, High Priest of the High Mountains. All agreed this was fitting. At the conclusion of the prayer to the Sun at the close of the ceremony, Vita stood by his side and told him what we wished him to take as his full name. This touched him, because he had difficulty in giving voice to his thanks. Later in the day, the cooks prepared fresh llama meat and a special soup with our favorite hot chili peppers. In addition, they made sweet cakes unique for the occasion. In mid-morning he left, with all of us crowding close to have him touch our foreheads again. What an experience! Unforgettable.
- Apani: And I recollect, also, the special prayer he said for us. Although many years have passed, I can still recite it:

O Creator, Creator O. Have mercy upon the men whom thou hast made and are gathered here, for they honor you as our Creator. Grant them continued good health as they labor on a task that is most pleasing to you. Make them and their children to walk in a straight road, without thinking any evil. Grant that they may have a long life, and not die in their youth, as a reward for working on a lasting monument to your greatness. O Creator, Creator O.

- Anco: That seems a unique prayer at a special moment. I am thankful to hear it. It now appears the moment has come to move up the great mountain.

- Apani: Yes, and this proved a propitious day – one in late October. Keep in mind, Vita and the *cunturs* wanted our efforts to take place in the month of November due to the favorable weather in that month.[100] Well, they received their wish! Here, Vita called the builders and told us we would not participate in lifting the rocks to the top, given that the success of the entire project depended on us and he wanted to lessen the risk of losing us to frostbite, injury, or sickness. Besides, he wanted us to finish work on the buildings at Main Camp before we left to assemble the huts.

- Anco: And did you?

- Apani: Yes. We finished our work before we departed for the top.

- Anco: How many hauled to the succeeding camp?

- Apani: Well, four *cunturs*, eighty-five rock-bearers, thirty carriers of food, dung, tents, and assorted other stores, and an extra twenty in reserve composed the entire unit. Each man carried, in addition to the weight of his load, a gourd of water, dried fruit, and *charqui*. They started from camp early, directed by the *cunturs*, one leading at the front, two at different positions within the file, and the fourth at the rear. They proceeded slowly, the *cunturs* keeping a steady pace and resting often. The course remained free of snow, but with the ground loose in places, as we builders found out when it came our turn, this made it difficult. Fortunately, the weather cooperated, with no storms

---

[100] On his many solo trips to this mountain, the author always traveled in either November or late March, early April. The days were usually sunny, but cool, with ferocious winds stirring up often in the afternoon and lasting into the night. At his base camps, anywhere from 14,500 feet to 15,000 feet, the weather was often so balmy that he took self-photos sitting outside his tent in a T-shirt! On one trip in April, however, a terrific wind and snowstorm blocked the way to the summit, a story he tells in Chapter 4 of his book, "Clawing for the Stars: a Solo Climber in the Highest Andes."

and only a slight breeze. They stayed within our sight until the long line finally disappeared behind a huge outcropping of rocks. It remains in my mind a grand and majestic scene and I have not forgotten it. In two hours, they reappeared from behind the rocks, in column, slowly wending their way back. Several appeared unsteady as they came towards us, a sure sign of breathing or headache problems.

- Pedro: And their condition when they made it back?

- Apani: Well, Vita went out to greet and congratulate them on their effort. They felt tired, no question about that, but the overwhelming mood of all remained cheerful and happy. A few, though, were sick and went to their tents to sleep. A friend saw me wave and came over to visit. He dropped to the ground and lay back to rest. "Well, how did it go?" I asked eagerly. He waited and then smiled and said, "Is that all there is to it?" He made a joke, of course. Physically, it had been demanding although within his ability. This is how most others felt too at the close of this first day, from what I heard and observed.

- Pedro: And the second loads went up the day following?

- Apani: Yes. The carriers left a little later in the day and planned to spend the night. Let me tell you how this all happened. They spent the night of the second lift at, let's call it First Camp, as it resided above Main Camp. The next day they made their initial carry to Second Camp, which lay below the summit of the mountain, and returned to First Camp for sleep. On the new day, they made their second haul to Second Camp, there to spend the night. A day later, they carried half the stones to the summit and returned to Second Camp to spend the night. After that, they took the remaining stones to the top and went back to Second Camp. The following day they returned to us at Main Camp.

- Pedro: Thus, the total number of days to carry the stones to the summit and return to Main Camp was seven?

- Apani: Yes. Now, when they exited Main Camp on the second day -- and here is the genius of Vita coming forward again

-- the cooks sent freshly cooked llama meat, cooked vegetables, and corn cakes to them daily. This is how the extra men Vita requested when we first attained the depot site proved their worth, for they helped carry the food to the camps. As a result, those above had enough to eat at their main meal every day instead of relying on *charqui*.

- Anco: And you and the other builders still worked on the ten structures in their absence?

- Apani: Actually, we finished all our work on them two days after the carriers left on their next haul to First Camp. We builders discussed among ourselves whether to ask Vita if we might follow the track to First Camp, to see how we felt there and return the same day. He assented, and so the following day we made the climb. By this point, the men resided at Second Camp, leaving First Camp deserted. It seemed an ideal site, large in area, the pond with fresh water, yet strangely unfrozen at such a height.[101]

- Anco: What of their condition when they returned?

- Apani: We knew the problems they had, as one or two came back to Main Camp suffering from freezing of their fingers, toes, or feet. In a day or two their toes and fingers turned black and hardened, as the flesh had died. In many cases, matters became worse when the skin blisters burst and infection set in. This required their feet, fingers, or toes to be cut off. If they remained in place, the man might die within several weeks. In addition, several returned who experienced breathing problems or headaches. Those who descended proved the lucky ones. Two died above Main Camp due to these illnesses.

- Pedro: And they brought the bodies back down?

- Apani: No. The *cunturs* buried them on the mountain. Trying to drag a dead body down to Main Camp would have been too difficult and dangerous.

---

[101] The author noted this phenomenon on other high peaks and believes steam vents inside the mountains warm the water pools.

- Anco: And now the builders' moment had arrived?
- Apani: Yes. After the *cunturs* rested for a day, we set out at daybreak. An icy breeze blew, which made matters uncomfortable. The *cunturs* had planned matters well. As an example, they left tents erected at First and Second Camp so we would not have to carry them. Moreover, they left enough food at the camps, which lifted the burden of carrying provisions from our shoulders. And certainly, not hauling the heavy rock loads served in our favor also. Our band included the four *cunturs*, eight builders, and ten who served our needs. Vita wanted to make sure we builders remained focused on our principal task of reassembling the huts.
- Anco: Any problems going higher?
- Apani: Yes. When we arrived at Second Camp, my friend Mayta became dizzy and could barely stand at all. He kept falling over and complained of severe headaches. The head *cuntur* told an extra man to take him down lower as this usually corrected the problem.
- Anco: And did it?
- Apani: Once he returned safely to Main Camp, yes, he did survive. On our journey to the summit, all went according to plan. Of course, it helped that the weather stayed benign, although the wind blew stiffly some mornings and evenings. It took us four days from Main Camp to Second Camp. The day following, we made the climb to the summit.
- Pedro: And your feelings?
- Apani: Well, to arrive at the top meant a great accomplishment. The *cunturs* hugged us, and this made us feel important. And the views from there overwhelmed us with their beauty. It is special to see the world from the top of a mountain, and particularly gratifying to see all our stones there stacked in four piles and arranged by their color codes.
- Pedro: And so you began reassembly?
- Apani: Yes. Mayta had been part of my builder team, so three of us now made up my party. Our hut was the one with the

lower stones marked in green, the upper ones in blue. Prior to beginning, we all looked over the site, to determine the best positioning of the structures. In the end, we decided a north/south arrangement the best, our hut's end wall separated by two feet from the other hut's end wall. When this had been resolved and settled, we went to work, with the *cunturs* helping when called on. We made quick business of it, with the lower half of each hut in place by early afternoon. The color-coding helped, of course. Also, we had chipped and shaped those rocks ourselves back at Angastu and we remembered their positions in the completed building.

- Anco: And you finished the succeeding day?
- Apani: Yes. When we positioned the last rocks of the upper halves, we stretched reed roof mats over the tops and paused to admire our work. The head *cuntur* recited a prayer Vita had spoken to him. Before we left, I took the small leather pouch that contained the lock of my mother's hair and placed it under my hut's corner foundation stone. So she received her wish -- her spirit now resides close to our Lord the Sun.[102] It turned cold and gusts of wind pummeled us as we returned to Second Camp, yet I felt too happy with what we had done to notice. It turned cold at night, the coldest since we had arrived on the mountain.

PHOTOS: Please see the pictures in the Ch. 8 folder, 8.16, 8.17, and 8.18 for what these structures look like today.

- Pedro: And did you all make it back to Main Camp?
- Apani: We had problems on the return. When we woke at dawn after the freezing cold of the night, our friend Chipana complained that he had no feeling in the fingers of his right hand or the toes of his right foot. Another builder and I massaged them, but failed to restore their color. We had to leave for Main Camp, so I remained with him and carried

---

[102] See Johan Reinhard's "The Ice Maiden" as to how the summit of Llullaillaco was used as a burial place for countless artifacts and three Indian sacrificial mummies.

282

his pack. We progressed slowly, made it back to First Camp, and rested there while we watched the remainder of our party move down the mountain below us. There is a place, where the path bears to the right, that a man lost his balance and began sliding down the slope. Seeing as the angle of sight from our position prevented a clear view, he disappeared quickly. We saw the others looking down the slope and doing no more, simply looking, as they could do little else. In fifteen minutes, they assembled and resumed their journey down, with no attempt at rescue. Chipana and I remembered the place as the most dangerous part of the route. At night, safely back at Main Camp, several of us continued massaging Chipana's fingers and toes. Unfortunately, he lost two toes and three fingers several weeks later when we returned to Angastu.

- Anco: And when did you leave the mountain?
- Apani: Vita and the *cunturs* planned to leave supplies in the structures we built at Main Camp. As an example, they left ten of each of the parts of warm clothing we used when climbing the mountain, so Anta-Aclla might have these for himself and his attendants when he conducted religious ceremonies in the future. They also placed dried fruits, nuts, and items such as that in one of the storerooms. Vita had ordered extra llamas so materials returning to Angastu and to Cuzco might have transport. Vita, the *cunturs*, we builders, and several others were the last to leave the mountain. We gathered at sunrise the next day. Vita said a prayer to our Lord the Sun and thanked him for the opportunity to serve him.
- Pedro: What transpired when you returned to Angastu?
- Apani: Well, Anta-Aclla and his priests conducted a ceremony thanking the Lord Sun for our safe return. Our general arranged a party in welcome with much food and drink. Many in the town attended also.
- Anco: Did they bestow honors on you and the others?
- Apani: Yes. Our general, as reward for our work on this project to bring honor and glory to our Father the Inca and to our

Lord the Sun, offered then and there to all those who actually performed work on the mountain, in whatever capacity, a release from service in the Inca's army, either to return home to Peru or to remain in Chile, in whatever town they wished to reside, and one hectare of land to cultivate.[103]

- Anco: It seems a grand and fitting reward.
- Apani: Well, many wished to remain in service. Those who did received extra wages from that point on. I decided, along with thirty companions, to stay in Chile and, to this day, I have never regretted having done so.

So ends the interview with Apani in de Merida's second letter. I present it in the hope that it may shed some light for the reader as to how the huts may have been placed on the top of Llullaillaco. Since the Inca never developed a form of writing, this incredible feat of human endeavor shall remain an enduring mystery.

To add another view, Dr. Johan Reinhard[104], in a personal note to the author, offers the following comment: "Without going into detail, the Incas made use of the stones that were available either at the site or nearby. Mountaintop sites vary in size and type (see my discussion of the building of platforms and burials in 'Inca Rituals') for many reasons, but one was the availability of stones. The stones weren't actually worked, at least not beyond a basic knocking off of sections to better fit the kind of roughly-made structures on Llullaillaco. Since the Incas used the available stones in their constructions, we don't see what the availability of stones was when the Incas first reached the summits. Also, they did gather sand and stones from hundreds of meters below in some cases, especially for the fill used in platforms. However, these were not well-carved stones carried from the base that were made for fitting together on top."

---

[103] One hectare is roughly equivalent to 2 ½ acres.

[104] His most recent book on his Andean archaeological finds is "Inca Rituals and Sacred Mountains," Cotsen Institute of Archaeology Press (2011).

Glossary of Terms

ACUTE MOUNTAIN SICKNESS (AMS)

The majority of people experience symptoms of AMS at elevations above 10,000 feet. Its occurrence depends upon the altitude, the rate of ascent, and the individual's personal susceptibility. Symptoms may include headache, loss of appetite, shortness of breath, and nausea. Diamox (see below) can moderate the symptoms. The author had headaches occasionally upon reaching a higher camp, but after drinking water or soup these dissipated within an hour or two.

ALMAGRO EXPEDITION

Please see the Introduction to Appendix C.

ALTIMETER

When the author began his climbing career in 1988, he used a small aneroid barometric altimeter. It determined the altitude by measuring atmospheric pressure. Wristwatch altimeters became available in the 1990's and are much more convenient to use today.

ALTIPLANO

The high desert plateaus of the Andes.

ATACAMA DESERT

The Atacama, known as the driest place on earth, lies in northern and central Chile and stretches from just below the Peru-Chile border to approximately 200 miles south of Copiapo.

CARABINEROS

The Chilean police.

COL

A low point in a ridge of mountains, often forming a pass between two peaks. The col between Tres Cruses Sur and Central is a perfect example.

CONDOR

The Andean condor is common in the Andean countries of South America. They are a member of the vulture family, have wingspans as wide as eleven feet, may weigh up to thirty-three pounds, and have been known to live for 100 years.

COULOIR

A mountain gully.

CRAMPONS

A framework of metal spikes strapped to the sole of the climbing boot to provide better traction on snow or ice.

CREVASSE

A deep crack in an ice sheet or glacier. They form as a result of the movement of an ice sheet.

DEXAMETHASONE

This prescription drug is used to ward off high altitude cerebral and pulmonary edema. The author never used it nor carried it with him on a climb.

DIAMOX

Diamox is a safe drug to take at altitude. It's a medication that encourages urination. That forces the kidneys to excrete bicarbonate, the base form of carbon dioxide; this re-acidifies the blood, balancing the effects of the hyperventilation that occurs at altitude as the body attempts to get oxygen. It also helps to lessen headaches and sleep disturbance.

EXPEDITION STYLE CLIMBING

There are several carries between camps as progress is made up the mountain. For example, on the author's first carry to the next camp he had a set list of items and gear to go with him. He dropped this load at the place chosen for camp, had something to eat and drink, and then returned to the lower camp to spend the night. The next day, he carried all his remaining gear to the higher camp and spent the night there. The following day, the routine began all over again toward the next camp. This style allows for the efficient movement of gear and it also permits the body to gradually acclimate to the higher elevation.

FLAMINGOES

One may see the Andean, Chilean, and St. James flamingo throughout the Andes. Each has different and distinctive coloring on their beaks, wing tips, body, and legs.

FROSTBITE

Severe trauma to skin and tissue of the extremities caused by intense cold.

GENDARME

A pinnacle of rock on a mountain ridge or slope.

GLISSADE

A controlled slide down a snow slope either crouching or sitting.

GORE-TEX

A water resistant and breathable fabric that has many uses in the mountains. The author's tent, windsuit, and climbing gaiters were all made of Gore-Tex.

HALLUCINATION

A feeling or perception without a stimulus, in this case, brought on by high altitude.

HIGH ALTITUDE CEREBRAL EDEMA (HACE)

HACE is a frequently fatal form of altitude sickness. Its symptoms include headache, loss of coordination, disorientation, loss of memory, hallucinations, irrational behavior, and coma. The only sure antidote is to get the climber at least 1,000 feet down the mountain as quickly as possible.

HIGH ALTITUDE PULMONARY EDEMA (HAPE)

HAPE is a life threatening fluid accumulation in the lungs. The symptoms are coughing, difficulty in breathing at rest, chest tightness, physical weakness, and the coughing up of blood and dark mucous. As with HACE, the climber must retreat at least 1,000 feet back down the mountain or this condition will prove fatal.

NIEVES PENITENTES

These are snow formations found in high, dry Andean areas. They are tall, thin formations of ice and snow and are normally found in fields of separate formations that may be as tall as fifteen feet. Some believe that they are formed by the wind. Others think that the position of the sun in the lower latitudes plays a part. Literally "snow penitent," named by the Spanish for their resemblance to a kneeling penitent in church.

NIFEDIPINE

This prescription drug is used to treat high altitude pulmonary edema. The author never carried it with him.

OJOS

An ojo in the Chilean-Argentine Andes is a source of water that springs from an underground water table.

REFUGIO

Through the years, the Chilean government has both erected small shelters or remodeled abandoned mine buildings to accommodate tourists passing through remote parts of the Chilean Andes.

SCREE

Small rock and sand debris.

SNOW BLINDNESS

A burning of the cornea by ultraviolet B rays at high altitude. Treatment consists of keeping the eyes closed. Sight usually restores itself in a day and a half.

SOLO MOUNTAINEERING

The author's personal definition is rather strict. If there is anyone else on the mountain, then he did not count the climb as a solo one. Actually, on his climbs alone, he never saw other climbers.

SPINDRIFT

Fine granules of snow blown by the wind.

SUMMIT REGISTERS

There are registers on several Andean peaks for climbers to sign. The author always declined to do so.

TALUS

Rock rubble.

TRAVERSE

To go up or down a slope diagonally or in a zigzag fashion.

WHITEOUT

A weather anomaly in which visibility and contrast are reduced or non-existent. The horizon disappears and there are no reference points, leaving the climber completely disoriented.

ABOUT THE AUTHOR

Bob Villarreal acquired a passion to climb at high altitude later in life, at 44. From that moment, until his last climb in November, 2009, at 65, he made thirty forays into the Andes. The majority of those climbs were solo ones. His driver, Giancarlo Fiocco or Patricio Rios, drove him to the mountain, dropped him off at Base Camp, and then returned in another two weeks. In one of the remotest parts of the Andes, along the lengthy border between Chile and Argentina, the nearest mine or Customs Station was 35 to 90 miles away. Should calamity strike the only recourse available to him was to walk out to safety.

Bob is a retired telephone company executive. He lives in Livermore, California with his wife of 40 years. They have two adopted daughters, one from Cuzco, Peru, and the other from Pasto, Colombia. He sees his children and three grandchildren several times a week. He plans one day to take his grandson, Alex, on a trip to visit the mountains of his dreams.

Acknowledgements

I am indebted to my wife of forty years for tolerating my frequent absences during my climbing years and the expense associated with each. She never complained about either and never acted in a way to discourage me from going, something for which I shall always be grateful.

Wayne Ferguson, my business mentor during our working days and a personal friend for forty years, read the chapters soon after I wrote them and before they were edited. He provided insights and suggestions about material and presentation that proved invaluable.

Sverre Aarseth, my friend of many years, also read the book when in its infancy and offered his observations and encouragement. Please see a brief rendering of his colorful climbing career in Chapter 9.

Chuck Huss, another friend, was kind enough to read the chapters and gave me encouragement to continue. He also graciously permitted the use of several of his photos for the book. I remain indebted to him for the use of his photograph of the Inca huts on the summit of Llullaillaco. Chuck also allowed the use of many of his photos from our climb together, as told in Chapter 9. (See also the website for more of his work.) For a rendering of Chuck's amazing climbing career, see the highlights in Chapter 9.

Mark Albrecht, my high school classmate in Catholic seminary for several years, kindly agreed to function as my editor. He was a perfect match for the job and he will edit my second book as well.

Nick Ward, one of my classical Greek and Roman literature students, designed my website and helps to maintain it. It is a superb piece of work.

Laura Kang Ward, Nick's mother, functioned as my proof editor. Her ability to spot the smallest and most minute details was invaluable.

Johan Reinhard, the preeminent Andean high altitude archaeologist, granted permission to use several of his Andean photographs in the "Photos" section of the "Clawing" website.

Alex Currie, my grandson, for asking me to write the book! He also suggested recording Google Earth Tours for each chapter, a notable addition to the website.

Maria Ester Rodillo, Giancarlo's widow, for her friendship through the years. Readers who intend a visit to Copiapo should plan to make her hotel, La Casona, their lodging for their stay.

Lightning Source UK Ltd.
Milton Keynes UK
UKOW03f1904170614

233618UK00001B/19/P